tree of strings
crann nan teud

a history of the harp in Scotland

KEITH SANGER

&

ALISON KINNAIRD

KINMOR MUSIC

"Strange that a harp of thousand strings
Should keep in tune so long."

Dr. Isaac Watt's "Hymns and Spiritual Songs"

The publisher acknowledges subsidy from the Scottish Arts Council
towards the publication of this volume

Published by   Kinmor Music
                    Shillinghill
                    Temple,
                    Midlothian EH23 4SH
                    Scotland

British Library Cataloguing in Publication Data

A catalogue record for this book is available
from the British Library.

ISBN 0-9511204-3-3 Hardback
ISBN 0-9511204-4-1 Paperback

Cover painting "Harp" by John Haxby
Cover design by Graham Ogilvie

Typeset from disk by Alphaset Graphics, Edinburgh
Printed in Scotland by Scotprint, Musselburgh

CONTENTS

PHOTO ACKNOWLEDGMENTS

Chapter 2
Stone at Dupplin. By permission, Royal Museums of Scotland
Stone at Aldbar. By kind permission of T.E. Gray (F.S.A. Scot)
Stone at Lethendy. By kind permission of T.E. Gray (F.S.A. Scot)
Stone at Ardchattan. Photo: Keith Sanger
Stone at Kilchoan. Photo: Keith Sanger

Chapter 4
Iona Psalter. By permission, National Library of Scotland
Kinloss Psalter. By permission, the Conway Library, Courtauld Institute of Art
King David, Dean House Ceiling. By permission, Royal Museums of Scotland
Music, Dean House Ceiling. By permission, Royal Museums of Scotland
Muses Ceiling, Crathes Castle. By permission, National Trust for Scotland

Chapter 5
Lamont Harp. By permission, Royal Museums of Scotland
Queen Mary Harp. By permission, Royal Museums of Scotland

Chapter 7
Extract from the Treasurer's Accounts. By permission, Scottish Record Office

Chapter 8
Detail of woman harper, Crathes Castle. By permission, National Trust for Scotland
"Musica" — Garden at Edzell Castle. Photo: Keith Sanger
Hill House. Photo: Keith Sanger

Chapter 10
Urquhart. By permission, Royal Museums of Scotland
Cawdor. Photo: Keith Sanger. By kind permission, Lord Cawdor

Chapter 13
William McMurchy's M.S. By permission, National Library of Scotland

Chapter 14
Ap Huw M.S. By permission of the British Library
Port Robart. By kind permission, Lord Strathnaver. Transcription, Courtesy Bill Samson
Detail of Fireplace, Castle Huntly. By permission, Royal Commission on Ancient
    Monuments, Scotland
Air by Fingal. John Bowie Collection
Lament for the Bishop of Argyll — MacFarlane M.S. By permission, National Library of
    Scotland
Clarsach Salute — MacLean Clephane Manuscript By kind permission, Capt. A.C.
    Farquharson of Invercauld

ACKNOWLEDGMENTS

Many individuals have given us their knowledge, support and encouragement throughout this project. The authors would like to record their warm appreciation for this help. We also wish to thank the staff of the national organisations whose assistance made possible the research and production of this book.

Thanks to   John Bannerman
Mike Billinge
Ronald Black
David Caldwell
Robert Evans
Ann & Charlie Heymann
Morag MacLeod
William Matheson
Colm O Baoill
Father J. M. Senes
Bill Samson
and to Joyce McMillan

Staff of   Scottish Record Office
National Library of Scotland
Edinburgh Central Library, Scottish Room
Edinburgh University Library
Royal Museums of Scotland
National Trust for Scotland
and to An Comunn Gaidhealach

FOREWORD

Most histories of music in Scotland tell us that little is known about the harp in that country. We have been led to believe that the names of only one or two native harpers can be found, and that virtually none of the music has survived. It seemed extraordinary that so little trace was left of instruments which had been played in Scotland for a thousand years or more. In the course of around thirty years of research it became obvious to us that a great deal of material relating to the harp did exist in sources which previously had not been examined. A number of long-accepted traditions do not survive objective evaluation, or have been mis-quoted. It is also important to look at the facts critically from a background of practical knowledge of the instrument, and of Scottish music. Gradually it became clear that the harp had played an important part in the nation's cultural life over many centuries. So much material was uncovered, indeed, that it was necessary to confine the objectives of this study.

This book, therefore, sets out to present the history of the harp in Scotland, in both Highlands and Lowlands, from the earliest evidence of the 8th-century Pictish stones to the present day. The historical background to the music is discussed in general terms. However, space does not allow us to enter into a detailed examination of practical playing techniques, nor to print more than a few examples of the many surviving harp tunes. Titles and sources of the music, given in an appendix, will hopefully allow interested students to pursue their own researches. It is clear that there is still much fascinating information lying buried, awaiting discovery, and the enthusiasm of present-day musicians for the harp in Scotland is evidence that the story of these beautiful instruments is by no means at an end.

Keith Sanger and Alison Kinnaird
Edinburgh, April 1992

1 Myth & Magic

Rycht as stringis ar reulit in a harp
In ane accord, and timyt al be ane uth,
Quilk as a king then curiusly thai carp,
The sang is sueyt quhen that the sound is suth;
Bot quhen thai ar discordand, fals and muth,
Thair wil na man tak plesance in that play:
Thair mycht weil thole the menstrale war away.

Bot, and the stringis be nocht al treu and traist,
Quhat sal we say? Sal we the menstral wyt?
Yha, bot he bent and pruf thaim with his wraist;
Be thai untreu, pul out and mak al quyte,
And utheris treu put in thair stedis als tyt,
And changis ay sua quhil he find treu acord;
Than wil men say he is worth til a lord.[1]

When the fifteenth century poet uses the harp as a symbol for the Kingdom of Scotland, he draws on the imagery of romance and magic which has surrounded one of our oldest national instruments for hundreds of years. It is a noble instrument of royal dignity and high standing. It is an instrument of beauty : in its form, its sound, and its craftsmanship. It is an instrument of harmony and accord, holding tension in perfect balance. It is a mysterious instrument, always rare; an instrument of glamour and glamourie; an instrument of the other world, pagan or Christian, as well as of our own. It can cast a spell of love or of evil intent, or soothe troubled minds in sleep. It has been played in Scotland for over a thousand years and has its place, not only in the native music but in the art, poetry and folklore of the different peoples that make up the Scottish nation. Later chapters will deal with the historical evidence pertaining to the harp in Scotland, but it is also important and fascinating to examine the special aura of enchantment and romance which surrounds it. The harp is a peculiarly romantic instrument.

The Scottish harp was never a 'folk' instrument. The word 'folk' suggests that an instrument would have been used for the native music throughout all strata of society, including the lower, less educated, levels. On the contrary, the harp was always a professional's instrument, and an instrument of the aristocracy. As such, it would not have been found in croft or bothy as some other instruments, such as whistle, jaw-harp or fiddle, might have been. The harper's skill and training were highly prized, and they themselves were regarded as being of high social standing. (The harpers also tended to esteem themselves highly, compared with other musicians. A certain amount of snobbery was sometimes involved.)[2] They often travelled around a great deal and, like all itinerant musicians, acquired a colourful image of excitement and mystery, especially among audiences who would seldom have been exposed to their art. Thus their music was seen as extraordinary, magical or even supernatural, as the references to harping throughout folklore and legend demonstrate. In the aristocratic households where a harper was employed, his presence emphasised the noble character of the family, and provided a link with the great deeds of his patron's ancestors, real or mythical. The image that the mention of harp music conjured up was that of a rich tapestry of abundant wealth and feasting, rare wines and precious metals, silk and satin, friendship and generosity — an idealization of a society no longer in existence or fast disappearing, but still as powerful an image as any description of Heaven purveyed by the Christian Church.

> Gu aros nach crion
> Am bi gairich nam piob
> Is nam clarsach a ris
> Le dearrsadh nam pios
> A' cur sasaidh air fion
> Is ga leigeadh an gniomh oircheard
>
> (To the dwelling that is not niggardly
> Wherein is the roar of pipes and
> Anon the sound of harps
> With the gleam of silver cups
> Making wine flow free and pouring it
> Into the goldsmith's handiwork.)[3]

Although the Church had adopted and adapted many pre-Christian beliefs, incorporating them into its rituals and ceremonies, there seems to have remained a suspicion and mistrust of the native music. The priests and ministers often found it difficult to reconcile themselves with its pagan connotations. This was most strongly seen in the strict Presbyterian areas, in some of which all non-religious music and dance were forbidden as being the Devil's music. Even today there is still a strong disapproval of them in some quarters. The stories of the 18th and 19th centuries which tell of musical instruments being thrown on bonfires do not mention harps, and indeed by that period the harp had gone out of general use in both the Highlands and Lowlands.[4] It may also have escaped condemnation because it was regarded as a 'heavenly' instrument since it was associated with Biblical characters such as King David and the Angelic Host. The harp does not survive with its reputation completely unscathed, however — it was often linked in legend with practices of the Old Religion.

A tale which was found in both the islands of Eigg[5] and of Skye[6] relates "How Music first came to the Western Isles". It tells how a boy found a strange musical instrument floating in the sea. When he pulled it out and held it so that the wind caught the strings, it made a wonderful sound. The boy sat fingering the strings, day after day, but could not find the way to make the magical music again. His poor mother, in desperation, went to a "dubh-sgoilear" — a practitioner of the Black Arts — to beg him either to give her son the skill of harping, or to quell his desire for it. "Give me your soul", said the "dubh-sgoilear", "and I will put the skill of music into your boy; or give me your body and I will quench his longing for it". "My soul is to you here and now", said the woman, " and the skill of music for my boy". When she went home she found her son, his face lit up with joy, making wonderful music on the harp. But when he found what his mother had sacrificed in order that he should receive the gift, he was torn with horror and remorse. The Eigg version of the story says that ever after, during the daytime, the happiness of his music would draw the eagle from the dove, but when night fell the boy's harping would sob with the agony of his mother's lost soul. The Skye tale, however, tells that when he discovered his mother's pact with the powers of darkness, from that moment he played only music so sad that the birds in the air and fish in the sea stopped to listen … "and that is the reason that it is impossible for anyone at all to draw joyful music from the harp or the clarsach".

The area around Loch Ness was also well-known as the centre of a powerful coven of witches. Castle Urquhart, the ruins of which stand brooding on the western shore, is said to have been built — and cursed — by these witches who dragged the stones for it from Abriachan and Caiplich at the behest of Conachar MacNessa, a semi-mythical character of the 12th century. Near the farm of Tychat, at the edge of the Loch, is a rock known as An Clairsach, the Harp. It was here that the witches gathered to celebrate their Sabbaths and, on the great rock itself, Satan would sit and harp as they danced for his pleasure.[7]

The harp appears again in a pagan context in the Life of St. Kentigern written in Latin, in the mid 12th century by Jocelin of Furness.[8] He tells how an Irish entertainer (ioculator) visited the court of Rederech Hael, ruler, in the 6th century, of the Kingdom of Strathclyde, and famed for his generosity. During the Christmas season the Irishman played with his hand on the "tympanum" and harp, and so pleased the King that after Epiphany, when it was the custom to give presents to the musicians, he offered the harper gold, silver, garments or horses as a reward. The man refused, saying that he had sufficient of these in Ireland, but the only thing that he would accept from King Rederech would be a dish of fresh brambles. His intention, of course, was to shame the Scottish King by making an impossible demand, and thus to "carry off his honour". Rederech, in despair, sought advice from St. Kentigern, who asked him if he remembered the place where, during a hunting expedition in the height of summer he had tossed off his outer garments because of the heat. Rederech assented that he could remember the place and the occasion. "Go", said the Saint, "straightway to the place and thou shalt find the garment still perfect hanging over a bush of thorns, and below that thou shalt find brambles sufficient, still fresh and fit for the gathering".

Just as Kentigern had told him, the King found the brambles and, his honour saved, gave them to the Irishman, adding an invitation to stay and enjoy the hospitality of his court as long as he pleased. The harper was obviously impressed since he not only stayed on, but joined the followers of Kentigern in the service of God, renouncing his frivolous trade.

Pre-Christian religion and myth have been distilled and preserved in a unique way in many of the ballads of Lowland and Highland Scotland. Sometimes the pagan beliefs have become overlaid with a patchwork of 'civilization', and sometimes the mystical elements have been rationalized by later generations who did not accept, as a matter of course, the whole complicated pattern of supernatural, faery and magical superstition. The older threads, however, can be clearly seen, and the harp and its music and special powers of enchantment feature in many of the songs.

Mortal men or maidens were likely to succumb to the charms of faery harp-music. The evil Knight in some versions of 'Lady Isobel and the Elf Knight' begins his seduction of the earthly princess by playing his harp to bind the rest of the household in sleep.[9]

> "He's taen a harp into his hand
> He's harped them all asleep
> Except it was the King's daughter
> Who one wink couldna get."

The seer, Thomas of Ercildoune — True Tammas — as he is enticed into the arms of the Faery Queen is invited to:

> "Harp and carp wi' me, Tammas,
> Harp and carp alang wi' me
> But if ye daur tae kiss my lips
> Sure of your body I will be."[10]

The music of the harp is again used to seduce, but it is the physical contact with the faery which seals his fate.

Mermaids, whose power to lure seamen to their doom with their songs is well-known, are sometimes represented in Scottish carvings playing the harp.[11] The siren-like attractions of the mermaid, the enchanting nature of the instrument; the golden hair, the shining harp-strings; the similar actions of combing their locks or caressing the strings, may all have combined to account for the harp appearing as an attribute of the sea-maiden.

Certainly mermaids seem to have enjoyed harp music, as is illustrated by the Gaelic tale "A' Mhaighdean Mhara", collected in South Uist by J.F. Campbell.[12]

The King's daughter is trying to find her vanished husband. "And she took her harp to the shore and sat and played and the sea-maiden came up to listen, for sea-maidens are fonder of music than any other creatures, and when she saw the sea-maiden, she stopped. The sea-maiden said 'Play on'; but she said 'No, not till I see my man again'. So the the sea-maiden put up his head. (Who do you mean? Out of her mouth, to be sure. She had swallowed him.) She played again, and stopped, and then the sea-maiden put him up to the waist. Then she played again and stopped and the sea-maiden placed him on her palm. Then he thought of the falcon, and became one and flew on shore. But the sea-maiden took the wife". Happily, the King's daughter was eventually rescued in her turn.

Mortals often employed the magical effects of harping to their own advantage. A Scottish manuscript of around 1585 tells the story of King Orphius, a version of a medieval romance descended from the tale of Orpheus and Eurydice.[13] The Auchinleck manuscript version of the same story relates how, when the harpers of Britain heard this marvel, they made a lay thereof, which they called after the King, "Lay Orpheo".[14] In the Scottish version, King Orphius plays the harp rather than the Orphean lyre, the King of Faery takes the place of Pluto, and Faeryland supplants Tartarus. In search of his stolen queen, Orphius travels to Faeryland. This portion is missing in the Scottish manuscript fragments but in the Ashmolean manuscript version Orpheo, when challenged by the King to state his reasons for daring to enter his realm, states that, as a harper, it was his duty to offer his music to Kings and nobles if they desired to hear it.[15] His peerless harping so delights the otherwordly King that he is rewarded by the return of his lady. The Scottish version continues with an account of Orphius's return to his own country, in disguise, to test the loyalty of his steward and his nephew, left as regent. He gains access to the court by requesting in the name of Orphius (foir orphius your emis saik) to be allowed to play for the ruler. His nephew, impressed by his wild appearance, orders his own musicians to give way to him — and then recognises Orphius's harp. He demands to know how it came into his possession. When Orphius tells him that he found it by the bones of a man who had died in the wilderness, his nephew weeps, swearing that he will never be merry again. Having assured the regent's loyalty, Orphius reveals himself, and his nephew and subjects rejoice at the safe return of their King and Queen. Which version of the tale is earliest is difficult to tell, but it certainly was known in Scotland in the fragmentary ballad version sung in Shetland until the 20th century.[16]

The Gaelic Arthurian romance "Am Bron Binn" which has survived to the present day as a waulking song, also demonstrates the potency of the harp.[17] It tells how the King of Britain saw a beautiful woman in a dream. Enamoured, he sends Sior Bhoilidh on a quest to find her. After travelling through many dangers, Sior Bhoilidh discovers her, held prisoner by a giant. The maiden suggests to the ogre that he lay his head in her lap (a position which gives her the opportunity to cast a spell) and that she should play her harp to him.

> "An cuir thu do cheann air mo ghluin,
> 'S gun seinneam dhut ceol is cruit?"

Having lulled him to sleep, she and Sior Bhoilidh draw the giant's sword from his belt and cut off his head.

A harper's duties in a noble household did indeed include playing his master to sleep. This ability, though it might arise simply from the calming nature of the instrument and its music, led to the development of a superstitious awe of its effects on the listener's mind — to enchant, to bind in sleep, to seduce, to call spirits or fairies, or to raise the dead. Reality and folklore could become confused, as in the story of the death of King Fethelmak contained in the 'History and Chronicles of Scotland" written in 1527 by Hector Boece, a principal of King's College, Aberdeen. It was translated by John Bellenden (c. 1490–c. 1550), and gives this account of a royal murder.

> "King Fethelmak hapnit to pas to Carrik, quhare he was in gret sollicitude all that day. At even he went to his bed, and commandit ane harpar to sing ane soft sang, to draw him of of hevy materis on sleip. Als sone as he was fallin on sleip, the two Pichtis afore rehersit was convoyit be the harpar quhare he lay, and slew him sleipand in his bed, the thrid yeir of his regne. The wache hearand the granis of ane deand man, enterit haistely in the chalmer quhare the king was liand bullerand in his blude : incontinent, thay follit on his slayairis sa scharply, that thay war all tane; and quhen thay had confessit all the manner and circumstance of this treasonabill slauchter, thay was all punist maist cruelly to the deith, and drawin sindry with wild hors. This slauchter of Fethelmak hapnit in the fift yeir of Constantius, Emprioure."[18]

Although this passage is fiction, as was much of Boece's history, it seems to draw on some of the events surrounding the death of Angus Og of the Isles c. 1490 for some of the details. We will give an account of the actual murder later in the book.[19]

There often seems to have been a feeling of mistrust and suspicion of musicians who could wield this powerful art. Some tales depict harpers as threatening and opportunistic, as in "Ridere na Sgiatha Deirge" (The Knight of the Red Shield), a story from Colonsay.[20]

> "Then he (the Knight) was stretched out on the battlefield, blood and sinews and flesh in pain, but that he had whole bones. What should he see but a musical harper (cruitire ciuil) about the field. 'What art thou seeking?' said he to the harper. 'I am sure thou art wearied', said the harper. 'Come up and set thy head on this little hillock and sleep'. He went and he laid down; he drew up a snore, pretending that he was asleep, and on his soles he was brisk, swift and active. 'Thou art dreaming', said the harper. 'I am', said he. 'What sawest thou?', said the harper. 'A musical harper', he said 'drawing a rusty

old sword to take off my head'. Then he seized the harper, and he drove the brain in fiery shivers through the back of his head. Then he was under spells that he should not kill a musical harper for ever, but with his own harp. (Bha e'n seo fo gheasan nach marbhadh e cruitire ciuil gu brathach ach le a' chruit fhein.)"

In a Barra version of the same story, there called "The Son of the Green Spring by Valour", the hero is the son of the Red Knight.[21] He encounters many adventures and dangers, including armies of enchanted warriors, three giants with several heads, the sons of darkness, and a witch, and also "tri cruitairean na cruite bige", the three harpers of the little harps who could set the whole world asleep. When the harpers come, he gnaws his fingers till his mouth is full of blood in order to keep himself awake, and at last kills the magic harpers with their own harps.

This soporific effect of harp music was well-known, and is frequently mentioned in the ballads. "Glenkindie" can choose to play a sleeping spell which will affect the entire company except for his lady-love.[22]

> He harpit a fish out o saut water,
> Or water out o a stane,
> Or milk out o a maiden's breast,
> That bairn had never nane.

However, the charm is used against him when his serving man, in pursuit of the same lady, harps his master asleep in his turn. While in "The Harper of Lochmaben"[23] and its Aberdeenshire variant "The Harping Mannie",[24] the harper lulls the courtiers of King Henry to sleep thus giving him the opportunity to steal the King's favourite horse.

A more eerie use of harp music is demonstrated in the familiar motif of harping and weeping on a dead lover's grave in order to recall them to this world. In "The Twa Brothers", for example, Lady Margaret harps the small birds from the briars and her true love from the grave.[25]

The sound of the harp is often associated with otherworldly apparitions. A ghostly harper, said to have been murdered by the troops of the Duke of Montrose in pursuit of Campbell enemies, haunts the Castle of Inverary in Argyll. He appears most often to women visitors and has been seen, dressed in dark tartan, most frequently in the Blue Room of the Castle. His music, when it is heard, sometimes presages the death of one of the Dukes of Argyll, or sounds at the time of their funerals.[26]

Writing from his native Skye, to which he had returned as a tutor in Sleat and Dunvegan after studying in Edinburgh and Leyden, Martin Martin gives this account of supernatural beliefs in the Western Islands, c. 1695.[27]

"There were Spirits also that appear'd in the shape of Women, Horses,

Swine, Cats and some like fiery Balls which would follow Men in the Fields; but there has been but few instances of these for forty Years past.

These Spirits us'd also to form Sounds in the Air, resembling those of a Harp, Pipe, Crowing of a Cock, and of the grinding of Querns : and sometimes they have heard voices in the Air by Night singing Irish [i.e. Erse or Gaelic. Ed.] Songs; the words of which Songs some of my Acquaintance still retain. One of them resembled the Voice of a Woman who had died some time before, and the Song related to her State in the other World. The Accounts I had from Persons of as great Integrity as any are in the World."

One of the most striking ghostly appearances of the harp in balladry is contained in the fine song "The Twa Sisters".[28] The young maiden, wooed by a knight, is drowned by her jealous elder sister. Her body is found by a harper who in some versions makes a harp from her bones; in others he uses her finger bones for tuning-pins; and, in some, strings his harp with locks of her golden hair. At a feast, which is sometimes the wedding feast of the elder sister and the knight, the harp then magically accuses the murderess.

> "He leant his harp against a stane,
> And straught it began to play its lane.
>
> O yonder sits my faither the king
> And yonder sits my mither the queen.
>
> And yonder sits my brother Hugh
> And by him my William, sweet and true.
>
> And the lasten tune that the harp did play
> Was 'Wae tae my sister, wha drooned me'."

The motif of musical instruments being constructed from a tree which had either grown from a corpse, or had been told a guilty secret, is quite common, and a relic of pagan tree-cults. However, the imagery of a harp fashioned from bones, or hair used as harp-strings, is very potent. The soul was thought to reside in various parts of the body — frequently in the bones or hair.[29] A small finger bone, or even the cutting from a finger nail, or a lock of hair, which fell into the possession of an ill-wisher could give them power over its owner. In stringing his instrument with three locks of her hair, the harper had transferred the soul of the dead girl to it, and given it a musical voice with which to tell the truth.

The harp in Scottish folklore was thus an instrument not only of enchanting sweetness, but also of a chilling, dangerous beauty. Both sides of its character are represented fully in song and story. A delightful description of the power of its music is given in the account of a harping contest in the Islay tale of "The Slim, Swarthy Champion" (An Ceathairneach Caol, Riabhach). It takes place between an unlikely Scottish hero — the Champion — who has travelled to Ireland, and the finest harpers of that land.[30]

"What", said O'Domhnuill, "canst thou do, oh Champion? Surely, with all the distance thou hast travelled, thou canst do something".

"I was once", said he, "that I could play a harp".

"Well, then", said O'Domhnuill, "it is myself that have got the best harpers in the five-fifths of Eirinn, or in the bridge of the first of the people, such as — Ruairidh O'Cridheagan, Tormaid O'Giollagan, and Thaog O'Chuthag".

"Let's hear them playing", said the Champion.

> 'They could play tunes and "uirt" and "orgain",
> Trampling things, tightened strings,
> Warriors, heroes, and ghosts on their feet.
> Ghosts and spectres, illness and fever,
> They'd set in sound lasting sleep
> The whole great world,
> With the sweetness of the calming tunes
> That the harpers could play.'

The music did not please the Champion. He caught the harps, and he crushed them under his feet, and he set them on the fire, and made himself a warming, and a sound warming at them.

O'Domhnuill took much lofty rage that a man had come into his court who should do the like of this to the harps.

"My good man, I will not believe that thou art not taking anger", said the Champion.

"Well, then I am, if I did but know at whom I should let it out".

"Back, my good man; it was no easier for me to break thy harps than to make them whole again", said the Champion.

"I will give anything to have them made whole again", said O'Domhnuill.

"For two times five marks I will make thy harps as good as they were before", said the Champion.

"Thou shalt get that", said O'Domhnuill.

O'Domhnuill gave him the marks, and he seized on the fill of his two palms of the ashes, and he made a harp for Ruairidh O'Cridheagan; and one for Tormaid O'Giollagan; and one for Thaog O'Chuthag; and a great choral harp for himself (agus clarsach mhor, choirealach da fhe).

"Let's hear thy music", said O'Domhnuill.

"Thou shalt hear that, my good man", said the Champion.

The Champion began to play, and och! but he was the boy behind the harp.

'He could play tunes, and "uirt" and "orgain"
Trampling things, tightened strings,
Warriors, heroes, and ghosts on their feet,
Ghosts and souls, and sickness and fever,
That would set in sound lasting sleep
The whole great world
With the sweetness of the calming tunes
That the champion could play.'

'Sheinneadh e puirt, agus uirt, agus orgain,
Nitheanna tearmad; teudan tairteil;
Curaidhean, laoich, as aoig air an casan;
Aoig, as ainn, as galair, as fiabhrais.
'S gun cuirte 'nan sion sioram suain,
An saoghal mor gu leir,
Le binnead a' phuirt shiogaidh,
A sheinneadh an Ceathairneach.'

"Thou art melodious, oh Champion!" said O'Domhnuill.

When the harpers heard the Champion playing, they betook themselves to another chamber, and though he had followed on, still they had not come to the fore."

It has always been assumed that the Scots "followed on" the Irish in adopting the harp from the Gaelic incomers of the 6th century. On the contrary, we hope to show the possibility that the three-cornered harp may have been a native Scottish instrument. The historical facts behind the Scottish harps are no less mysterious and romantic in their way than are the myths.

2 SHAPES & STONES

"Clarsach bheag: tri-oiseanneach, is tri troighean anns an teud mhoir
Clarsach mhor: tri-oiseanneach, is tri troighean anns an teud bhig.
A little harp: three-cornered, and three feet in the big string
A big harp: three-cornered, and three feet in the little string."[1]

Before examining the earliest evidence of the harp in Scotland, it is useful to draw a brief sketch of the historical background of the country up to the 8th century when representations of the instrument first appear.

There have been many successive waves of settlers into Scotland in the eight thousand years during which it has been continuously populated. We have no idea as to the language of the inhabitants up to the Bronze Age, but around this time, or at least by the 4th century B.C., there is evidence of the arrival from the Continent of a people speaking a P-Celtic language. The Celtic peoples, who are thought to be of Indo-European origin, spread through Asia Minor across Europe, reaching the western fringes around 600 B.C. The Celts are divided linguistically into two groups. The Q-Celtic languages, which include Irish Gaelic, Scottish Gaelic and Manx, are so-called because they preserved the Indo-European "qu" in their speech; whereas in the P-Celtic languages, i.e. those related to British, Welsh, Cornish and Breton, this is transformed into "p". The other branch of the Celtic peoples, the Q-Celts, appear to have reached Ireland about the 6th century B.C. but did not make recorded incursions into Scotland until some centuries later.

The first maps of Scotland survive from the Roman historians of the 2nd century A.D., and these give the names of fourteen different tribes. We do not know if these were Celts or earlier peoples, but over the next three centuries they seem to have formed confederations which absorbed the smaller tribes. This creation of more unified groups was probably in response to the Roman invasions of the 1st and 4th centuries, and their attempts to subdue the native inhabitants.

By the 4th century A.D. there were two main peoples living in Scotland: the British, speaking a P-Celtic language which was an ancestor of Welsh; and the Picts, divided into two confederations of Northern and Southern Picts. The Pictish language has never yet been satisfactorily deciphered, but Kenneth Jackson suggests that it seems to have been basically a P-Celtic language containing an admixture of elements, including British. In his study of 11

'Archaeology and Language', Renfrew also cites the evidence of the Pictish personal names and place-names — that they "would not contradict the view that they represent a northern dialect of Brithonic, perhaps not unlike that spoken further south before the dominance of the Romans".[2]

The Q-Celts, the Gaelic-speaking Scots who eventually gave their name to the country, had made various forays from Ireland into the west coast of Scotland during Roman times. By the 6th century they were firmly entrenched in their kingdom of Dalriada — in Argyll and the neighbouring islands, and south-west Scotland. These Scotti were Christian, and their first monastic community in Scotland was established on the island of Iona by Columba and his followers in 563. Christianity had been introduced to those Britons living south of the Forth-Clyde valley through Roman influence from the 4th century onwards, but there is no firm evidence that it had spread to the Picts until Columba, it is said, converted King Bridei, son of Maelchon (554-584). Even after this only the southern Picts, that is those living to the south of the Mounth, the range of mountains which stretch across Scotland ending just south of Aberdeen, seem to have been fully converted, while the Picts in the north retained their pagan traditions.

In the 7th century the Angles of Northumbria advanced up into south-east Scotland to the Forth estuary and across it into Southern Pictland. Over the next few hundred years the balance of power frequently changed as these four peoples formed constantly shifting alliances and fought between themselves. The other main direction of influence was from the islands of the north and west — Orkney and Shetland and parts of the Hebrides, where Norse occupation was established by the 9th century, and was another important cultural factor.

The significant events which led to a more unified Scotland can be represented by the conversion of King Bridei by Columba; the battle of Nechtansmere in 685 when the Angles were defeated by the Picts; the subjugation of the Dalriadic Kingdom in 741 by the Pictish King Oengus, son of Fergus; and in 843 when Kenneth MacAlpin became king of both Picts and Scots by right of matrilinear succession to the Pictish throne, and by succeeding his father as ruler of the Scots.

By the 8th or 9th century, the time of the earliest iconographical representations, there seem to have been several different stringed instruments being played in Scotland and Ireland. There is academic debate whether these should be described as "lyres" or "harps". The two names seem to have been used indiscriminately by early writers and this, added to the fact that the sources of our information have sometimes been translated from Gaelic into Latin and subsequently into English, compounds the confusion. It also seems likely from the evidence of the sculpted stones that the instruments were changing and developing over hundreds of years and, in cases such as this, the nomenclature may remain static while the instrument alters — alternatively, an archaic name may be retained and applied to a "modernised" instrument. Many of the writers were also foreigners and were ignorant of musical terminology, particularly that of the alien culture that they were attempting to describe.

To clarify the words we use in discussing the instruments we will define them in 20th century terms, the principal difference being the relationship of string to soundboard.

A harp, therefore, has the strings running away from the soundboard, exposed on both sides. Harps are basic international instruments — it is almost inevitable that any culture which uses a bow and arrow will eventually invent some harp-like instrument. Many different forms exist in every Continent. We are using the word "harp" as a generic term in the early chapters to cover all the different forms of this instrument. The nomenclature for specific types of harps will be discussed in full at a later point.

A lyre has strings which run across the board, often over a bridge.[3]

The carved stone crosses of Ireland show instruments which seem to be either quadrangular harps or versions of the lyre with either an oblique slanting top, or a round top. The carving on the South Cross at Castledermot, which probably dates from the 9th century, includes a musician holding a quadrangular harp on his knee. Rimmer suggests that the soundbox of the harp appears to be the horizontal shape at its base, "a curved 'arm' or 'neck' ... rises from one end of the box and overhangs it.", and a forepillar joins the end of the curve to the horizontal box. It seems to have six strings, as do the quadrangular harps on the crosses at Ullard, and the North Cross at Castledermot. Rimmer relates these to the remains of the harp found in the Saxon ship burial at Sutton Hoo in England which also had pins for six strings, and suggests that they may have been similar instruments.[4]

A round-topped lyre is shown on the 10th century cross of the Scriptures at Clonmacnoise. The box of the lyre is clearly shown with two arms rising on either side of it, joined across the top by a curving string-holder. The strings run across the box from a central point at its base, fanning out to join the curving bar at the top. It, too, is played on the knee of a seated figure.

The musicians on another 10th century Cross, that of Muireadach, at Monasterboice include a seated figure playing what Rimmer describes as an "oblique topped lyre". The soundbox with two arms at the side can be seen, as well as what appears to be a bridge over which the strings run, to join a string-carrier which this time is angled from the top of the outer arm, down towards the arm nearest the player. A bird perches on top of the instrument (possibly representing the human soul), and a player of the triple-pipes also appears on this stone.

There are numerous examples of these stringed instruments on crosses throughout Ireland. What is striking, as Rimmer points out, is that "there are few which can be regarded as harps and no triangular-framed harps at all".

There are no representations on the Irish crosses of the triangular-framed harp as we know it. That is, a harp with a fore-pillar bracing the frame between string-carrier and box.[5]

In Scotland the situation is quite different. Triangular framed harps are found first in the Pictish carvings on the East Coast. Later they appear on the crosses of the Gaels of the Western Highlands and Islands. These early crosses were carved by the Irish Christian immigrant community in Iona. They predate the crosses in Ireland, and early examples illustrate instruments similar to those on the Irish stones. On St. Oran's Cross, which probably dates from the mid to late 8th century, a figure is shown seated on the ground, again playing a quadrangular harp, a vertical quadrilateral with two rounded angles. The other figures on this side of the cross are too worn to draw any conclusions about the story which was being illustrated unless the musician represents an isolated "David" figure.

St. Martin's Cross, also on Iona, is fortunately much better preserved, and here too is found a harper playing on an instrument of the same type — quadrilateral with two rounded angles. He appears to be seated on a small stool with his legs out-stretched, and faces a player of multiple pipes. The stone is too worn to distinguish whether they are double or triple pipes. They apparently represent David and his musicians, and the stone dates from the second half of the 8th century.

The Royal Commission on the Ancient and Historical Monuments of Scotland (1982) puts forward the theory that the differing and developing methods of construction of the several Iona crosses would suggest that they are "an early and experimental group, not derived from any established tradition of stone-carving." While the decoration itself, though using subject matter and a basic style of carving which are similar to Irish crosses, also shows other features, such as the lack of frames dividing the scenes — "a Pictish rather than an Irish characteristic". From this we might infer that Irish immigrant sculptors may have been training native craftsmen in their skills while allowing them some freedom to express their own traditions in the decoration. These two crosses include the only depictions of quadrangular harps in Scotland.[6]

All the other iconographic representations of stringed instruments on Picto-Scottish stones are of a three-cornered, triangular-framed harp. Most of these occur in areas which were former Pictish strongholds and thus subject to primary or residual Pictish cultural influence, and most are in eastern Scotland in the territory associated with the Southern Picts. They are likely to date from about the 8th-10th century and do not seem to pre-date the period of the introduction of Christianity to any great extent. Having become Christianised, it appears that the people who carved the stones were using the harp as a symbol of their faith, either in association with Biblical figures or, unlike the Irish carvings, simply as an independent motif.

Pictish carved stones seem to have been erected from about the 6th century to the 9th century. Anthony Jackson in his fascinating study "The Symbol Stones of Scotland" suggests that they have a genealogical and territorial significance, and tabulates them into three classes — Class I inscribed only with Pictish symbols; Class II which show the Pictish symbols and figures; and Class III which depict mainly figures. Class II and III stones date from the late 8th and 9th centuries onwards and are the stones which feature the harp in their carvings.

The earliest may be the 8th or 9th century stone at Nigg in Easter Ross where the harp is used simply as a "David" symbol, without a player. This is clearly a three-cornered harp with a rounded curve between neck and soundbox, and a straight forepillar. The box is deep at the base and tapers towards the neck. There is no sign of a joint between the box and the string-carrier, which stands out from the box at more or less 90°. There appear to be seven strings carved on it.

A similar harp is depicted on a 9th or 10th century stone at Monifeith in Angus, this time being played by a harper who sits on a chair with the harp

Stone at Dupplin

Stone at Aldbar

resting on the ground by his feet. The top of the forepillar, which may be slightly curved, is level with the crown of his head. It is a three-cornered harp, apparently of fairly light construction, with eight strings shown.

On the stone at Dupplin in Perthshire, which probably dates from the 10th century, a very similar harper plays a harp which closely resembles that on the Nigg slab. Again he is seated, playing a large harp which is set between his feet on the floor. The forepillar rises slightly higher than the head of the figure. The pillar, which is slender, shows a very slight curve towards the top. The harp is represented as having eight strings, and appears to be played on the left shoulder, where the rounded curve as the box meets the string-carrier at the neck can be clearly seen. The chair or throne on which the harper sits has a carved back and this, added to the fact that chairs were not a common item of furniture but were reserved for those of high rank, may signify that this is a royal "David" figure, or may indicate the esteem in which harpers were held.

The harp which is carved as a "David" symbol on a stone (9th or 10th century) at Aldbar, in Angus, has much the same proportions as those at Nigg and Dupplin but appears to be of rather sturdier construction. The joint between soundbox and neck is a sharp 90° angle. The straight string-carrier projects slightly beyond the forepillar, which has a definite shallow curve. It is not possible to make a guess as to the number of strings due to the weathering of the stone.

At Ardchattan, in Argyll, an early Christian cross-slab shows a vertical row of three ecclesiastics, including a harper. This stone was unfortunately damaged when it was retrimmed at a later date, possibly for use as the lid of a coffin. The forepillar of the harp is missing but the box and string-carrier look much like those on the Nigg and Dupplin stones, while the harper is in a similar pose to that on the stone at Monifieth. This harper, though, appears to be sitting on the ground rather than on a chair. Below the harper another musician plays triple-pipes, while yet another may be playing some kind of horn or, it has been suggested, may hold a crown.

The triple-pipe occurs again in conjunction with the harp on a 10th century Picto-Scottish stone at Lethendy in Perthshire. The harp in this instance is triangular with a straight forepillar. Both musicians are depicted as standing. The piper is similar to those on other Scottish stones, and also to some in Ireland. He fingers the two outer pipes, while the centre pipe appears to act as a drone. This resembles the Sardinian Launeddas, which was probably a precursor of the bagpipe. The appearance of the triple-pipes on carvings which also feature the harp may be of significance, which we will discuss later in the chapter.

At this point there are still no triangular-framed harps to be seen in any of the Irish carvings. Some of the illuminated manuscripts which were produced in monasteries founded on the Continent by Irish monks do indeed illustrate harps, but these appear to be of the Middle Eastern-influenced angle-harp type

without a pillar. None of the manuscript illustrations show a harp with a
clearly defined forepillar until the 11th
century.[7]

The first undoubted example of a
triangular-framed harp in Ireland is
found on the Shrine of St. Mogue,
which probably dates from the 11th
century. Another harper appears on
the Shrine of St. Patrick's Tooth,
dating from around 1376. These cas-
kets were reliquaries, which demonstrate
the skills of the Irish craftsmen working in precious metals. On the Shrine
of St. Mogue a robed, bearded figure
plays a triangular-framed harp set on
his knee and resting on his left shoulder. It has a light soundbox, a narrow
neck leading to a slightly curved string-
carrier, and a slender but T-shaped
pillar. It appears to have 9-10 strings,
though 10-11 tuning pins are shown.
Above it we see again a little bird like
that on Muireadach's Cross.

The harp on the cover of Fiacail
Padraig (The Shrine of St. Patrick's
Tooth) is also played by a seated, robed

Stone at Lethendy

figure. It has a curved forepillar, though this one has no clearly visible T-
shaped formation. The soundbox is shallow, with a projecting block at the base,
and the harmonic curve seems less substantial than that on the St. Mogue's
harp. The instrument is shown with 23 strings and is played on the musicians's
left shoulder, with both of his hands clearly visible.

The earliest Irish triangular-framed harp carved in stone may possibly date
from the late 12th century. It occurs on a frieze in Ardmore Cathedral, Co.
Waterford. A figure seated on a throne faces two women who rush towards
him, one of them holding a baby — the judgement of Solomon. At the back
stands a harper who is obviously the King's court musician. He holds a small
triangular harp, but the scale of the sculpture and the weathering of the stone
make it difficult to distinguish any details.

This instrument appears similar to one on the capital of a pillar in the south
choir of Iona Abbey. It shows an angel playing on a triangular-framed harp
for the Virgin Mary. The harp is small, with a curved forepillar, but the string-
carrier is a straight pin-bar. There is no clearly defined soundbox. If the

instrument is more than a product of artistic licence, it is possibly an example of the small harps said to have been carried at their belts by early churchmen. The Iona carving is probably the work of Donald O'Brolchan whose signature is found elsewhere in the sculpture. He was apparently a craftsman of Irish descent working in the Abbey during the 15th century.

Reilig Odhrain, also in Iona, once contained a 14th–15th century grave-slab — now in the Abbey Museum — which shows a mounted horseman and a harper who is seated on what appears to be a small boat. The carving of the harp that he is playing is too worn to give more detail than the outline shape of the instrument, which has a strongly bowed forepillar and a pronounced harmonic curve. Surviving harps do exist from this period, and this slab shows a harp which is consistent with these in its basic size and shape.[8]

Similarity to an existing harp is striking in the 16th century carving found in Jerpoint Abbey, near Kilkenny in Ireland. It is the effigy of a man with a small harp lying at his side. This instrument bears a close resemblance to the Lamont Harp, which we will describe in detail later in this book. The tomb appears to be that of a William O'Banahan or O'Habrahan, according to Armstrong, or O'Houlahan, according to Canon Cerrigan, but the inscription is too worn to decipher much detail. The harper almost certainly would have served the Butler Earls of Ormond. The Butlers were consistently loyal to the English interest, and unlike other Anglo-Irish families, were not Gaelicised to any great extent. Only in 1515, when the succession moved sideways to the branch represented by Sir Piers Butler did the Ormond Earldom move closer to native Gaelic influences. It is likely that the harper's tomb dates from this period. It is unique in Ireland.[9]

The last stones which are carved with harps of this period are found in Scotland. One, at Kilchoan burying ground at Glasvin in Skye, is badly worn. It was reset, upside down, as a headstone to a modern grave but has now been restored to an upright position. The upper portion shows a kneeling man playing a relatively large harp with a sharp peak at the junction of the forepillar with harmonic curve. The rest of the slab shows a sword, a long stemmed chalice and the front view of a mitred ecclesiastic holding a crozier. Glasvin was in the area held by the MacLeods of Harris and Dunvegan, but the identity of the owner of the slab is unknown. The depiction of a religious figure is noteworthy because many churchmen of the period did indeed maintain a harper.[10]

The most interesting Scottish carving of a harp, dated to the end of the 15th century, is that on a grave slab at Keills in Knapdale. Most of the detail of the carving is poorly defined, except for the soundbox which showed, clearly, ornamentation which is closely similar to that on the Trinity College and Queen Mary Harps. The worn inscription on the stone indicates that it commemorates a man whose name is no longer readable and his son Allan, who had the slab made. It has been suggested that Allan and his father were members of a family of hereditary harpers attached to the MacNeils of Gigha,

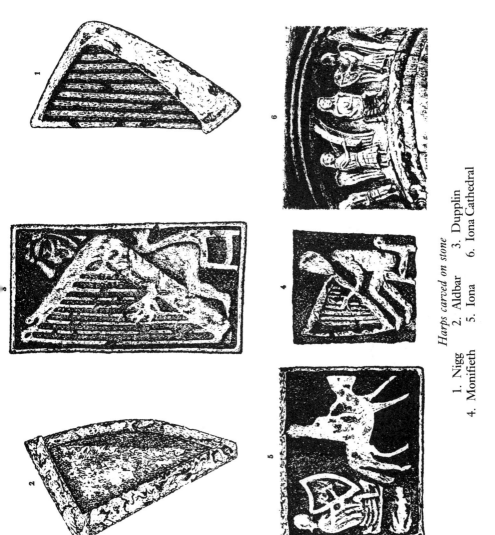

Harps carved on stone

1. Nigg   2. Aldbar   3. Dupplin
4. Monifieth   5. Iona   6. Iona Cathedral

at that time one of the principal families in the area. The slab was drawn by T.P. White in 1873 when it was in a much better condition, but now the carving is quite worn and the finer details of the strings and soundbox decoration are no longer visible. It has been suggested by Steer and Bannerman that the slab still lies in its original position inside the church, which has now been re-roofed to protect the collection of grave slabs from further weathering.[11]

These carvings represent all the known, clearly recognisable, examples of triangular-framed harps (though there are other less well preserved Scottish stones which may include them) which exist in Scotland and in Ireland between the 8th and 15th centuries.

It appears that in Scotland the first carving in stone of figures with musical instruments was instigated by Irish immigrants, either because they had the necessary artistic skills or because they made the concept of representing these elements acceptable, or both. Carving on stone of formalised and abstract symbols had been a tradition amongst the Pictish tribes for at least two centuries before figurative carvings appear.

The earliest examples of triangular-framed harps occur on stones which were furthest from the Scottish centres of Christianity and Irish influence. These are in areas which were under Pictish rule, particularly in Southern Pictland, and contain strong pagan, i.e. native Pictish, elements. It is possible that in this large triangular-framed harp the sculptors were representing, not an imported accessory of Christianity, but an instrument which already existed in their own native culture.

It is unlikely that this harp could have been imported from elsewhere through trade links since no recognisable triangular-framed harps are depicted or found in Europe, or indeed anywhere else in the world, before these 8th-9th century Picto-Scottish carvings. We suggest that the Irish sculptors, who had been brought to Iona, trained or were an example to native craftsmen who spread their skills across the country. As they did so, they adapted elements of their own Pictish culture to Christian symbolism, including the indigenous harp. Had this been a native Irish instrument, it would seem extraordinary that there are no representations of it on Irish stones of the early period and, even then, not until 300-400 years later than the first Scottish examples. It cannot simply be that it was regarded as a pagan instrument because the lyre or tiompain features even more strongly in the pre-Christian myths and legends of Ireland, and yet occurs frequently there on the Christian crosses. In Scotland, however, it appears that the introduction of Christian iconography added considerably to the vocabulary of the existing Pictish artists, and to the range of subject matter that they felt it appropriate to portray. The triangular-framed harp therefore appears to have its origins in Scotland, amongst the Picts, and possibly also among the other P-Celtic-speaking British tribes of Scotland.

The other instrument which is found on the stones, the triple-pipes, often

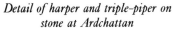
*Detail of harper and triple-piper on
stone at Ardchattan*

Stone at Kilchoan

appears alongside the quadrangular stringed instruments on Irish crosses. In
Scotland it only occurs on three stones: one at Iona with the quadrangular harp;
one in Argyll; and one in Perthshire — in both of the latter cases along with
a triangular-framed harp. The frequency of Irish examples and the western
orientation of the Scottish stones with this combination of musicians suggests
that the triple-pipe was likely to have been Irish, and spread into Scotland from
the west coast. The Scottish stones which show the two instruments may
represent areas where the Christian Irish influence overlapped with the native
Pictish culture.

Does the iconographical evidence of the stones give us any information
about the nature of the triangular-framed harp and its construction?

The earliest Picto-Scottish stones show an instrument which reaches from
the floor to the top of the head of a seated player. This is considerably larger
than any of the early Irish representations, none of which appear to be played
with the harp resting on the ground but instead are played on the knee, or even
held by a standing player. The early Scottish examples are fairly consistent in
showing a slender forepillar which is straight or only very slightly curved; a
strong straight string-carrier which comes from the top of the soundbox
without a narrowing at the neck and in most cases without an apparent joint;

and a soundbox which in some cases is distinctly deeper from front to back at the base.

Irish depictions, and the later Scottish ones, show an instrument which is somewhat smaller (in most cases very much smaller), with a strongly bowed T-shaped pillar, a string-carrier which is usually a harmonic curve, and a box which often narrows from front to back at the base, or at least remains the same depth, while widening considerably across the soundboard.

Irish harps commonly had a one-piece soundboard and box carved out of a solid block of wood which was hollowed out from the back. The strong curved pillar developed a T-shaped section at the mid-point to add extra strength. The heavy triangular-section harmonic curve also usually had a metal band along each side which not only acted as a brace, but also helped to hold the tuning pins firmly against the pull of the strings.

We know from early Irish literary references that metal strings were habitually used on all their stringed instruments. There is no mention of any other material being used to string either harps or tiompans. The compact, sturdy construction of the existing early harps was necessary to withstand the pull of the metal strings, which was considerable. The tension of the strings in fact held the joints at each of the three corners of the harp together without the use of glue. Even so, few harps have survived simply because the tension of a metal-strung harp kept up to pitch will eventually break the soundboard through fatigue. Despite their robust construction, the existing examples still show how the belly of the harp was raised markedly by the pull of the metal strings.

The Picto-Scottish examples, as far as we can judge from the stones, do not appear to show this characteristic shape and may therefore have been constructed in a different manner. The relationship between the top of the box and the string-carrier on stones like those at Nigg and Dupplin in fact suggests a one-piece construction — that the maker would have chosen a log of wood with a branch growing from it at the appropriate angle, and carved the string-bar and box all in one. There is clearly a joint, on all the harps, at the extremities of the pillar. If a harp were to be carved in this fashion it would probably be easier and more logical to hollow out the soundbox from the front.

In the history of musical instruments it is very uncharacteristic for an instrument to shrink! Almost invariably, over centuries, the succeeding versions of any instrument will tend to grow in size in response to improvement in techniques and materials, and to the demands of ambitious performers. It would be most unlikely for a floor-standing harp to first shrink to the size where it could be played on the knee in the 12th to 15th centuries, and then to grow again in the 16th century until it was more or less back at its original dimensions. A marked lessening in the size of the instrument is likely to be due to substantial change in the needs that the construction of the instrument has to fulfill — for example, a change from light to heavy tension stringing.

It is possible, of course, that different artists were depicting large and small versions of the same instrument, which existed contemporaneously. However, it is clear that if the Picto-Scottish stones are accurate representations of instruments of that period, they simply do not appear to be substantial enough to withstand the pull of metal strings. A harp as large as those shown on the stones at Dupplin or Monifieth would need to have been of massive construction to sustain such tension.

It seems likely, therefore, that a large Pictish harp would not only be differently constructed, but would have been strung with a material other than the metal wire of the Irish harps. What, then, might have been used? The other early harps to be found in the British Isles were in Wales. They are mentioned in the Llyfr Du o'r Waun Manuscript which records the ancient Welsh Laws. The manuscript was written down in about the second quarter of the 13th century, but the Laws that it contains are probably considerably older. Several of these Laws refer to the harp and, in every case, the word 'telyn' is used — the word which still commonly means 'harp' in Wales today.

The word is interesting because it appears to derive, not from the root 'ten', meaning 'tension', as has sometimes been suggested, but from an Irish word 'teilinn' meaning the humming or buzzing of a bee. This word survives today in Scottish Gaelic as 'seilleann' — a bumble bee. Eugene O'Curry in his work "On the Manners and Customs of the Ancient Irish" (1873) put forward this explanation and it is convincingly supported in his paper "Telyn a Chrwth", by A. O. H. Jarman.[12] The legend which is told about the origin of the expression is that it was originally a derisive nickname given in contempt to the Welsh instrument by the Irish harpers brought to Wales by Gruffydd ap Cynan in 1075. They were comparing their own harps favourably with those of the Welsh. All the early Irish stringed instruments were strung with metal, giving a clear resonant note which was apparently quite different from the tone of the Welsh harps. These, we are told on numerous occasions, were strung with horsehair, and produced a low, buzzing sound. There are references throughout early Welsh literature to 'horsehair harps' to 'glossy hair' or to 'black hair'. The horsehair was apparently twisted or braided to form the strings. Research by Dr. Robert Beck suggested that the horses depicted on the Pictish stones are of the breed now known as Eriskay ponies. According to Beck, these were the horses ridden by the Picts at the Battle of Nechtansmere. The Eriskay pony is the last survivor of these native ponies of the Highlands and the Hebrides. They stand between 12 and 13 hands high, with a dense coat, usually black or grey, and a long, thick mane and tail, from which there would have been no difficulty in procuring single hairs of at least 40" in length. It would thus have been possible to twist even the longest strings on a harp of the size indicated on the Pictish stones from a number of single strands. Experiments by Robert Evans show that one particular method of twisting the horsehairs, similar to rope-making, gives a very pleasing note, very comparable to that of a gut string, when used with a light wooden sound-board. The tone is quite clear, suggesting that 'humming' might be a better description of the sound, or perhaps bray-pins were sometimes used, which indeed change the tone to an angry buzz.

Andrew Borde, an Englishman, who published a book in 1547 or 1548, which described many different countries and nations, introduced each section with a little poem in which he makes a native of each country describe his homeland. The Welshman says:

> "If I have my Harp I care for no more.
> It is my Treasure, I keep it in store;
> For, my Harp is made of a good mare's skin;
> The strings be of horsehair, it maketh a good din.
> My song, and my voice, and my Harp doth agree,
> Much like the buzzing of a humble bee:
> Yet in my country I do make pastime
> In telling of prophecy, which be not in rhyme".

If Borde was not aware of the derivation of the word 'telyn', and it is unlikely that he would be, this description is an extraordinary confirmation that the 'buzzing' effect of the horsehair strings was as obvious to this English onlooker as it had been to the Irish incomers who had given the Welsh harp its apparently mocking name. Borde's mention of the harp 'made of a good mare's skin' concurs with other descriptions of Welsh harps as having soundboards of leather. Edward Jones writes "It seems also that the body of some of the ancient Harps were covered with leather; (somewhat similar, perhaps, to the ancient Corwgl, Coracle or British boats, which were made of hoops and covered with horses' hides, as mentioned by Caesar and Pliny.) I am informed by Mr. William Williams that, when a boy, he had an old leather harp which he used to play upon. The body of it was hollowed, or scooped out of a piece of wood and covered over with an ox's skin, which was sewed extremely tight at the back; and the pegs, which the strings were screwed with, were made of bone, or of ivory".[13]

Leather soundboards are common on instruments throughout the world, and could indeed be a suitable match for horsehair strings. William William's harp sounds exactly like the one described in a poem by Sion Phylip which dates from about 1580:

> "The sweet polished trunk, fair and light the load,
> the form of a heart, between the breast and the arm;
> a tone and sound the strings produce:

To effect this tone, four things concur;
wood, skin and hair, lovely and complete the gift;
which with bone must be tightened".

Again, the harp apparently has a hollow wooden soundbox with a leather soundboard stretched across it, lightly strung with horsehair from bone tuning pins (or perhaps a bone tuning key was used).

Another poem by the 14th century Welsh poet is scathing in its criticism of a new harp, apparently Irish, in which he particularly detests its curving shape — its 'form of a bent bow', its 'bow and horrible stooping thing' and its 'bent column', which indeed sounds much like a description of the Irish harps of this period. The poet urges young musicians to seek out the horsehair harp, as in the days of their ancestors — a noble instrument. Confusingly, the poem seems to suggest that both gut and metal strings were used on the new harp, played with the nails (which technique is most often used nowadays on wire strings but in early music was also used with gut), and that it was covered with leather. It has been suggested that this particular harp was a hybrid instrument. However it may be that the poem intended to describe *two* new foreign imports — one a metal strung harp brought into Wales by the Gaels, and the other a gut strung harp of the type used in England by the Middle Ages. Both cultures were exerting pressure on the native Welsh traditions at this period. Gut strings were certainly used on some instruments in Wales by the 14th century, but were obviously regarded by traditionalists as much inferior to horsehair.

What we can gather from the literary references is that these old Welsh harps were wooden. Some of them had a soundbox which may have been hollowed out from the front, with a leather skin stretched across it, secured probably with sewing or lacing of some kind. (Strikingly, some Scottish grave slabs and existing instruments show what appears to have been a traditional pattern of criss-cross lines decorating the sound box of the harps.) Welsh harps apparently had straight forepillars and bone tuning pins, (as mentioned in the ballad of "The Twa Sisters"). They were strung with twisted horsehair, which produced a softer tone with shorter decay than the ringing metal strings of the Gaelic harp.

Where did these harps come from? As Osian Ellis points out "Early Welsh literature is noticably reticent in references to the harp and crwth, which is surprising in view of their later popularity".[14] Some scholars have suggested that the harp was introduced into Wales from England. But there is no sign of a triangular-framed harp in England before 900-950, the probable date of the mythological poems in which the name 'telyn' occurs. The Laws are probably equally old and, though both they and the myths were not written down until around 1200, they specifically mention how the younger musicans were abandoning the older horsehair harps. This would lead one to believe that the instrument was ancient, even by the end of the 12th century. The word 'telein' is also included in a Cornish vocabulary collected about 1100, and may have been borrowed from Welsh. For the name to be widespread in Wales by 1200, and to have spread beyond it by the previous century, suggests that the instrument must have been in established use for a long time. It seems unlikely that the contemptuous nickname, said to have been given to it by Gruffydd ap Cynan's men in 1075, should have been in use as the normal (and formal) expression for the harp such a short time afterwards. Clearly, the instrument, and its name, must have arrived in Wales in some earlier period. Here, once again, we find strong links with the Picts and the other British tribes of southern Scotland.

During the late 4th and early 5th centuries many of the tribes of Britain were on the move. The Northern Picts spread north through Caithness and Sutherland into Orkney and Shetland, and west as far as Skye. The Southern Picts consolidated their territory from the Mounth down through Forfar into Fife, and their influence, at least, may have extended as far south as Hadrian's Wall. Isolated examples of Pictish stones can be found from Lothian and Roxburghshire to Galloway. The Caledonii, who seem to have been a confederation of smaller tribes, and the Maeatae skirmished in the Central Highlands and across to Buchan and the Mearns. The Novantae held Nithsdale and Galloway, and the Selgovae the mid and upper Tweed Valley. The Romans had found some allies — the effects of Christianity were spreading from the south, and from St. Ninian's community in Whithorn during the 5th century. These allies were the Damnonii of Upper Clydesdale and Ayrshire, and the Votadini, whose territory lay in the south east of Scotland, from Clackmannan to Northumberland. All these tribes are likely to have spoken dialects of the P-Celtic Brittonic language.[15]

The Irish, too, were sending waves of settlers to the mainland of Britain, first from east central Ireland to the Lleyn peninsula of Caernarvonshire in North Wales. These invasions were probably in response to gaps in the Roman defences left by Maximus. Most of the Deisi tribe and part of the Ui Liathain also moved from southern Ireland into south west Wales where they founded a local Irish dynasty which continued for some centuries. In the late 5th and the 6th century, the Irish settlers in Pembroke and Carmarthen also spread into east Cornwall, north Devon and parts of Somerset.

Perhaps to counterbalance the influx of Irish immigrants in Caernarvonshire, the Votadini, possibly acting as 'foederatio' of the Romans, were persuaded to migrate en masse from southern Scotland to North Wales. There are many legends about these people and their leader, Cunedda, who is said by some to have been a Pict, by others that he may have been of Romano-British descent. Tradition has it that they expelled the Ui Liathain and Deisi from south Wales, but the archaeological evidence is really only strong enough to connect them with the re-occupation of some north Wales hill-forts at this time.

Other descendants of these Votadini — the Gododdin — remained in Scotland, occupying territory in Lothian and Berwickshire and at least as far south as the Wear, if not to the Tees. During the 6th century the Gododdin were, like other British tribes, pushed north and west by the encroaching Angles of the Bernician and Deiran kingdoms of North East England. A poem in Old Welsh, or Brittonic, was composed about the year 600 at the Gododdin court in Edinburgh by the poet Aneirin. It commemorates the desperate and ill-fated battle between British tribes and Angles in an attempt to contain the spread of Anglian power. Aneirin relates how Mynyddog of Gododdin met his enemies at the head of an army which included British tribesmen from Ayrshire, from Elmet (or Elfed in Yorkshire) and some from 'beyond Bannog' who would have been Pictish.[16] The site of the battle, named as Catraeth, was suggested by philologists to be Catterick in the North of England. However, recent examination of the internal evidence of the poem makes it clear that the confrontation must have taken place within about sixty miles of Edinburgh — possibly near Loch Macatterick in Carrick. McDiarmaid points out that this is beside the fortified Loch Doon and the Hooden hills — possibly the hill "Hyddwn" in the poem. Almost all Mynyddog's warriors, outnumbered many times by their enemies, are said to have fallen in the battle. The odds against the British, described as 10,000 against 300, were no doubt exaggerated for heroic effect, but the defeat described by Aneirin was certainly a turning point in the balance of power between Angle and Briton. The word used for "minstrel" in the Gododdin poem is "Gerdawr" — the root of "cerddor", which is still used in that sense in Welsh today. In Scottish Gaelic, the word as "ceard" now normally means a "craftsman, smith or tinker", but W. Matheson points out that it is also used specifically to describe a "harper", in folk tales which contain poetic "runs". These "runs" tend to preserve formulae of some antiquity because they persist in the memory. The run describing poet, bard and harper is usually "fili, bard is clarsair",[17] but also occurs as "bard is ceard is fili".[18] This might indeed demonstrate the entry of a Pictish word into both languages.

Yet another series of poetic fragments found in the Historia Brittanica, and some poems ascribed to Taliesin, tell of the fall of the British Kingdom of Urien of Rheged. This lay between Yorkshire and Galloway and eventually passed into Northumbrian hands, apparently through a combination of inter-dynastic marriages and the aggressive leadership of Ecgfrith of Northumbria. He met his death in 685 at the hands of the Southern Picts as he tried to push his frontier still further north.

Between 682- 709 mercenary bands of British warriors appear in the Annals of Ulster, serving first in Antrim, then as allies of the Ulstermen in Co. Louth, and subsequently in the army of Cellach Cualann, King of Leinster. The progress of these mercenaries, from the north down the east coast of Ireland, implies that they crossed the Irish Sea as a result of major political disturbance in northern Britain. Smyth suggests that these warbands represented the dispossessed elite warriors and nobles of the Kingdom of Rheged. The fact that in 684 Ecgfrith launched an attack on eastern Ireland, where his exiled brother had also sought safety, would serve to confirm that the Northumbrians saw the area as a base for their enemies and a source of potential danger. Their hold over the British who remained in Galloway was not complete, or very strong. It was not until about 731 that they felt sufficiently secure to appoint a Northumbrian bishop to the diocese of Whithorn.[19]

Christianity had been introduced into south west Scotland, at least as early as the 5th century, through the community at Whithorn which was said to have been founded by Ninian. It had spread throughout Strathclyde, Southern Pictland and the territory of the Gododdin, who indeed are portrayed in the poem as Christian heroes attacking a heathen Anglian foe. Christian cemeteries dating from the early 6th century onwards are distributed from Lothian and coastal Fife to southern Angus. The long cist sarcophagi found in these have antecedents in the pre-Christian burials of the Celtic Iron Age, and also relate to the trench-like graves in the cemeteries of the Galloway and Carlisle region. The cult of St. Kentigern, whose ancestry is said to stem from a royal house of the Votadini, flourished throughout Fife, Clackmannan and south east Pictland, as well as the Forth-Clyde valley. The evidence of written records, archaeology and place-names show that the influence of this older Celtic Christian Church remained strong in these areas. Indeed, there was some antagonism between it and the Roman Christianity which the Angles attempted to impose on their newly conquered territories.[20]

A fundamental cultural unity existed between the southern Picts, Strath-clyde and the Gododdin, which resisted Anglian influence throughout the Dark Ages until their absorption into the Kingdom of Scotland. Briton and Pict united effectively to repulse the Dal Riatan Scots in 642, and the Angles at Nechtansmere in 685. Overlordship of this confederacy appears to have been held by the kings of Strathclyde, a dynasty which came to an end only with the expulsion of Eochaid in 889, after which the succession passed to the Scottish royal line. This assumption of power by the Gaelic-speaking Scots marked the end of British culture in southern Scotland.

It is to this period that Jackson dates the transmission of the earliest extant Brittonic poetry, including the "Gododdin", some in manuscript form, and most of the oldest historical traditions, from southern Scotland to Wales. That these had been preserved in Strathclyde is evidenced by the significant inclusion in the "Gododdin", which otherwise deals with historical events of the Lothians around 600, of a single verse of Strathclyde poetry relating the victory of Owen of Strathclyde over Domnall Brecc in Strathcarron in 642.[21] The Welsh "Chronicle of the Princes" (Brut y Tywyssiogion) tells us that in 890 a group of the Men of Strathclyde were forced "to depart from their country and to go to Gwynedd". The Chronicle says that this was because they refused to unite with the English, but it seems likely that the pressure came not only from the Angles, but from the newly established Scots-Gaelic ascendancy. The British nobles and warriors of Strathclyde, and their learned followers, could not co-exist with a Scottish ruling class, or be absorbed into their service as could the lower orders of British society. As we see, for example in the writings of the 9th century Welsh historian, Nennius, the scholars of Strathclyde had had continuous contact with their counterparts in Wales for hundreds of years. Their migration to Wales would therefore have been in response to the danger that they posed as potential claimants to the royal line and the loyalty of their tribesmen. Their choice of refuge was due not only to ties of blood and kinship, but to the essential cultural unity which existed between their peoples.[22] Along with their traditions of poetry and literature, it is to be expected that the Britons would also have carried with them their music.

With the aid of the archaeological, iconographical, historical and literary evidence, we can suggest some conclusions about the origins of the harps of the Celtic nations. The triangular-framed harp appears to have its origins in Pictland, and possibly also amongst the other British tribes of Scotland. Unequivocal representations of the instrument feature on Picto-Scottish stones at least 200-300 years before they are found elsewhere in Europe, or indeed anywhere else in the world.

It may be useful at this point to summarise the main points of the evidence that these stones offer us.

1. All the early stones in Scotland, except two, depict triangular-framed harps.
2. The two exceptions, which depict quadrangular harps, occur in an Irish immigrant community and date from the 8th century.
3. All the many early Irish stones depict quadrangular instruments — there are no triangular-framed harps represented.
4. The earliest triangular-framed harps on Picto-Scottish stones occur from the 8th century.
5. The first Irish depictions of triangular-framed harps occur, on metal, on a reliquary in the late 11th century, on stone in the late 12th century.
6. The two Scottish examples of the quadrangular harp are on the west coast.
7. The distribution of the other six early Picto-Scottish stones showing triangular-framed harps is strongly biased towards the east side of the country.
8. Between the 8th and the 15th centuries there are two depictions of quadrangular harps on stones in Scotland.
9. Between the 8th and the 15th centuries there are 10 (13) depictions of triangular-framed harps on stones in Scotland.

10.   Between the 8th and the 15th centuries there are many quadrangular stringed instruments depicted on stones in Ireland.

11.   Between the 11th and 15th centuries there are two triangular-framed harps depicted on stones in Ireland and two on reliquaries.

12.   The first representations in Scotland are of large, lightly built instruments, apparently floor standing.

13.   The later instruments in both Scotland and Ireland appear to be smaller and more strongly constructed.

The general picture appears to be of a large, floor-standing instrument which may well have been strung with horsehair. These harps were probably introduced to Wales by British tribesmen during the waves of migration between the 6th and 9th centuries, when the earliest Brittonic poetry that survives was also transmitted from southern Scotland to Wales. There, the harps were given the mocking nickname of "buzzing thing" by Irish settlers, a name which was adopted (perhaps with some humour!) by the Welsh. Meanwhile, between the 8th and 10th centuries, the Irish had come in contact with the Pictish harp through their Christian communities in the west of Scotland, and perhaps also through the exiled mercenary warriors who fled across the Irish Sea from the failing British Kingdoms of south west Scotland. The size and construction of the triangular harp was altered in order to carry their customary metal strings, and it became what we recognise today as the Gaelic harp, the "cruit" or "clarsach".

3 CLARSACH and CRUIT

Siod mar a dh'ordaichinn dut iad,
'S nighean righ 'ga posadh riutsa,
Le sioda, le srol, 's le trusgan;
Nuair theid i mach, seinnear cruit dhi,
Seinnear clarsach nan teud druidte.

It is so I would have ordered:
Princess should be your betrothed one,
Silk and satin to be her robing,
When she goes out, "cruit" is played for her,
"Clarsach" with tightened strings entoned too.[1]

We are concentrating primarily on the harp in Scotland, but we will refer to Irish sources where appropriate. There are many important links and comparisons to be made between the two countries as we look at the early literary evidence.

A description of the instruments used in Ireland, Scotland and Wales was included by Gerald de Barri in his "Topography Hibernica" c. 1188. De Barri, or Geraldus Cambrensis (Gerald of Wales, 1146-1223) was a Norman ecclesiastic of mixed Welsh descent. After studying in Paris, he served as a royal clerk to Henry II, and accompanied Prince John to Ireland in 1185. Following a passage in his book on the musical expertise of the Irish (one of the few positive impressions they made on him), he continues : "It is to be observed that Scotland and Wales — the former by virtue of trade and affinity, and the latter by propagation — strive in practice to imitate Ireland in their melodies. Ireland uses and takes delight in two instruments : the *cythara* and the *tympanum*, Scotland in three, the *cythara*, *tympanum* and *chorus*, and Wales in the *cythara*, *tibia* and *chorus*. Moreover, they play upon 'bronze' strings (Aeneis ... chordis) rather than strings made of gut. In the opinion of many people, Scotland has not only equalled her mistress, Ireland, in music, but today excells and surpasses her by far. For that reason, people look upon her now as the fountain of the art."

What did Gerald mean by 'Scotia'? In another section of the "Topography" he explains that the Irish are called Scotti, and the northern part of the island of Britain is also called Scotia because it is inhabited by a people originally 31 descended from these men. "The affinity of language and dress, of arms and customs even to this day, proves this." This would suggest that he was referring to the Scottish Gaels who, although in retreat from the position held at the beginning of the 12th century, were still the dominant cultural force over the greater part of Scotland except Lothian and the Norse-controlled Northern Isles. It is likely that 'cythara' means a harp, almost certainly a triangular-framed harp, and that 'tympanum' is the 'tiompain' or lyre. 'Tibia' and 'chorus' may represent wind instruments, perhaps even a form of bagpipe or a bowed stringed instrument. With regard to the stringing of the instruments, however, the Latin text is very ambiguous. When he says that "they play upon 'bronze' strings", does he mean just the Irish, or the Scots and Welsh as well? That sentence can in fact also be translated as "They play upon 'bronze' strings *more than* strings made of gut", which would suggest that both were in common use. One might even read into the last two sentences of Gerald's text, a possibility that the Scots' superior performance might have derived from a long-established native tradition of harping (though on a rather different instrument) which had been absorbed by the Gaelic Scots. Geraldus Cambrensis leaves us with many questions unanswered, but his lack of detail probably reflects the fact that, although he was familiar with Ireland and Wales, he never actually visited Scotland.[2]

The lyre, the 'tiompain', has been shown by Dr. Anne Buckley in her comprehensive study to have continued in use in Ireland until after the 15th century, but specific references to the instrument in Scotland invariably have an Irish connection.[3] There is very limited evidence for its use in Scotland, although Irish sources describe some of their players, such as 'O cerbaill' and others, as being 'pre-eminent' or 'Ollamh' of both Scotland and Ireland. The 'Conchoir o hanglyne tympanyt' (Conchobhair O hAnnluain tiompanach) who features in the lists of entertainers in the "Book of the Dean of Lismore" would have been of the same Irish family as Fionn Ua h 'Angluinn, chief tiompain player of Ireland, whose death in 1490 is recorded in the "Annals of the Four Masters".

An example of a possible wrest-plank of a round-topped lyre found at Dun an Fheurain, Gallanach, Argyll, is inconclusive. Made of deer antler with five perforations, it is included in a report of the excavation published in P.R.S.A.S. Vol. 103, with no other suggestions for its use, but with conclusions left open.[4]

The word 'tiompain' features in several Scottish place-names, usually in its geographical sense of 'gully' or 'knoll'. The Gaelic proverb "'S mairg a loisgeadh a' thiompan rithe', (Cursed that I burned my tiompain for her) with its story of a musician who had made a fire from his tiompain to save his wife from exposure during a winter journey, only to have her decamp with another man, is well known in Scotland and in Ireland. In Scotland it is linked with the pass of Mam an Tiompain, above Glen More in Mull. It is possible, however, that the proverb became attached at a later date to the place-name, which probably describes the geographical configuration of the valley.

We know of no references to the tiompain in Scottish Gaelic poetry, but it does occur in stories with an undoubted Irish association, such as the legend of Clach an Tiompain in Ross-shire. This stone is near the wells of Strathpeffer, and when struck, makes a hollow sound (perhaps indicating a confusion between the words 'tiompain' and 'tympanum' -a drum). It is said to have been originally put in place by Fionn Mac Cumhaill to keep the waters of Loch Ussie in check while he leapt across the valley. The Brahan Seer, Kenneth Mackenzie, prophesied that should the stone be moved after it has fallen three times, the waters of the loch will flood the valley below, until ships sail up Strathpeffer and tie up to Clach an Tiompain. (So far it has fallen twice!)[5]

The earliest Gaelic word for a stringed instrument was 'cruit', a generic term which could be applied to any instrument which was strung with metal wire. It may be that in Scotland the expression persisted in this older sense so that a player of the tiompain or the quadrangular harp may have been referred to as a "cruitear". This would explain the puzzling lack of native "tympanists" in Scotland, in spite of the fact that Gerald de Barri and other literary references make it clear that the tiompain was played there. Tiompains, or other lyre-type instruments, using this old name of "cruit" may be the ancestors of the bowed-lyre found in Wales and elsewhere in Britain, called "crott" or "crowd". By 1200, in Ireland, the name "cruit" seems to have become more specifically associated with the triangular-framed wire-strung harp. This narrowing of the meaning mirrors the change in the definition of the word 'harp' in the Germanic languages. Most sources agree that the term derives from the Anglo-Saxon 'hearpa', the Old German 'harapha' and the Old Norse 'harpa', which stem from the root 'harpan', to pluck. There also seems to be a consensus that it originally applied to the various forms of the North European Lyre.[6] By the 12th-13th centuries, the word had become transferred to the triangular harp, but the evidence of how and when this happened is very vague. The earliest mention of a 'harper' is found in the English Royal Rolls of the late 13th century relating to Edward I's administration in Scotland.

A Latin charter from the time of David II contains the first definite references to players of the "cruit" in Scotland. It is dated 6 May 1346, and grants land held by his father in the Earldom of Carrick to "Patricio, filio quondam Michaelis Cithariste de Caryk", whose descendants were called in Gaelic 'M' Churterr' (MacChruitear — a name now Anglicised as MacWhirter). They seem to have been a family of hereditary harpers, since Michael's grandson, Duncan McChurterr, appears in a document of 1385, and also probably played the "cruit". Whether the instrument was a wire-strung harp or a tiompain in this case we cannot tell.[7] The Royal Exchequer Rolls, which have preserved much valuable information, were kept in a quasi-Latin, with the added use of the odd Scots or Gaelic term. By the 15th century the Rolls were also using "cithariste" to describe players of the "clarsach".

This name for the harp appears first in a 13th century poem in praise of one of the O'Brien lords of Thomond in Munster. It was composed by a poet called Giolla Brighde Albanach, who, as his name suggests, was a Scot. (In another poem he describes the woods of Scotland, which he says he loves by birthright.) He uses the phrase "chlar shoileach" to describe how "fair hand never played on *willow board*, strings as musical as his speech". "Clar" meaning a "board" is the root of the commonly-used Scottish Gaelic word for harp — "clarsach". As well as "board", it has several other alternative meanings, including a "deck" or a "table". Dwelly also, interestingly, gives as a less usual definition the word "trough" suggesting a hollowed-out piece of wood. Willow itself was one of the sacred trees of the pagan tree-cults, which would give a magical significance to an instrument built from it, as well as having practical qualities of lightness, density and resilience, ideal for constructing harps. The word "clarsach" may indeed have come into being as a contraction of "clar shoileach". Both the "clarsach" and the "cruit" appear to have been metal-strung harps.[8]

A praise poem addressed to a new harp by the Irish poet Gofraidh Fionn O'Dalaigh contains the first example of the word "clarsach" itself. The oldest section of the poem dates from 1382-1387, and comprises ten quatrains, though a further twelve verses were later added to it. The source is the Book of the Dean of Lismore, compiled in Fortingall, Perthshire, between 1512-40, which contains the earliest examples of Scottish Gaelic poetry — the songs and poetry of the itinerant bards. The O'Dalaigh's were a family of poets which had branches in both Ireland, in West Meath, and in Scotland. The Scottish side of the family had been founded in 1220 by Muireadach Albanach O'Dalaigh, who fled there after killing the steward of O'Donnell of Tir Connell in an argument over tribute which the steward was collecting. In a subsequent poem, attempting to reconcile himself with O'Donnell, Muireadach states that they should not have parted over the death of such a churl! It appears that Muireadach also was acquainted with Giolla Brighde Albanach — they are said to have both gone on a Crusade together, as poets often did, accompanying a patron to record and extol his exploits on the trip, much as press reporters do today on a State Visit abroad. The O'Dalaigh's are also the reputed ancestors of the great Scottish family of the MacMhuirich poets. Clearly, they had many contacts with that country and ample opportunity to become familiar with the word "clarsach", if the term is of Scottish origin.[9]

Scottish "clarsach" players appear no later than the word is found in use in Ireland, which points to the fact that the name had been established in Scotland for at least a generation. It had apparently spread from Gaelic into Scots as well, which also suggests continuous use of the term for some time.

The Scots records mention Eugenio Klerscharch in Glassary in 1434, and Duncan Clarescheouch in Strathdon in 1438. These Exchequer Rolls also use the term "harp". A lone example of "clarsaghours" occurs in the Anglo-Irish Annals of Henry VI, in 1435, giving orders for the banning of Irish musicians and poets as a subversive influence. Apart from this, the Annals speak primarily of "harpers", with the "cruit" featuring occasionally.[10] Generally speaking, in poetry which is identifiably Scottish Gaelic, the expression for the harp is much more frequently "clarsach" than "cruit", whereas in Irish sources there is a definite preference for the word "cruit" which continues to the present day. Geographically, we have further evidence in that, according to Bannerman, most Irish references to the clarsach belong to the north of Ireland, which has always had strong economic and cultural links with Scotland. These links are still apparent today, for example in the style of the traditional music of Donegal, which relates closely to that of Scotland. All these factors would tend to tip the balance in favour of a Scottish origin for the word "clarsach".[11]

It may have crossed the Irish Sea during one of the most marked early periods of Scottish influence in Ireland, which began around the year 1260, when a new, hard, political feeling of resistance sprang up amongst the Irish against their Anglo-Norman invaders. This was pithily expressed in the phrase : "better a castle of bones than a castle of stones". The native Irish had always been at a military disadvantage compared with their opponents because their social system simply was not geared towards lengthy wars. Unlike the trained knights and regular army of the Normans, the Irish chiefs had depended on raising a levy, at short notice, from the small farmers and peasants on their lands, who would be armed with whatever weapons were available, would fight a single pitched inter-tribal battle, and would then return home. Very different tactics were needed to resist the professional Anglo-Norman troops. It was necessary to bring in mercenaries, and these came from West Scotland and the Hebrides. They were called Gallaglach, or galloglasses, meaning "foreign soldiers". In Professor Eoin MacNeill's opinion, it was the recruitment of these mercenaries and the Irish regulars who at a later date were modelled on them, which enabled the Anglo-Norman invasion to be held in check for the next three hundred years. These men were of Norse-Gaelic descent, an elite band of fighting men, heavily armed, whose bravery and loyalty were legendary. In his paper on "West Highland Mercenaries in Ireland", McKerral says "They have been described as 'janissaries of Ireland, who up to the battle of Kinsale in 1602, remained the one part of an Irish army that could be entrusted to stand its ground to the end'". Recruits for this "corps d'elite" came from some of the most notable families of the west of Scotland. Many had forfeited their lands to King Robert the Bruce after the Wars of Independence, and had been forced to seek employment and patronage abroad. The galloglass captains usually pledged loyalty — to the death — to one particular Irish chief, who would grant them lands on which they then settled, built castles and established themselves as minor nobility. The principal galloglass commanders were MacSween, MacDougall, MacDonald, MacRory, MacSheehy and MacCabe. They gradually spread through Ireland, the MacDougalls settling mostly in the north, where the name became MacDowell, Moyle or Coyle; the MacDonalds in Ulster, Connaught; the MacRuaries in Tyrone and Connaught; the MacSheehys in Munster; and the MacCabes through Leitrim, Cavan, Monaghan and Meath. These are only the names of the most important families, and many lesser ones were also involved, but there is no clear information on the number of galloglasses who migrated at this period. However, there is no doubt that they must have had a marked effect, culturally and linguistically, on the Irish people. If "clarsach" was originally a Scottish Gaelic word, this is the most likely route for its introduction into Ireland.[12]

One of the most famous images of Irish life in the Tudor period is a woodcut by John Derricke, 1581. This shows a chieftain, sitting at a feast, being entertained by a bard and a harper. The chieftain who is depicted is none other than MacSweeney — one of the Mac Sween family who had come to Ireland as the foremost of the galloglass captains. The Sweens were Norse-Scots who had entered into a treaty with the English king Edward II, against John, Earl of Menteith, in 1310, in an attempt to regain their ancestral lands in Knapdale. The attempt failed, and the family fled to Ireland, where they became established in Ulster, Munster and Connaught, and lords of a quarter of Tir Connell (Donegal), as MacSweeney or Sweeney. John Derricke's woodcut shows a scene which was typical of a celebration of the cultured Irish nobility. After more than two hundred years amongst them, the MacSweens would obviously have become naturalised, but the customs in Highland Scotland were very similar at this period to those in Ireland.[13]

In the ancient schools of Irish poetry, the classic arrangement was that the "fili", highly-trained and highly respected, composed the poetry but did not perform it. It would instead be chanted or recited by a "reacaire", to accompaniment from a harper. An occasion of this sort is illustrated in MacSweeney's feast. The harper, in a typically Irish furred mantle, sits on the ground, accompanying a "reacaire" whose performance is directed by a "fili", standing behind the chief. He wears the Celtic tonsure, with the hair shaved back from the brow, a custom which goes back to the pre-Christian cropping or shaving of the head as a symbol of thralldom, and denotes that he was a man who had a special calling. (A Scottish Gaelic tale mentions Mac Gille Mhaoil na Cruit — Macmillan the Harper — whose name translates literally as "the tonsured devotee of the Harp".) Another "fili" sits on MacSweeney's left, which indicates that the scene may even depict a poetic contest.[14]

The hierarchy of fili, reacaire and harper was customary in Ireland, and also known in Scotland where poets and musicians would tour round the great houses, even up to the 17th century. It is illustrated in the story of the exploits of Father Cornelius Ward, an Irish priest who belonged to a famous family of poets, the Mac a' Bhairds. He was sent to Scotland in about 1620 as part of an attempt by the Catholic Church to recover lost ground. Practicing Catholics were grudgingly tolerated at this period in Scotland, but priests were definitely regarded as undesirable and were likely to be hunted down if their presence were discovered. In order to gain access to Campbell of Cawdor (who also held land at Muckairn in Argyll), Ward disguised himself as an itinerant Irish poet on the Scottish circuit, travelling accompanied by a singer and a harper *"as was the custom"*. He composed a poem in praise of Campbell, which had the desired effect — he was invited to stay as a guest for three days during which he disclosed his identity and succeeded in converting his host, as he relates to the Vatican in the account of his visit.[15]

In Scotland, however, there are no traces of the post of "reacaire" or reciter, but there are references to a "bard". The bard apparently was not as highly trained as the fili, but composed lesser forms of poetry and performed them himself. He sometimes also played the harp, thus blurring the distinctions between the various offices. The Scottish bard may also have performed the fili's poetry, if the fili himself did not do so. It may even have been sung by the harper, or it might have been recited by one of the fili's entourage — in other words, a trainee poet. It is possible that the office of "reacaire", unlike those of fili and harper, was not a heritable one, and so was not considered worth recording, but it is noticable that there is no mention of it in any of the accounts of the composition of Gaelic poetry in Scotland. The best description of one of the Irish Colleges is contained in the Memoirs of the Marquis of Clanricarde, published in 1722, detailing the methods of training poets in Ireland in the 17th century and presumably, since the practices had not changed for many years, for some centuries before this. Students were only admitted from the families in which the profession was hereditary, and were selected on their ability to read and write in Gaelic, and their "strong Memory". Every evening the professors would set a subject and stipulate the syllabic structure of the poem they were to compose, and the students would lie all next day in a dark and windowless cell. Martin Martin says of the Scottish Gaelic poets' methods of composition that "... with a Stone upon their Belly and Plads about their Heads, and their Eyes being cover'd they pump their Brains for a Rhetorical Encomium or Panegyric". In the evening the students would write down the results of their mental labours, congregate for a meal, and present their poems to the teacher and their fellows for correction and criticism. It seems that the comradeship thus engendered resembled that of University life, and that the students were even said to be sorry to return home when the colleges' year ended in early summer.[16]

The usual length of study was for 6–7 years, during which time the student fili would learn the different formal patterns of syllabic verse which were regarded as the highest form of poetry. In the 15th and 16th centuries the "amhran" metre of poetry appeared. It is one of the basic metres of folk-poetry, and seems to have swept across the whole of Europe, carried by the music of the travelling minstrels and troubadours. Its use became increasingly common in Scotland, where the attitude to the strict rules of the Irish poetic schools seems to have been rather more relaxed. However, its introduction certainly led to the decline of syllabic verse as an archaic form of poetic expression. The role of the fili began to disappear — a decline speeded by political events which in effect destroyed the traditional Irish and Highland Scottish social structure.

In Ireland the Flight of the Earls in about 1607 led to the almost immediate collapse of the poetic colleges. Disappearance of their major patrons left them with no real economic support and without a discriminating, cultured audience. The Scottish training of bards survived for a further hundred years, perhaps because of their less strict interpretation of the poetic rules. Even in 1699 the Rev. John Fraser of Coll was still describing the orders of poets as comprising "Bardi", "poetici", "seneciones" (genealogists) and "symphoniaci" (musicians).[17]

In Scotland one of the crucial shifts of power from the north, southwards, occurred with the dissemination of the powerbase of the Lords of the Isles between the mid-15th and mid-16th centuries. The Lords of the Isles derived their power in the first place from their ancestors, Gofraidh and Somerled, Norse-Gaels who established rule first over Argyll and then over the Norse-held Hebrides. Their descendants, Clan Donald, Clan Ruari and Clan Dugall, took different sides in the Wars of Independence, after which Clan Dugall forfeited large parts of their territory or were exiled. Clan Donald, which eventually absorbed Clan Ruari, owed allegiance to the Scottish Kings for their lands and widespread sphere of influence, but maintained considerable independence from the Crown. Firmly entrenched as Lords of the Isles, the MacDonalds consolidated their power through inter-dynastic marriage and military strength throughout Argyll and the Hebrides, and laid claim to the Earldom of Ross, around 1400. This brought them into direct conflict with the Scottish Crown, as did their readiness to enter into treaties with Edward IV of England whenever it seemed to be to their advantage. In 1475 and 1493 John, Lord of the Isles, forfeited lands to the Crown as a result of charges including treason. His title was usurped by John Mor, Lord of Dunivaig and the Glens, who appears to have been a more effective leader until, in 1499, he, with his son and grandsons, was captured by the King of Scots and executed in Edinburgh. A long series of risings took place in the Western Highlands on behalf of the heirs to the title, which were not finally suppressed until 1545. The Crown, however, was not strong enough to enforce its authority over such a wide and intransigent territory and, though the MacDonalds never completely lost their status or a great part of their lands, other clans, notably the Campbells, stepped in to fill the vacuum created by the extinction of the Lordship.

As Lords of the Isles, the MacDonald chiefs had been well-known as patrons, not only of the Christian Church in the West Highlands — they had a close association with Iona — but also of the native traditions and arts. Their period in power coincides with a flowering of West Highland stone carving, particularly the practice of erecting stone crosses, a custom not found elsewhere at this time. They also maintained the great MacMhuirich family of poets on lands in South Kintyre, and neighbouring lands were granted to their family of hereditary harpers, the Mac Ghille Sheanaichs. (This proximity would suggest that it was convenient for poet and harper to be in close contact with each other.) With the fall of the Lordship, their role as patrons was taken over by the Campbells, whose own hereditary poets were the MacEwens. While the MacDonalds may have given the MacMhuirich and Mac Ghille Sheanaichs their lands rent-free in exchange for their services, the Campbells allowed them to remain in their accustomed holdings during the late 15th century and up until the 1630's, but by this time the Exchequer Rolls record that they were having to pay rental for the land. This does give us an interesting insight into the relative status of poet and harper. The MacMhuirichs held 8 merklands, while 4 merklands, which is still a sizeable area of property, were held by the Mac Ghille Sheanaich harpers. The harpers, however, were obviously somewhat lower down the hierachy.[18]

The harper bridged the worlds of the highly-trained but archaic fili, and that of the more versatile minstrel. He had provided the prime support for the fili's words, playing as they were sung or chanted, acting simply as an accompanist, though in Scotland he may have also been permitted to present the fili's poetry. On a less formal level, he probably performed solo instrumental music and song to his own accompaniment. That a harper, in Scotland, could also be a bard, is illustrated by two poems by Giolla Criost Bruilingeach, who lived in the mid 15th century. Derick Thompson has identified him with the Mac a Bhreatnaich, or Galbraith, family of harpers from the MacDonald lands in Kintyre. Giolla Criost may have been of the branch serving the MacNeills of Taynish. The family seems to have been well-known in Scotland and in Ireland at this time. There is a reference in a poem by Donnachadh MacCailein, the Good Knight of Glenorchy, who died at Flodden in 1513, to a harper called Lachlann, who also fell in the battle, whom he describes as "MacBhreatnaich bhinn" (sweet voiced Galbraith). MacCailein makes fun of him because he is notorious for demanding all sorts of gifts. Coincidentally, of the two poems by Giolla Criost Bruilingeach, which are included in the Book of the Dean of Lismore, one is soliciting the gift of a clarsach. This poem, composed around 1458, is addressed to the Irish noble, Tomaltach MacDiarmaida of Moylurg. Giolla Criost says that he has come to Ireland especially to make this request, that he be rewarded with a harp for the poem that he is presenting.

> "Clairseach ar leath dom dhan damhsa
> tabhair mar iarraim, a ri;
> ghnuis mar bhlath na h-abhla abaigh,
> o 's ni tharla agaibh i".

> "A harp in special grant me at my request, thou king, thou whose countenance is as the ripe bloom of an orchard, for it is a matter that thou hast by thee".

It seems that he was successful because another poem, which contrasts the generous MacDiarmaida with another Irish lord, Maguire the Unruly, he says that he received the harp. He was clearly a harper, but is also described in the Book of the Dean of Lismore as a "bard in Leymm", which Thompson identifies as Leim in Gigha. Apparently the poetry produced by a bard/musician was rated considerably lower than that of a fili. One of the Irish poets, contrasting the "genuine" forms of poetry of the fili, with inferior kinds, refers to one of them as a "Bruilingeach" — the name given to Gille Criost as a nickname. It seems that his compositions were typical of the Scottish harper-poets of his times.[19]

4 HARP and CARP

"To harp or carpe, whare-so thou gose,
Thomas, thou sall hafe the chose sothely:
And he saide, Harpynge kepe I none,
Ffor tonge es chefe of mynstralsye."[1]

By the late Middle Ages the wire-strung clarsach was established as the characteristic instrument of the Scottish Gael. In the non-Gaelic areas of Southern Scotland the development of the harp seems to have been somewhat different. If our hypothesis is correct, and the triangular-framed harp of the Picts spread southwards, it would appear that, in the territory dominated by the Angles, horsehair strings were replaced by gut. This was certainly happening in Wales between the 10th–12th centuries.

The southern movement of the instrument may be marked by the 9th century stone at Masham in North Yorkshire. In this, an area of mixed British and Anglian influence, the stone is carved with both a triangular-framed harp, which is too worn to decipher much of the detail, and an Anglo-Saxon lyre — an instrument which, confusingly, was referred to as a "hearpe". This is the only representation of David playing a round-topped lyre which occurs in pre-Norman carvings in England. Indeed, these scenes of King David and his musicians are rarely found in early English sculpture and are uncommon even in Anglo-Saxon manuscript illustrations. The lyre which David plays bears some similarities to the Sutton Hoo instrument, though it also appears to be slightly waisted, unlike any other early English examples or representations. Below him, another musician plays a small triangular-framed harp, the only example of the instrument at such an early date in an English context. All these factors, and the unusual portrayal, in semi-profile, of David, make the Masham stone atypical of other Anglo-Saxon carvings, and point to outside influences in its design.[2] Bower's "Scotichronicon" written in Latin around 1440 describes how a group of disaffected Pictish warriors fled to England having quarrelled with Kenneth MacAlpin and Domnall, his brother, who succeeded him in 854. There they allied themselves with the Saxons and harrassed the Scottish king until he eventually succeeded in wiping them out. The massacre was also mentioned by Fordun. Although the histories of Bower and Fordun have been regarded by some scholars as unreliable, unless they can be verified 41 elsewhere, it does seem likely that there were military and cultural contacts between Picts and Saxons during the 9th century.[3]

It was customary for Anglo-Saxon instruments to be strung with gut. This material was used for almost all European stringed art-instruments up to the Renaissance, with the exception of the metal strings of the psaltery (the ancestor of the family of stringed keyboard instruments) and the Gaelic harp. Horsehair may also have been sometimes used on the continental "viella". Jean de Bries's "Le Bon Berger" of 1379 recommended, in a comprehensive list, that gut-strings are best for "vielles, harpes, rothes, luthz, quiternes, rebecs, choros, almaduries, symphonies, cytholes and other instruments that one makes to give sound by means of the fingers and of strings". Metallic stringing was regarded as characteristic of Irish instruments, and elsewhere as an exceptional material to employ.[4] We might therefore suppose that Anglo-Saxon influence encouraged the adoption of their gut strings for the triangular harp, while in the Scotto-Gaelic areas the preference was for wire strings after the Irish fashion. Both types of string sustain a higher tension than horsehair, making smaller size and sturdier construction a logical development for the instruments. More compact harps would naturally be easier to transport, which may have aided their rapid dispersal through England and the rest of Europe. Triangular-framed harps appear in manuscript illustrations dating from the late 10th or early 11th century from St. Gallen in Switzerland (possibly produced by Irish monks), in a manuscript in the Vatican Library which dates from the same period, and in an 11th century manuscript in Cambridge University Library.

The first player of the harp who is named in a contemporary source in Scotland is found in a Lowland context. The Chronicles of Melrose, written in Latin around 1260, describe "Adam, a native of Lennox. It is reported that so great was his holiness that during the twenty years which he spent at Old Melrose he was never seen or known to go into bed nor out of bed. The plain proof of this was, that it was clearly perceived that the straw, over which were placed the sheets of that pretended sleeping place of his, remained constantly in the same unchanged condition for the whole of this space of time. But since it was God's good pleasure that this most excellent man should not fall into the sin of hypocrisy, the straw which was laid upon his bed sometimes — though rarely — crumbled into dust from old age; and then the man of God commanded that new straw should be laid upon the top of the old, just as if it was his intention to break through his custom and to sleep upon his bed. He did, however, go to sleep; but the little time that he spent in sleep was passed by him in a sitting posture, or prostrate before the altar of the blessed Virgin, the mother of God; where also it was his custom to spend the greater part of the winter nights in playing upon the harp and singing songs which are called "Motets" (in citharizando cum cantilenis que vocantur "motete"), written in honour of the holy virgin-mother. During the daytime he sat for the most part near the church-door, going daily through the psalter according to custom, and close by his hand there always stood a basket, in which there was such an abundant supply of loaves, that no poor man was permitted to go away from his presence either complaining or unrelieved, but he always carried something away with him. Therefore, as he himself used to say, he thought himself fortunate in having such a full store of provisions laid up for him by those poor persons who kept flocking to him; and this by means of the bread which he distributed to them. The rich also came to him, and even the king of the land, that Alexander who lies buried within the church of Melrose, as well as many others, drawn by respect for his holiness, earnestly entreating that he would take as much of their wealth as he thought fitting, but this he very seldom consented to do; however, he sometimes accepted a few of their cows, that he might supply the poor with milk when they came to him. He himself had two cows belonging to the monastery, and they afforded a supply of milk sufficient for himself and his associate (praebentes sibi et socio suo lac ad sufficientiam). The immediate cause which brought the nobles of the land to him, was that they might confess their sins to him and receive his blessing; and many persons thought that his holy benediction would profit them much".[5]

Adam's years at Melrose must have been spent in the earlier part of the century, because in 1252 we are told that "John, abbot of St. Edward's (i.e. Balmerino in Fife) resigned his office and Adam, the porter of Melrose, succeeded him". The monastery of Balmerino or Balmerinach, was inhabited by a colony of monks from Melrose. It was especially favoured by Alexander II, who granted to the monks of that house, lands subsequently called Steadmuirland, Friarmyln, Kincraige, Pitgorno, Craigford or Freeland, Drumdriel and Gaitside. At Gaitside the monks afterwards built a chapel to the Virgin Mary. Interestingly, these lands span the countryside between Balvaird, which is later associated with Master Elyas, Harper to Alexander III, and Harperleas Reservoir to the south. In 1260 the Chronicles record that "A., abbot of Balmurinach, resigned the government of that establishment (which he could no longer retain, in consequence of his infirmity) to this successor Adam, a monk of the same house".[6]

Abbot Adam's connection with Lennox may be significant. The area known as the Lennox is around Loch Lomond, western meeting point of the old kingdoms of the Dal Riadan Scots, the Picts and the Britons of Strathclyde. It is the territorial home of the Mac a' Bhreatnaich (son of the Briton) clan, now Anglicized as Galbraith. Could Adam indeed have been a Mac a' Bhreatnaich? In around 1200 a Gillecrist Bretnach witnessed a charter to Melrose, which would point to a possible family link with the Abbey. In the 15th century this family provided a number of harpers to the Crown, and there may well have been a long tradition of practising the bardic arts in this area. Derick Thomson suggests that when Muireadach O Dalaigh was exiled from

Ireland around 1213-1216, he fled to Lennox, where he composed one poem
to Alun, Earl of Lennox, who died c1217 and another to Amhlaoibh, probably
the son of Alun. This poet, also known as Muireadach Albanach, may also have
been based in the area — Thomson identifies the Kathil Mac Murchy, witness
to a transaction at Dumbarton in 1259, and described as a man of substance
of Lennox, as Muireadach's son.[7] Slightly later, in the Book of the Dean of
Lismore "The only Scottish poet ... who was certainly not a native of the area
dominated by the Lords of the Isles, is the only one for whom the compilers
saw fit to record his place of origin, namely Donnachadh Mor from Lennox".
Donnachadh's poem describes a poet who has lost his voice, who can no longer
sing nor play his harp, and whose verse is not understood. It would appear that
in the Lennox there may have been, as later in Perthshire, a cultural meeting
point and centre of patronage which stimulated the bardic arts — perhaps even
a school of poetry and music. Abbot Adam might well have had a relationship
with the families or scholars emanating from there. As for his harp or "cithara",
there is no clue whether this was a wire-strung or a gut-strung instrument.
Coming from Lennox, there is the possibility that either might have been used
in that area. Adam's native background might suggest that he played a clarsach,
but his religious education, and the "motet" form of music that he sang, would
seem to weight the balance in favour of a small gut-strung harp, of the
Romanesque type illustrated in some of the early manuscripts.[8]

The Treasurer's Accounts of the Royal Court in Scotland are extant from
1471 and indicate that a distinction was being drawn at this date between the
two different types of harp then in use in Scotland. One type was known in
both the Highlands and the Lowlands by variants of its Gaelic name of
"clarsach". These include "clareshaw, klarsheow, klairsheough" and many
other versions of the spelling. The name appears to refer specifically to the
wire-strung harp. The possibility that both gut and wire strings were in use
contemporaneously in Scotland is suggested, as we have noted, by Gerald of
Wales, and confirmed in 1521 by John Major, in an account of the Highland
customs of his own day. He writes ... "for musical instruments and vocal music
the Wild Scots use the harp, whose strings are of brass and not animal guts,
and on this they make most pleasing melody". John Major, or Mair, who lived
from 1467-1550, was born in East Lothian. He studied at Cambridge and Paris,
and taught at St. Andrews University. While there is no evidence that he ever
travelled in the Highlands, he would have had ample opportunity to see and
hear the clarsach. As we see from the Royal Accounts, Highland harpers were
frequent visitors to the Lowlands during this time as musicians at the Kings'
Courts, and in the train of wealthy nobles. In almost all cases, it is specified
that these were "harpers on the clarsach". Slightly later additional evidence
comes from George Buchanan. In 1561, describing the harps of the Highlands,
he says "some are strung with brass wire, others with the intestines of
animals".[9]

Other written material is scarce in Scotland for the period up to the mid 15th century, which reflects the unsettled political situation. In Gaelic Scotland the MacPhees were the record-keepers to the Lords of the Isles, but much of the knowledge that they held in trust would have been retained by memory and transmitted orally. Little of it has survived. The early Campbell papers are not yet fully available. Nor are the Papal papers, which relate to Gaelic Scotland and, though some of these have been examined, there is as yet no known mention of a harper.

The evidence of harping that we do have at this period comes mostly from English language sources. With this we run into the usual problems of nomenclature. It is clear that when the name "clarsach" was used, it referred to a wirestrung instrument. "Harp", however, could mean either a wire- or gut-strung instrument, depending on the situation in which it occurs. If English or Scots was the language of a particular document, the word "harp" is quite likely to be used, even in a Gaelic area, although background and context clearly indicate the use of metal strings. The Treasurer's Accounts fortunately are usually specific about which instrument was being played. Sometimes it was a necessary distinction in order to differentiate between two harpers of the same name. For example, there were two musicians called "Pate Harper" (an embryonic surname) — who both received payment on the same occasions. One Pate (or Patrick) apparently played the clarsach, while the other played the harp.

> 1501 April 13th, Pate harpar on the harp, Pate harper on the clarsach, James Mylson harpar, the Ireland clarsach, and an English harpar, each received … xiijs.

> 1502 January 1st, James Mylson, Pate Harpar, Alexander Harpar, Pate Harpar clarsacha, and the blind harper, each … xiijs.

From what little evidence remains, the "harp" played within the Lowland Scottish sphere of influence appears to have been a version of the gut-strung harp which was common to most of the European courts of the period. Medieval Scotland was part of an international community linked by a common language, in Latin; by frequent and widespread travel by the aristocratic and intellectual classes, which disseminated elements of culture and religion from country to country; by active trade; and by inter-marriage, conquest, and the consequent exchange of territory between the royal dynasties of Europe.

Whatever may have been happening in indigenous harping in Scotland during the 11th–14th centuries, the gut-strung harp was certainly widely used among the Norman families who were influential, not only in England, but also north of the disputed Border. After the Conquest of 1066, the Normans spread throughout Britain, and many came to Scotland during the reign of Malcolm III (1057–1093). Some supported the claims to the English throne of Malcolm's Saxon queen, Margaret, and her brother, Edgar Atheling; some were disillusioned by William's tyranny; and some were attracted by grants of land from the Scottish kings. The Bruces (de Brus in Norman French) gained the Celtic Earldom of Carrick through the marriage of Robert Bruce to Marjorie of Carrick, mother of Robert I. With these estates, it is likely that they inherited the retainers associated with the older titles — the MacChruitears appear to have been the hereditary musicians of the Earls of Carrick, playing the 'cruit' of the Irish Scots, rather than the harp of their new Norman masters. The land given by the Bruces to these musicians was at Dallellachan in Ayrshire, and was eventually sold by their descendants, circa 1385, for twelve cows with calves. Robert the Bruce is also said to have given lands at Gattonside near Melrose to a French harper named Bastoun. Local legend has it that Bastoun was with Edward's army at Bannockburn, and was captured by the Scots, but his playing so pleased Bruce that he was rewarded with the land on which stands a house now known as 'Ardenlea', but formerly known as 'Boston House'.[10]

Several Norman nobles held lands in Scotland and in England, as indeed did the Scottish kings themselves. David, the younger son of Malcolm and Margaret, gained the Honour (or Earldom) of Huntingdon, which included a claim to Northumbria, as a result of his marriage to Matilda, grand-niece of the Conqueror. For these estates he paid homage to the English king. Some Norman nobles appear to have more or less commuted between the two countries, along with their household servants. The St. Clairs, one of whom, William, had been appointed cup-bearer to Queen Margaret of Scotland in honour of his "wisdom", were influential in both domestic Scottish and international politics. William's great-grandson, another William St. Clair, aided Robert the Bruce in his contest for the Scottish Crown against John Balliol in 1292, but also swore allegiance to Edward I of England for his English lands. An entry in Edward's Wardrobe Accounts in 1285–86 notes a payment to William le Harpur, minstrel of Lord William de St. Clair. In 1279 Henry of Rosslyn, whose daughter may have married William St. Clair, resigned his lands in favour of St. Clair. The St. Clairs, or Sinclairs, later demonstrated their wealth and power by building Rosslyn Castle and the nearby Rosslyn Chapel, begun in 1446. Among the spectacular stone carvings in the Chapel is a series of musicians on the capitals of the pillars, including a figure, presumably King David, playing a harp.[11]

The harpers would have travelled regularly with their masters as valued members of their households, and were sometimes entrusted with other duties. In 1325, the "harpour" of Walter Fitz-Alan, the Steward of Scotland, was arrested in London despite the fact that he held a safe conduct from the Warden of the Marches, and was only freed by the intervention of King

Edward himself. In Scotland, as in Ireland, harpers were often used as spies or secret envoys since the itinerant nature of their profession did not arouse suspicion as they travelled from place to place — perhaps this was the reason that he was apprehended. The Fitz-Alans, who later became known as Stewart, were of Breton origin, and held the office of Stewards of Scotland between 1325-1390. They owned estates on the west coast of Scotland at Kyle-Stewart north of Ayr. There is a "Harperland" recorded there by 1373, which was probably held by their harpers in return for their services. In the same area, near Kirkoswald, a Harperland, also known as Slaphouse, features in a later document signed by Robert Jolly, its owner, in 1580. A broken fragment of the seal, still attached, bears a representation of a harp which resembles some Irish instruments of the 17th century. Robert le Harper, who paid homage to Edward I at Ayr in 1296 may also have been a tenant of one of these "lands". In this case, his name, which is of English origin, would suggest that he played a gut-strung rather than wire-strung instrument. Harpers in Scotland appear frequently in the English documents of this period. A seal which is attached to a fragment of a homage document bears the device, though rather worn, of a harp. It was the seal of "S' Walraun Le Harpeur" and dates from around 1290. "Ughtred le Harpur and his heirs" lived in Berwick on Tweed before the town was forfeited by John Balliol to the English. He was a tenant of William de Moravia (or Murray) in 1296. The Murrays were a family of Flemish origin, which reflects the fact that trade with Germany, the Low Countries and Norway was an important factor in Berwick's predominance as a major East Coast port. Like Ughtred, Rogier le Harpur of Hom paid homage to Edward in Berwick in 1296. "Hom" is Home near Coldstream, and between Kelso and Coldstream, by Stichill, lies Harpertoun.[12]

A pattern seems to emerge from these records which links harpers whose names are of non-Gaelic derivation, or families descended from them, with "Harper" place-names on estates often held by landowners of Norman or Flemish origin. Another who is mentioned in the Ragman Rolls of 1296 is Erchebald de Harpenfeud, whose name is almost pure Saxon. The derivation of the name "Harpen-Feud" comes from an Anglo-Saxon word "feud" meaning "a fief, the right to lands or hereditaments held in trust or on condition of performing certain services". It is obviously, in this case, a specific word used to describe the terms on which the lands were occupied. The area, now called Harperfield, seems to have been part of a grant of land by the Abbot of Kelso to Theobald, a Fleming, in about 1147-1160. Between 1160-1180 part of it, called Cultersegill, was granted to a Waldeve Fitz-Bodin, whose name is evidence of his Anglo-Norman ancestry. Whiting le Harpour also paid homage in 1296 at Lanark and may be associated either with Harperfield, which is 4 miles south of Lanark, or Harperhall, near Elsrickle, 12 miles to the east. "Harperleas" is found near Loch Leven, in Fife, while Harperfwate

(Anglo-Saxon for 'Harper's clearing) is recorded in 1376, among the lands of the Earl of Morton.[13]

William le Harper de la Lawe probably lived near Edinburgh since that is where he paid homage to Edward. "Law" is Old English for a hill, which gives many possible locations for his home. However, surrounding Harperrigg in the Pentlands, just outside Edinburgh, are Capelaw, Castlelaw, Scald Law, Bavelaw, and Greenlaw, which must make it a likely contender. As if in confirmation, a neighbouring place-name to "Harperrigg" is "Over Williamston". To the south-east of Edinburgh two harpers are associated with place-names near Haddington. John le Harpour de Saulton had his lands restored on 8th September 1296. Saltoun lies just west of Haddington, while the "Harperfield" nearby the town may be the lands gained by Thomas Citharist at the forfeiture of Gilloc de Camera during the reign of David II.[14]

The consistent relationship between personal names and place-names, being of Anglo-Saxon rather than British or Gaelic origin, suggests that these harpers were part of the non-Gaelic culture of the Lowlands of Scotland. Harpers moved quite freely between Scotland and England. In 1294 Edward I's harper, Adam, accompanied him on a visit to Berwick. On this occasion it is recorded that "Hugh, Adam's boy" was accused of stealing a sword from his master and attempting to sell it. Another English harper, "Willelmo Sithariste Anglico" was paid xxs in the Scottish Exchequer Rolls of 1360. It is clear that these harpers travelled widely, that they were highly respected, and that they could take their place within the cultured society of their day. Because of the international nature of this society, it is probable that the harps that they played were typical of those used elsewhere in Europe at the time.[15]

A pictorial record of these instruments exists in the illustrated books made for religious use. Curt Sachs describes the small rounded harps of the 12th and 13th centuries as "Romanesque", while by the 14th and 15th centuries they had narrowed and elongated into the elegant shape defined by Sachs as "Gothic".[16] These harps frequently appear in illustrations which depict King David. It was common practice, in the international community which was the medieval world, to commission religious books from one of the centres which specialised in their production. Manuscripts found in Scotland are often, therefore, not of Scottish provenance but were painted in "scriptoria" elsewhere. An example of this is the late 12th or early 13th century Iona Psalter which was made in Oxford for an Augustinian canoness with a special interest in the saints associated with Iona, including S.S. Columba, Baithene, Adamnan, and Oran. A marginal notation gives the name Beota, which is possibly a form of the Gaelic name Bethoc or Beathag. A daughter of Somerled, son of Gilbride, and Lord of the Isles, was Behag, the first prioress of Iona. The King David, drawn within the letter 'C' of the word "Cantare" plays a harp on his left shoulder and resting beside his knee. It has a light frame with a curved forepillar, which is being bitten on this occasion by a small blue dog!

The inclusion and arrangement of the Saint's Days in the manuscript indicate that the book was specifically intended for use on Iona. Oxford, at this period, was quite cosmopolitan with both a Scottish and an Irish contingent in residence. This cultural melange may have some significance in the spread of the triangular-frame harp southwards through England and into Europe. In a survey of stringed-instrument makers in late medieval English documents, it is noteworthy that, of the nine harpmakers listed, between 1366–1467, four are to be found in Oxford.[17]

Iona Psalter

Kinloss Psalter

A tiny "David" figure appears within the "Beatus" initial in a Scottish Psalter which was written at Culross under Abbot Richard Marshall between 1450–70, but his harp is not drawn in sufficient detail to distinguish more than the general triangular shape of the instrument. On the contrary, the painting of King David in the Kinloss Psalter, though small, is exquisitely detailed and shows a harp of Sach's "Gothic" type. This manuscript was made in about 1475 for use within a Cistercian monastery in the North of Scotland, and the inclusion of S.S. Ninian and Adamnan, according to Eeles, point conclusively to Kinloss.[18] The instrument illustrated in the Psalter is a relatively large,

50 Harp and Carp

King David, Dean
Hous ceiling

Music, Dean
House ceiling

Muses ceiling, Crathes Castle

lightly-built and gracefully pointed harp. Wood's manuscript Psalter, written in 1562-66, also illustrates several harps, among other instruments. In a secular context, the "Tale of Rauf Coilyear", a book printed in St. Andrews in 1572, includes a small woodcut of a harp, apparently as a purely decorative motif since there is no mention of the instrument within the text itself.[19]

Two harps are painted on the panelled ceiling of Dean House which dates from the early 17th century. The David figure, in this case, is similar to that in the Kinloss Psalter but his harp, though quite tall and slender, has a distinctly curved forepillar. A harp of the same shape is also depicted in a group of instruments behind the figure representing "Music" elsewhere on the ceiling. It is unfortunately impossible to say whether or not these harps were painted from life. It was common for artists to use copybooks, which resulted in similar motifs appearing throughout Europe. In Scotland, for example, the painting of Cain and Abel, from a ceiling originally in Dean House, closely resembles the illustration in the Cologne Bible, while the beamed ceiling of Rossend Castle includes designs taken directly from copybooks — an ostrich from Rollenhagen's "Nucleus Emblematum Selectissirorum" (1611-13) and a goat from Whitney's "Choice of Emblems" (1586).[20]

The fine ceiling painting at Crathes, in Kincardineshire, which dates from the late 16th century also shows a harp of the same type. It is played on the left shoulder of a lady and rests on a table. The ceiling illustrates the Muses, and other female musicians perform on viol, bass viol, lute, cittern, a small portable organ and a sideways-blown bell-ended flute.[21] Several instruments performing in consort were a popular feature of the art and music of this period. That gut was customarily used for all the stringed instruments can be seen in an account of 1612 which describes "Strings called Harpe, Lute or Citterne strings, the groce xii s". The same account lists the duty payable on instruments imported to Scotland at that time. Though many of the common European instruments are included, such as lutes, "whissillis" and virginals, harps and bagpipes do not appear, which may point to the possibility that the production of these instruments centred in Scotland itself.[22]

One might suggest that, in the more rounded shape of the Dean House and Crathes harps, it is possible to find echoes of the earlier Romanesque instruments which had been superceded in most of Europe by the Gothic style harp. In Scotland the art and architecture of the Gothic period contained strong elements of vernacular tradition, which made the native examples of this style less distinctive and exaggerated than those of England or the Continent, where Gothic Art reached its full flowering.

5 HARPS OF THEIR OWNE SORTE

"Musica maxime delectantur, sed sui generis fidibus, quarum aliis chordae sunt aeneae, aliis e nervis factae, quas vel unguibus praelongis, vel plectris, pulsant".

"They delight much in musicke, but chiefly in Harpes of their own fashion, of which some are strung with brasse wyar, others with sinews; which strings they stryke either with their nayles growing long, or with a plectrum".[1]

While no specimens of the medieval gut-strung harps survive in Scotland, we are fortunate that three fine examples of the clarsach still exist, one in Ireland — the harp in Trinity College, Dublin; and two, significantly, in Scotland — the Lamont Harp and the Queen Mary Harp. The latter two instruments were handed down in the Robertson family of Lude, in Perthshire, and are now in the National Museum of Antiquities, in Edinburgh. All three harps are thought to date from the mid to late 15th century.

The Lamont and Queen Mary Harps are unique among surviving instruments in that they are constructed entirely from hornbeam. The wood from this tree is hard and capable of withstanding abrasive wear, the name coming from the Anglo-Saxon for "horny (wooded) tree". It does not seem to have been native to Scotland at this period, being found in the South East of England and very locally in a few westerly districts of England and South Wales. Timber was, however, regularly imported into Scotland during the Middle Ages and Renaissance. There are records of wood being brought from England for ship-building — there were well-known shipyards at Kishorn and at Inverness which were taking orders from foreign customers during the 13th century. A galley for the Crusades was ordered, by an Englishman, from yards in south west Scotland, and tradition has it that the timber for this ship came from Norway. In 1475 a Scottish merchant whose name, interestingly, was Duncan Lamont, was given a safeconduct to trade throughout the realm of England, sailing out of Dumbarton in his ship the "Trinity". There were thus many opportunities for this wood (which would be relatively exotic at that time) to reach Scotland. It would be inferring too much to say that the use of hornbeam for both harps points conclusively to a common source of origin, but it is certainly a coincidence that both were constructed from the same unusual foreign wood.[2] The makers of both harps must therefore have had 53 access to a source of imported timber. The Trinity College harp has a harmonic curve and soundbox of willow, and a later forepillar which may be of oak. Willow and birch were the native woods traditionally said to have been used for harps in Gaelic poetry and legend, but it would appear that the harp makers tended to use any suitable block of wood which was available. The use of an uncommon wood like hornbeam suggests, however, that the two Lude harps were instruments of importance, for which a special and highly prized wood was selected.

The three harps do not differ markedly in size and structure, the Lamont Harp being the largest. Their sound boxes are formed from one solid piece of wood, hollowed out from the back, to leave a fairly thick soundboard. The back of the boxes is closed by a solid panel. The holes for the strings, in the raised rib which runs down the centre of the soundboard, were reinforced with decorative metal fittings to prevent the metal strings from cutting into the wood. From the bottom of the box, a block of wood projects downwards to form a junction with the lower end of the forepillar or "bow". This is deeply curved, with the outer face widened to form a 'T' cross section, giving additional strength. The upper end of the forepillar is morticed into the underside of the harmonic curve, which projects forward beyond the junction. The other end of the harmonic curve sweeps upwards towards the treble, before curving over and downwards to mortice into the top end of the soundbox. The lower part of the harmonic curve is pierced with a line of holes reinforced on either side by two metal bands, through which pass the tapered metal tuning pins. A cross section through the harmonic curve where it commences at the junction with the soundbox, is almost oval in shape, changing above the highest tuning pin to a deeper section with a flat bottom, almost parallel sides, and becoming triangular at the top. The slight "hump" which occurs at this point is most pronounced on the Lude harps, especially on the larger Lamont Harp. This led Armstrong to the conclusion that what he called the "Highland Hump" was a feature unique to Scottish harps.[3] The hump is, however, common to all three harps, the difference being one of degree, with the hump on the Trinity College instrument being the smallest. It seems likely that, since the purpose of the hump was concerned with structural strength, its size was related to the size of the harp, and not to the style of a particular geographical area. Unlike modern harp construction, the harmonic curves for Gaelic instruments were cut from a single piece of wood. The strength of wood varies according to the direction of the stress in relation to the direction of the grain. With the sweeping shape of the harmonic curve, weak points will occur unless dimensions at these points are increased to compensate. The Lamont Harp has a crack running along the grain under the hump, which has been repaired by metal reinforcement at an early period, suggesting that the hump, despite its size, was still insufficient to compensate for the stress created by the tension of the metal strings.

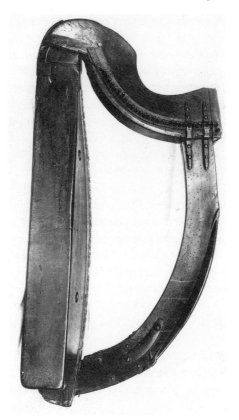

Lamont Harp

The presence of small areas of wear on the soundboxes of the instrument, caused by the friction of the players' arms, indicates that the clarsach was, like its Irish counterparts, played on the left shoulder, with the left hand playing the upper register. This method of playing, may, as Ann and Charlie Heymann suggest, have had a symbolic function, in that the left side of the body — the side of the heart — is traditionally the female side, and thus played the treble strings while the stronger right hand played the deeper, masculine strings. This is a neat and convincing argument but the use of the left hand for the upper strings was at least partially a result of the solid construction of the neck and harmonic curve. The stringholes at the ends of the tuning pins were not directly above the stringholes in the soundbox, being further to the left (as viewed by the harper). The shorter the string, the further its departure from the perpendicular became, creating a fan-like effect with the higher strings which made them difficult to reach with the right hand. This problem could, of course, easily have been reversed by changing the direction of the tuning pins, but there is no evidence to indicate that this was ever done. We might therefore assume that the clarsach was played on the left shoulder for some particular reason. Practical experience shows that, for a right-handed player, it is easier to guard the left-hand nails from being broken, since one naturally performs mundane tasks with the right hand. Thus the important melody-playing nails — and the means of earning the harper's livelihood — were more likely to remain intact, if the left hand was used for the treble strings. The nail-playing technique may also be the reason why there were so many blind players of the clarsach. While music was the obvious profession for a person blinded by illness or at birth, it would be much more logical for them to take up singing, or one of the other instruments such as bagpipe or fiddle where the fingers remain in more or less the same position while playing — and indeed some blind pipers and bards are found. But the harp is much more difficult to play without sight. It may be that it was easier to keep all the nails long if one were blind, and not expected to perform manual tasks of any sort. Nails were crucial to the style of music played on the wire-strung clarsach. Certainly the Irish evidence would support this view, the harpers there continuing to play on wire strings in that manner until the introduction in the early 19th century of the "neo-Irish" harp with an off-set, cut-away neck and gut strings played with the fingers. This was a new and substantially different instrument, and by then the era of the old Irish harpers was past.

Dimensions of the three harps are given in Appendix A. The metalwork and decoration of the instruments merits close examination. The Lamont Harp has brass shoes on each of the string-holes. All are of the same simple pierced triangular design, except the three highest and two lowest mounts, which are horse-shoe shaped, with quatrefoil terminations. Rimmer suggests that these may be the five surviving original mounts.[4] There are metal braces at the foot of the pillar, and smaller decorated brass plates at the hump of the curve, marking later repairs. The original brass strips on either side of the harmonic curve have holes for 32 pins, 30 of which survive. These stringbands are decorated with a geometric pattern, with the letters SIII incised at the end nearest the hump. The string pins have a simple cut decoration on their ends. Four of them have slots, rather than holes, for the strings.

The triangular termination of the harmonic curve is faced with a brass mounting, which measures 6" high x 2¼" wide, with sides 3/16" deep. It was apparently made separately from the harp, since the underside of the base has had to be cut and folded back to accommodate the forepillar, interrupting the engraved pattern. The sides of the mount are incised with geometric interlacing, while the triangular face is covered with a rather free, foliaceous design, which surrounds a large oval boss, intended to imitate a cabuchon jewel. The three sides of the triangle are edged with a twisted border and the mount is fastened to the harp by three studs with decoratively cut heads. There are also two brass straps which link and strengthen the joint between pillar and curve. These, too, are engraved with foliaceous patterns, and terminate at each end in an animal head. Armstrong suggests that these were later additions. They appear, however, to be contemporary with the triangular mount.

Brass mountings for a harp, which were found at Ballinderry in West Meath, Ireland, also show a strap which would have been fixed to the instrument at the same point so it seems to have been common practice, when these were made, to include these straps in the metalwork for a harp. These Ballinderry mountings were intended for a harp of similar shape to the Lamont Harp, though slightly larger. They have holes for 36 pins. They appear never to have been used on a harp since their condition is extremely fine. As we have already mentioned, the brass mount on the Lamont Harp was made by a craftsman who did not have the actual instrument before him. It appears that there were centres of craftsmanship in Scotland and in Ireland, which specialised in the production of fine artifacts. Although these mounts are said to be of a somewhat later date than the Lamont Harp, the engraved designs certainly relate closely to those on the Scottish examples. The Ballinderry mountings have much in common with those on the Lamont Harp — the single curve of the stringbands; the animal head which terminates the upper end of the strap; the interlaced patterns on the ends of the studs and on the pins. On one side of the mount, and in the peak of the face, they also show patterns of palmette leaves closely similar to those carved on the Queen Mary Harp.[5]

The Queen Mary Harp is the finest example of an early clarsach still extant, and having been least altered over the years, is probably closest to its original condition. The back panel is original, and has been worn away at the back of the shoulders, and at the lower left corner, as has the animal head which is carved on the projecting block at the base. This shows how the harper would have lifted the instrument after performance, with his right hand under the back of the shoulders, and his left hand holding the forepillar. He may have placed it on the ground or surface where it was to rest, so that the block and left back corner first made contact and then were slid forward until the clarsach was safely resting on its back, thus wearing these two points away. It is also likely that the harps would have been played balanced on one corner of the keel, tilted backwards. This makes a substantial difference to the amount of tone which is produced. The Irish harper in a portrait from the 17th century royal court of Denmark may be seen to tilt his harp at such an angle.[6] The brass stringbands have holes for 29 pins, in addition to which, a further hole has been made through the wood just below the front end of the band, for a string which appears to have been attached at the lower end of the centre ridge by a metal loop. The string pins are plain. Praetorius, writing of the Irish harp in 1619, describes the strings as being of "great thick brass". It seems likely, however, that all three of these existing clarsachs would have been strung relatively lightly. Modern brass is an alloy of copper and zinc, but medieval brass was closer to the modern bronze — i.e. an alloy of copper and tin, sometimes with the addition of a little zinc or lead. This made the alloy somewhat harder than

Queen Mary harp

modern brass. We do not know if any of the original strings were on the Lude harps when they were sent to Edinburgh to be examined in 1805, but at this time the Queen Mary Harp was again strung, first with brass wire. When it was realised that a completely different technique would be necessary to play the metal strings, it was decided, under the direction of Joseph Elouis, a Swiss harpist domiciled in Edinburgh, to restring it yet again, this time inappropriately with gut. Elouis then performed upon it, but, though the upper register was declared sweet and delicate, it was thought that the lower strings (not surprisingly) lacked tone.[7]

To give a rough guide as to the gauge of wire strings which might originally have been on the Queen Mary Harp, it is possible at least to test for the greatest diameter of wire which can be passed through the hole in each of the string pins.[8] This varies from 0.018" (0.46 mm) to 0.039" (1mm) although, judging by the hole sizes, the pins do not seem to be still in their correct order. However the spread of sizes seems to be consistent with measurements taken from the metal strings on the reproduction Queen Mary Harp thought to have been made by Glen, now in the Highland Folk museum at Kingussie. (see Appendix A)

The patterns on the front, sides and base of the box of the Queen Mary Harp were burned into the wood, and are of the compass and rule type — crosses of several designs, between which run criss-crossing diagonal lines. The patterns on the curve, of semicircles at intervals along the upper and lower edges, linked by double lines which follow the shape of the curve, are of the same type. These also appear on the small triangular face at the end of the curve. There are fine foliaceous scroll patterns carved at the top of the box, on the side of the pillar, and the top of its front face. Faint traces of pigment in some of the carving suggests that it may at some point have been picked out with colour. A roundel with a pelleted border is carved on either side of the pillar, at top and bottom, each showing a mythical beast.

Fabulous beasts did not enter the vocabulary of the heraldic artist until around 1400, and were not in widespread use in heraldry until the 16th century. We have examined the possibility of the designs having some family or clan significance but they do not seem to have any apparent links. In religious art, however, the symbolism of mythical beasts, with their atavistic echoes of pagan beliefs, was widely used and understood. Similar beasts appear on many of the West Highland graveslabs of the 14th and 15th centuries, especially those of the Iona school of carving, which are also found on the mainland. In the case of the Queen Mary Harp, then, the animals appear to be religious symbols — the Lion is associated with the Resurrection since medieval natural history states that young lions are born dead, only coming to life three days after birth, when breathed on by their sire. A lion frequently represented Christ as Lord of Life. The Griffin, which has the fierce nature of both lion and eagle, was often used as a symbol of Christ the Conqueror. The Dragon, in Christian art, usually represents the Devil, which may account for its position at the base of the forepillar. It is sometimes portrayed at the foot of the Cross, signifying that Evil has been overcome, as did the Dragon's head carved on the croziers of the Scottish bishops of this period. However, among the Celtic peoples, the Dragon has a more benign significance since it was well known in pre-Christian times as a symbol of a war-leader. The Dragon on the Queen Mary Harp is two-footed, as one would expect, since four-footed dragons did not begin to appear in heraldry until after 1400, and were not in common use until much later. The last roundel is interesting because it depicts a group of beasts. The largest, horse-like animal is clearly a Unicorn since it has cloven hooves, a small horn (on its nose rather than on its forehead) and

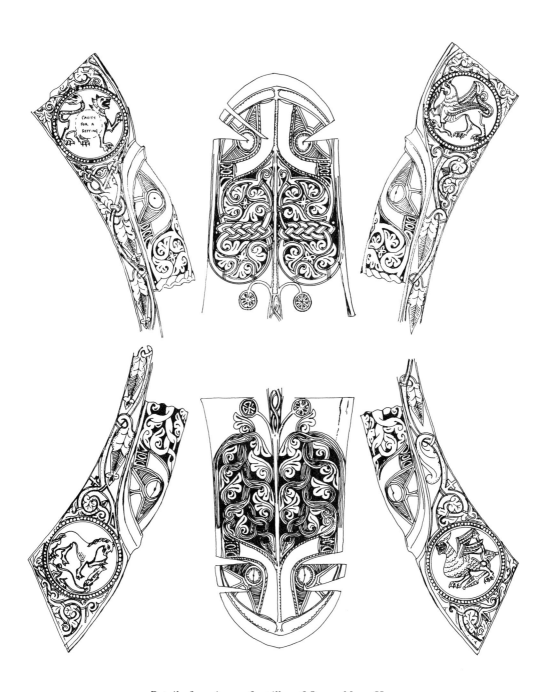

Detail of carving on forepillar of Queen Mary Harp

an oddly twisted tail. The Unicorn was one of the most common, and potent, symbols of Christ in the medieval world. Its strength and white colour represented purity, and the belief that though it was extremely wild and fierce, it could be captured by a virgin of spotless character, made it easily linked with the Incarnation of Christ through the Virgin Mary. The paramount religious symbolism of the Unicorn was so overwhelming that it was seen as too holy for ordinary secular use in heraldry and it only appeared very occasionally during the Middle Ages. Even in the royal arms of Scotland it was rarely used as a supporter until the end of the 15th century. Under the Unicorn's feet lies a Wyvern, a two-footed wingless dragon. The heraldic name for this beast comes from the Middle English word meaning "serpent", and the animal often represented the Serpent or Devil. This group, therefore, may symbolise Christ overcoming Satan. The Unicorn appears to be feeding the Serpent with a fish — yet another symbol of Christ, but one which had a further significance in Celtic myth as the Salmon of Knowledge. The speckles on the sides of the fish are clearly visible. Another Christian motif may been seen in the plant form twisting up the sides of the pillar. The leaves do not have the typical palmette shape of the more stylised designs, and since the stems sprout small crosses, this too may be intended to represent Christ, as the "true vine".[9]

The central portion of the pillar has six silver studs down the front of the bow, and is strongly carved with two fish or snake-like heads facing away from each other, with a complex design of palmette leaves and knotwork intertwined on their necks. The letters "D.O." are carved behind the reptiles' eyes. These probably represent the inscription "Deo Oblata" (Offered to God).[10] This, along with the large number of crosses which are included in the design, strongly suggest that this harp was made for a religious purpose, or for a layman with some ecclesiastical connection.

The Trinity College instrument bears many similarities to the Queen Mary Harp. It has been much tampered with, however, since its original construction. It has been recognised for a number of years that the forepillar, at least, is not that of the original harp.[11] Since these clarsachs were usually held together simply by the pull of the metal strings, it would be a straightforward matter to replace any of the three sides, were they to be damaged. The harmonic curve and box are made of willow, and probably date from the mid to late 15th century. The top of the curve has been damaged at some time, judging by the incomplete decoration at the point of the hump, which seems to have been cut away. The box has the same construction as the other harps. The centre ridge has holes for 29 (30?) strings, all but four still protected by horseshoe-shaped metal shoes. The burnt-on line and compass decoration shows similar geometric patterns to the Queen Mary Harp, and to the harp on the stone at Keills, but a later craftsman has altered and added to the original designs. Armstrong regarded the decoration on the left side of the box as being that of the original decorator. The terminations of the T-shaped section in the

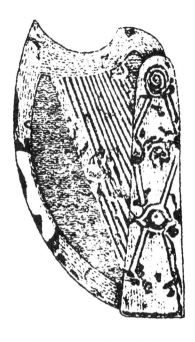

Harp on graveslab at Keills

centre of the forepillar are, like those on the Queen Mary Harp, carved to resemble the heads of reptiles or fish, though the interpretation of the carving differs slightly — the eyes are not as prominently carved, while the turned-back lips of the reptiles are even more pronounced. Further incised decorations were added subsequently, covering most of the forepillar with a geometric step pattern on the inner curve, and the sides and front of the pillar with panels of interlacing. The rather angular style of these carved designs bears some resemblance to the patterns on the pillar and curve of the Castle Otway Harp, which probably dates from the early 17th century. The Trinity College Harp has four roundels at the top and bottom on either side of the pillar, illustrating pairs of wild or mythical beasts, but these do not appear to have a deeper significance than a purely decorative function. They, too, are common on West Highland graveslabs. Most of this later decoration was lightly engraved or incised into the wood, care being taken not to interrupt the existing carving of the reptile heads. Yet another layer of decoration was added to the harmonic curve where lettering — probably IHC (the monogram representing Jesus Christ) and geometric motifs were carved in between the original semi-circle and line designs. Altogether, there may be as many as 5 layers of decoration on this part of the harp. There is evidence that small silver bosses were removed from this area, allowing space for the later decoration, or have fallen

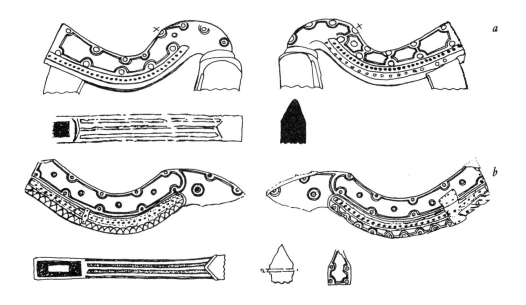

Decoration and moulding on and beneath the harmonic curves of:
a)Trinity College Harp; and b) Queen Mary Harp
x = point of hump damaged or cut away

off. Four of them still remain on the left side, and one on the right. Nineteen silver knobs decorated the space below the stringband on the right side. The moulding carved on the lower surfaces of the harmonic curves on both Trinity College and Queen Mary harps is virtually identical.

The pillar has been damaged in the centre of the T-formation, where a large hollow has been gouged out, apparently to take a setting for a jewel. The peak of the curve bears a metal mounting, finely made, still holding a cabuchon crystal in the upper setting, and in the three corners of the mount are bosses of star or blackberry forms. The front face is framed in a twisted rope, and the sides are of a battlemented design.

The general proportions and shape, and the original decoration on the boxes and harmonic curves of the Trinity College and Queen Mary Harps is so strongly similar as to suggest that they originated in the same workshop. The almost identical pattern on the harp carved on the slab at Keills supports the proposition that this was in the west of Scotland, and this is confirmed by the particular spiral arrangement of split-palmette leaves which appears on the upper part of the soundbox, and on the forepillar, of the Queen Mary Harp. This, according to Bannerman, is "one of the characteristic patterns of late medieval monumental sculpture in the West Highlands of Scotland, and has

West Highland graveslab,
Kilmory

no parallel in Irish art of this period". The split-palmette was used in Irish metalwork and carving during the 11th and 12th centuries, but never developed into the graceful, flowing patterns seen on the 14th and 15th century Scottish stones. At this time West Highland art was at its most vigorous and self-confident. In Ireland, indigenous artistic expression had suffered greatly from Anglo-Norman influence, and had become much debased since the superb metalwork, stone-carving and manuscripts of the 8th — 12th centuries. Bannerman makes the point that West Highland art represents what Irish art might have become by the same period, had it not stultified under the Anglo-Norman rule. The Trinity College Harp has long been held as an outstanding example of Irish craftsmanship. It is indeed outstanding because it is unique in the Irish situation. The craftsmanship, and the artistic style which this harp and the Queen Mary Harp demonstrate, are, however, typical of work produced in the West Highlands at this period.[12] This evidence strongly suggests a Scottish origin for both harps.

During the 14th and 15th centuries the Lords of the Isles were at the height of their influence as patrons. This patronage drew together craftsmen of many disciplines who appear to have been centred on the area around Keills and Kilmory. Bannerman points to the concentration of graveslabs there, which are carved with the tools of the artisans — carpenters, smiths and clothmakers — whom they commemorate — as well as those of the stone masons who carved them. The graveslab at Keills on which the harp is represented shows not only the instrument itself but also what may be a tuning-key, as well as other symbols. "Ailean" who commissioned the stone to be made for himself and his father may have been one of a family of harpers, harp makers and even harp tuners. (A reference in the Irish Annals to Aed O Shochlain who died in 1226 describes him as "master of canntaireachd and of harp tuning".) Excavations at Finlaggan in Argyll, the 15th century palace of the Lords of the Isles, yielded, in the first exploratory trench, a brass or bronze tuning pin. It is 52 mm long, with a rectangular end which shows the wear made by a tuning key. It is pierced at the narrower end for a string of less than 0.66 mm diameter.

The size of the pin is rather large for a lyre, and would suggest that it may have been made for a small, metal-strung harp. That the hereditary family of harpers to the Lords of the Isles, the MacGhille Sheanaichs, were active in the area is shown by the appearance, as witness, to a document signed at Finlaggan in 1456, of "Duncan Mcohanak". We know, from an Irish poem, written about 1640 in praise of a harp, that up to four different specialists could be involved in the construction of the instrument -a designer, a woodworker, a metalworker and a decorator. Obviously it would be convenient if all these craftsmen were based in the same area, close to their patrons and the harpers that they employed.[13]

There appears to have been just such a community around Knapdale serving, primarily, the Lords of the Isles. At this period they ruled what was virtually an independent kingdom from the Western Isles across a large part of the Highlands. It was independent culturally as well as politically. The Macdonald lords felt free to negotiate treaties of their own with the English kings — not only for military purposes, but also, significantly, to trade directly with the South of England. The Gaelic language and arts of the Highlands were developing their own character, while still showing, clearly, their Irish ancestry. The style of ornament typical of West Highland work stems from the roots of the 8th century Iona school and, indeed, outstanding exponents among the hereditary families of stonemasons bear the obviously Irish names of O Cuinn and O Brolchan. However, though the O Brolchans are recorded as working in Ireland in the 11th century, Steer and Bannerman show that the family had migrated to Scotland some time before the mid 14th century. It may, in fact, have been the flowering of native art, and the availability of patronage, which attracted Irish craftsmen to move to Scotland. It may also have been a response to the attitude of the Anglo-Norman hierarchy to the native idiom of artistic expression. In any case, by the 14th and 15th centuries the West Highland area had developed an artistic style which was quite distinctive and unique to itself.[14]

The decorative patterns on the Queen Mary and Trinity College Harps point to a West Highland origin for both instruments. The unique use of hornbeam for the construction of both the Queen Mary and the Lamont Harps suggests that the latter harp, too, emanated from the same part of the country, which was undoubtedly trading directly with the area where this tree was native. It is striking that the Scottish origin of the Lamont Harp, in particular, has never been in question, and that all the traditional and historical evidence places this firmly in Argyll. Despite this, the closest representation in stone to the Lamont Harp occurs on the tomb in Jerpoint Abbey near Kilkenny in Ireland. It is unique in that country. This harp resembles the Lamont instrument very closely, but also shows, at the lower end of the forepillar, a turned-back lip like those of the reptile heads on the Queen Mary and Trinity College harps. Presumably the upper part of the T-section also showed this feature, but it is now damaged as, unfortunately , is the peak of the harmonic curve. The carving is so accurate that the sculptor must have been working from life. There is no evidence that the harp he was copying was not made in Ireland. Its similarity to the shape of the Scottish examples, however, suggests Scottish influence in that area, probably through the galloglass warriors.[15]

Further evidence for Scotland as the source of all three existing harps is brought forward by Bannerman. In 1565 George Buchanan first published his . "History of Scotland" and, describing the customs of the western islands, he says "They delight very much in music, especially in Harps of their own sort, of which some are strung with brass wire, others with the intestines of animals; they play on them either with their nails grown long, or with a plectrum. *Their only ambition seems to be to ornament their Harps with silver and precious stones: the lower ranks, instead of gems, deck theirs with crystal".* As well as being an interesting confirmation that both gut and wire strings were in use at the same period, the description of the decoration is particularly significant. Buchanan was writing in Latin, however, which lays his assertions open to interpretation, especially since he uses the unusual word "fides", usually translated as "harp", but which is also a general term for any stringed instrument.[16]

In corroboration of his statements we have an early translation of Buchanan, published in Edinburgh in 1594 and reprinted in 1603, under the title "Certain Matters concerning the Realme of Scotland". This was the work of John Monipennie, who held lands at Pitmillie in Fife. One of his family, Mungo (or Kentigern) Monipennie, was Dean of Ross between 1546-1580, and is likely to have been based at Rossfearn in Easter Ross. Others of his relatives, probably through this connection, also developed marriage and business links with Ross. John Monipennie would thus have had opportunity to become familiar with Highland customs. His work, though based on Buchanan, differs in significant respects so that he appears to be attempting to clarify Buchanan's statements for his readers. He writes in English, and uses specific terms for different harps. "They delight much in musicke, but chiefly in Harpes and Clairshoes of their owne fashion. The strings of the Clairshoes are made of brasse wyar, and the strings of the Harpes of sinews; which strings they stryke either with their nayles growing long, or else with an instrument appointed for that use. *They take great pleasure to deck the Harpes and Clairshoes with silver and precious stones; and poor ones, that cannot attain hereunto, decke them with christall".* Monipennie's careful use of specific terms for the instruments shows that he was knowledgeable on the subject, and would also suggest that the rest of his statement is accurate.[17]

The two descriptions of the habit of ornamenting harps are particularly interesting in relation to the existing harps. The Lamont Harp bears a metal boss intended to resemble a cabuchon jewel. The mount on which it occurs was made separately from the harp, as we see from the adjustment necessary

before it would fit the top of the forepillar. The original decoration of the
Queen Mary and Trinity College Harps does not appear to have included any
such ornamentation. The Trinity College Harp, however, is now decorated
with a silver mount with two settings for stones, one still filled with a rock
crystal. This silver plate may well obscure original carving like that on the
Queen Mary instrument since the rest of the original semi-circle and line
pattern on both the curves matches almost exactly. The centre of the forepillar
on the Trinity College Harp has had a hole roughly made in it to take yet
another setting, now missing. Equally insensitive alterations were inflicted on
the Queen Mary Harp, where the centre of one of the animal roundels was
gouged out, apparently to hold a setting, while a ring of brass tacks high on
the outer face of the forepillar and three small nails on the outer edge of the
neck, which also interrupt the existing carved patterns, are further evidence
of subsequent additions to the ornamentation. According to Lude tradition,
these fastened gold and jewelled plaques which were affixed to the harp during
the reign of Queen Mary, showing the Queen's portrait and the royal arms of
Scotland. These are said to have been stolen from the harp during the Jacobite
Risings of 1745. The reign of Mary, Queen of Scots (1542-87), coincides with
Buchanan's description.

According to Bannerman, the vigorous West Highland school of carving
petered out around the middle of the 16th century, so it may be that the desire
to ornament harps with silver and gems was a substitute for the superb carving
of the previous century. Certainly the Trinity College Harp, judging by the
quality of its wood carving, was not the "poor man's harp" that Buchanan's
comments would suggest, but its owners still seem to have felt the need to make
it an object of conspicious wealth by the addition of silverwork and crystals.
So, too, did the owners of the Queen Mary instrument. It would appear that
the convention of decorating harps in this way was a fairly short lived fashion
which was characteristic of Scotland in the mid 16th century, and may
subsequently have been copied from time to time in Ireland.[18]

Although Irish poetry and legend may describe harps formed from precious
metals — sometimes entirely of gold — this seems to be purely romantic
invention. In the early poems which describe harps, Gofraidh Fionn
O'Dalaigh, though he speaks of the instrument itself as "breast jewel of the
High Kings", and, in detail, of the harp's colour and shape, makes no mention
of precious ornamentation on it. Nor do the additional twelve verses which
were added at a later date.[19] O'Curry's often-quoted version of a 13th century
poem, on a harp which had belonged to Donnachadh Cairbreach O Briain, is
flawed. The writer was Giolla Brighde Albanach, a Scot. Gerard Murphy
points out that a mistranslation by O'Curry resulted in the legend that the poet
was trying to buy back from Scotland his master's harp "which had previously
passed to that country". On the contrary, Giolla Brighde was asserting that
nothing would part him from the harp that was so dear to him. O'Curry also

translates "an chroinn tslabhradhuigh" as "this gem-set tree", where in fact the word "slabhradhaigh" does not infer jewels, but means a "chain" — more likely a description of the row of metal shoes which protect each string-hole up the centre strip of the harp. None of the surviving 16th or 17th century Irish harps bear mounts of precious metal, or jewelled or crystal settings. By 1640 an Irish poem mentions a craftsman who would decorate the harps with gold, but the evidence suggests that this type of ornamentation was not usual during the earlier period.[20]

All these clues point to the strong possibility that the Trinity College Harp may have been made in Scotland, and that it did not leave that country until, at the earliest, the second half of the 16th century. The history of this harp, of which surprisingly little is known, would tend to agree with this hypothesis.

6 FICTION AND FACTS

"Is mairg a bhristeadh teud cruite"
Woe unto such as break a harp-string — Gaelic proverb[1]

Although the Trinity College Harp has been widely known as the "Brian Boru Harp", it is generally agreed that any connection between this instrument and the High King of Ireland who died in 1014 was the invention of 19th century myth-makers. The first known Irish owners of this harp were a branch of the O'Neill family during the late 16th or early 17th century. Their coat-of-arms was engraved on a small silver badge which was fixed at that time to the front part of the carved reptile's head on the forepillar.

If the Trinity College Harp was indeed made in Scotland, the opportunities for it to have crossed the Irish Sea into the possession of the O'Neills at this period were many, varied and extremely colourful. In the first place, the trade route between Scotland and Ireland ran from Craignish in Argyll, a few miles to the north of Keills, across Jura and Islay, to Lough Foyle in Ulster, which leads directly down into the O'Neill lands of Tyrone. There were many links between the great families of the two countries. In 1565, Sorley Boy MacDonnell, who was one of the family of the MacDonalds of the Isles and, according to Pitcairn's Criminal Trials, was married to O'Neill's sister, was taken prisoner by Shane O'Neill, Lord of Tyrone. As ransom, Shane negotiated with MacDonald for reinforcements of 1,000 galloglasses in return for Sorley Boy's freedom, in 1566. In that year he also bargained with the Earl of Argyll for troops to resist the English. The MacDonnells later gained further territory in Northern Ireland when, in 1586, Sorley Boy and his cousin Angus were "denizened" and granted lands in parts of the Route and Glens of Antrim, respectively. These may have been given to them in return for their help, in 1567, in the eventual massacre of Shane and his followers.[2]

By far the most extraordinary story also concerns the exploits of the intemperate Shane. Catherine MacLean was a lady related to some of the foremost aristocratic families of the West of Scotland. She was sister to MacLean of Duart on Mull, and widow of the Earl of Argyll. As well as speaking Gaelic, she was "not unlearned in the Latin tong, speakyth good French, and is sayd some lytell Italyone". Her second marriage was to Calvagh O'Donnell of Tir Connell, or Donegal. In 1560, while they were at the monastery of Killodonnell on the shore of Lough Swilly, they were attacked 69 by Shane O'Neill, whose enmity with the O'Donnells was of long standing, and both O'Donnell and his lady were carried off. She is said to have been kept, chained to a small boy, and only released to satisfy her captor's drunken pleasure. She bore sons to both O'Donnell and O'Neill, and the acts of feuding, revenge and treachery between her Scottish relatives and the Irish clans continued for many years. This cultured and aristocratic lady, who was both a Scottish dowager countess and an Irish queen, might well have brought a harper in her retinue from Argyll. Whether she would have had much opportunity to enjoy music seems rather doubtful! Some sources say that she deserted O'Donnell for O'Neill, and may have betrayed him. Whatever the case, she eventually returned to Scotland and was married, yet again, to Stewart of Appin, one of Argyll's advisers.[3]

Any connection between the Trinity College Harp and these historical events is, of course, purely a matter of speculation. What they demonstrate, however, is that contacts (of all kinds!) between the O'Neills and the great families of Argyll, where the harp is likely to have been made, were frequent and constant, and involved a sizeable influx of Scots into the North of Ireland during the 16th century. The influence of the thousands of well-born galloglass warriors, recruited to aid the Irish chiefs at this time, must have extended throughout the entire country.

Definite records do exist, however, of one clarsach which has especially strong associations with the family of the Lords of the Isles, under whose patronage both Queen Mary and Trinity College harps may have been made — a family whose progress leads directly to Ireland and to the O'Neills. The Trinity College Harp is known to have been in O'Neill possession by the 17th century.

In 1490 an action was raised by Ninian Bannatyne of Kaimes in Bute against Agnes MacDonnell "his gudemother for the spoiliation and taking from him of ane pailzoun (a pavilion or tent), a brew cauldrone of xvij gallons, ane maskifat (a vat) and *ane clareschaw* ...". On 7th October 1491 it was decreed that she should keep the harp, but that she should compensate her stepson for it to the sum of xx shillings. Agnes or Agnetta MacDonnell was the daughter of one of the Lords of the Isles.[4] Her father, John Mor, had assumed the title and the leadership of the West Highland clans in the power struggle with the Scottish Crown. In 1499 John Mor, with his son Iain Cathanach and his grandsons, was captured and executed in Edinburgh. At least one of the grandsons, Alasdair, escaped this fate, and made his way to Ireland, no doubt hoping to consolidate support and fighting men for his cause. His great-great-grandfather, Iain Mor MacDonnell, had married Marjery, heiress to the powerful Anglo-Irish Bissett family. Through her the MacDonnells had inherited extensive lands in Northern Ireland, and were known as Lords of Dunniveg and the Glens of Antrim. Alasdair's sons, James, Angus, Colla and Sorley Boy, spent much of their lives in Ireland. It was Sorley Boy who married

Mary, daughter of Con O'Neill, Earl of Tyrone, and it is in the possession of the O'Neills that the Trinity College Harp is found later in the century. Sorley Boy's brother James also made an important dynastic marriage, to Agnes Campbell, daughter of the 3rd Earl of Argyll. On James's death in 1565, she was again married, this time to Turlough Luineach, who had succeeded Shane as chief of the O'Neills. She too brought with her a large dowry of galloglasses to serve her new lord, and thus, indirectly, once more linked the family of the Lords of the Isles with the O'Neills. It is certainly possible that Agnes MacDonnell's clarsach should have followed this path to Ireland as a token of friendship between the MacDonnells and the O'Neills, and that the jewelled mount and O'Neill badge were affixed to it in the mid 16th century to mark one of these unions. In a further alliance between the two families, in 1589, Angus, eldest son of James, late Lord of the Isles, came to Ireland and marked his commitment to O'Neill's revolt against Tyrone by an exchange of presents. The Earl and he "joined in great friendship, laying together in one bed for two nights". The Irish lord gave Angus seven of his best horses, and the Scottish chief, in return, presented O'Neill's men with all the plaids and armour he had brought with him.[5] Perhaps it is slightly less likely that a clarsach might have exchanged hands on an occasion such as this, rather than to mark a wedding or betrothal.

Nor is this the end of the tangle of relationships and co-incidences that surround Agnes MacDonnell. She was a widow when she married Thomas Bannatyne of Kaimes. Her first husband had been John Lamont, who died in 1488.[6] On his death, possibly at the battle of Sauchieburn, John Lamont's lack of a male heir led to the succession moving to his brother Duncan. According to McKechnie, Duncan (d.1515) was married c. 1498 to Giles Buchanan of that Ilk. This family, too, had an interest in harping. Giles's near relative, Walter Buchanan of Spittel, was himself involved in a dispute over a harp, and on 23 February 1533-4 he was ordered in a judgement in favour of Isabell Logan, John Lennox her son, and Thomas Napier of Ballekrinrain, to return "ane harp als gude as it was at the tyme it was taken fra the said Isabell".[7] Returning to the Lamonts, John and Duncan also had two sisters whose names were Lilias and Mary. It is Lilias who is said to have married Charles Robertson and to have brought the Lamont Harp to Lude in her dowry.

The known background of the Lude Harps is mostly dependent on oral traditions and, since there is usually at least a basis of fact behind these, they are worth examining in detail.

A letter from General Robertson giving the history of the two harps which had been handed down within his family was sent with them to Edinburgh in 1805, when the Highland Society commissioned John Gunn to examine and report on the instruments. This letter was unfortunately mislaid while he was writing the report, which accounts for a certain amount of confusion within it. The letter had been lost altogether by 1880 (possibly in a fire at the Society's rooms) when Charles Bell, on behalf of the Society of Antiquaries of Scotland, acquired the two harps from the Steuarts of Dalguise, to whom they had passed by marriage. Bell suggests, since Gunn's report was published during the lifetime of General Robertson, when it could have been contradicted, that its main particulars may be taken as authentic. The family tradition of Lude, recorded at the beginning of Gunn's report, states that the Caledonian (Lamont) Harp was brought from Argyllshire in about the year 1640 (changed in an erratum note to 1460), by a "lady of the family of Lamont, to the House of Lude, upon her marriage into the family of Robertson of Lude". Gunn later repeats this with the date changed to 1460, and with the suggestion that "we should therefore infer that the Lady was a performer on the harp". Bell, in his account, quotes Gunn, but with the date changed to 1464, and adds a quotation from Burke's "Landed Gentry", 1848, where it is stated that "Charles, the 5th Laird of Lude, married during his father's lifetime, Lilias, daughter of Sir John Lamont of Lamont, and it was with this lady there came one of those very curious old harps called the "Lamont Harp". John, grandson of the said Charles and Lilias, seventh of Lude, married Beatrix Gardyn, widow of Finla More, ancestor of the family of Invercauld, who was killed the same year at the battle of Pinkie".

It is with Beatrix Gardyn that the Queen Mary Harp is said to have come to Lude. Gunn's version of the tradition states that it was given to Beatrix Gardyn by Queen Mary, while on a hunting excursion to Perthshire, and that Beatrix had married into the family of Lude. The portrait of the Queen, and the Royal Arms, were said to have been fixed to the harp at this time. A footnote by Gunn claims to be quoting General Robertson's letter, but later in the report a further footnote correcting an erroneous statement made while the letter was mislaid, quotes the General's words, referring to Beatrix Gardyn — "from which lady both the families of Farquharson and this family (Lude) are descended". The footnote suggests that the harp then came with one of her female descendants to Lude. Gunn continues with a long description of a hunting party to Atholl in 1563, attended by Mary, Queen of Scots, but this appears to be an addition made by Gunn, himself, and not taken from General Robertson's own words. Bell (who obviously did not think much of Gunn's scholarship) states that, while the traditions may be accepted as correct if shorn of the "flowery antiquarian statements introduced (by Gunn) to make up a bulky, saleable and readable publication ... The story of the gift from Queen Mary to Beatrix Gardyn may have been told from generation to generation, but there has been more than one Queen Mary in Scotland, and in the course of the years became connected with the best known Queen Mary, probably before the marriage of John Robertson of Lude, the last performer on the harp, with Margaret Farquharson of Invercauld, the descendant of Beatrix, by whom it may be reasonably conjectured that the harp was brought to Lude".[8]

Bell's scepticism about the historical accuracy of Gunn's elaborations on the subject of the harp's origins is well-founded, especially when they relate to such a romantic figure as Mary, Queen of Scots. She, like other figures such as Bonnie Prince Charlie and Rob Roy, attracted a great deal of 19th century myth-making! However, to test the validity of these traditions, we can trace back through the history of the house of Lude, which has been linked for so long with both the harps.

Beatrix Gardyn, "daughter to Banchory", was indeed widowed by the battle of Pinkie in 1547 in which her husband, Finlay Mor, was killed. During this marriage she had bourne five sons and five daughters to continue the line of the Farquharsons. Beatrix Gardyn's second marriage was to John Terlachson (Charles' son). The Gaelic custom of using patronymics, as well as the family name, makes it possible to identify John Terlachson as John Robertson of ·Monzies, who was born in about 1485.[9]

His father was Charles Mac Ian (John's son) of Clunes. There are few contemporary references to this Charles Robertson, but he is likely to be the "Carlet Johnson", who witnessed an instrument of seisin in favour of the Earl of Atholl in Atholl in the year 1474. The Robertson family tradition, that the Lamont Harp came to Lude as a result of the marriage of Lilias Lamont to Charles Robertson in about 1460-64, could fit with the known dates of this "Carlet Johnson". A mid 18th century manuscript in the Lude papers mentions "John of Monzies, born about 1485, the son of Charles Mac Ian of Clunes, born 1455, the second son of John Donaldson of Lude, born about 1420". If this is correct, then the marriage of Charles to Lilias must have occurred later than Gunn's date of 1460. On the other hand, child-marriages were common at this period, which may account for the birth of their son more than twenty years later![10]

Apart from the Clan history, at present there is no known documentary evidence which refers elsewhere to Lilias Lamont, though this is indeed a common forename in the Lamont family. The Lamonts were one of the major clans of Argyllshire, who were associated with the Knapdale and Cowal areas in particular. In 1238 Sir Ladman (eponymous ancestor of the family) gave to Paisley Abbey the Churches of Kilmun and Kilfinan, and the Chapel of Kilmory on Loch Gilp. The Glassarie Writs also list two discharges on 26th January 1434 by John McKane of Kylman (John Lamont of Kilmun on the Holy Loch) to Sir John Skrymgeour, which was witnessed, among others, by Eugenio Klerscharch. (Eoghan or Ewen Clarsach).[11]

The MacEwens were a family of hereditary poets and genealogists who served the Campbells of Argyll and Glenorchy and, before them, the MacDougalls of Dunollie. They may also have had connections with the Irish bardic family of O'Hosey who, like the MacEwens, often used the uncommon forename of "Athairne".[12] After the middle of the 16th century, however, MacEwen harpers are found in the neighbourhood of Lude. An instrument of seisin 1588, in favour of John Tarlachsone alias Robertson, the son and heir of John Terlachsone of Monzie, lists among the witnesses, Anthony McEwin VcChlairser, a servant of the said John. Anthony is probably a scribal attempt at Anglicising the Gaelic name "Athairne". Traces of MacEwens continue with a "John" and "Neil" on record in Middle Dalguise in 1597 (two names which also run in the pedigree of the Argyll bardic line.) Another harper occurs in the Lude Barony Court Records for 15th August 1670. At a court held by Alexander Robertson of Lude, a claim was given by "John McEvin harper against Allan McDod for blooding him in the brow, the said Allan confest that he strak him with ane tree, and denyes not the bloodweik". The estate of Lude falls within the Earldom of Atholl, and shares a common march with the Atholl estate of Blair. Among the Blair papers is a commission signed by the Duke on 24th June 1709 nominating "John Robertson, alias Clarsair, at Poldornie, to be one of the poormen in the parish of Blair Atholl". This may indicate the presence of another harper, but it was common for clansmen to use the family name of their chief so this may well be the same "John McEvin" who, having survived the brawl in 1670, had fallen on hard times in his old age.[13]

In 1669, a Croft VcEwin is mentioned in the Lude papers and is likely to have been the land held by the family of harpers. It occurs again as Croft ic Kewen in 1704, when it is described as a 10 shilling land, and was still on record up to the end of the 18th century, but on these occasions it does not appear to have been held by anyone of the name of McEwen. It can probably be identified as the "Balinewen" near the site marked as a Druid temple on Stobie's map of 1783, close to the Bridge of Tilt, a little north of the modern village of Blair Atholl.[14]

If the information handed down in the Robertson family is true, and it was Charles of Clunes who married Lilias Lamont, a MacEwen harper with the "Lamont" Harp may have travelled with her from Argyll, where the harp was made, as part of her dowry. The suggestion that the harp was played by Lilias herself was an inference made by John Gunn, and was not derived from General Robertson. Indeed the strong, simple lines of the harp, and the lack of carved decoration, suggest that it may have been the "working instrument" of a professional harper, rather than a ceremonial or aristocrat's instrument.

What of the history of the Queen Mary Harp? In the main line, the Robertsons of Lude claim descent from Patrick de Atholia, son of Duncan de Atholia, in the 14th century. The line can be traced in the Lude papers, through Donald Patrickson, to his son John, who received a charter of the lands of Lude in 1448, and was married to Margaret Drummond some time before 1452. In 1507 their son, Donald Johnson, with the approval of his father, resigned the Lands of Lude to his own son, John Donaldson. In his turn, John Donaldson resigned the lands and barony of Lude, in 1518, into the hands of James, Archbishop of St. Andrews, and one of the Regents of Scotland, in favour of Patrick Ogilvy of Inchmartine, while reserving to Donald of Lude his life rent thereof. A manuscript of about 1800, amongst the Lude papers, contains the tradition that Ogilvy of Inchmartine was uncle to John Donaldson — whose mother may therefore have been an Ogilvy — and that he thus gained an unfair opportunity of possessing his nephew's lands. It is not made clear exactly how he achieved this. In any case, the main line of the Robertsons died out at this period, and Lude remained in Ogilvy hands for a further three generations.[15]

Not all the Robertson lands had been lost, however. John Donaldson and Margaret Drummond apparently also had at least one younger son, the Charles Mac Ian (John's son) of Clunes, already mentioned. His son, John Tarlachson, received a charter in 1510 for the lands of Easter Monzie, and a charter in 1513 for Wester Monzie in the lordship of Lude, from John Donaldson of Lude, his cousin. Sometime between 1547 and 1564 either John Tarlachson or his son, also named John Tarlachson, married Beatrix Gardyn, and at this time laid claim to the estate of Inchmagrannoch. His claim to these lands was ratified by Mary, Queen of Scots, and her husband Henry, Lord Darnley.[16]

The lands at Inchmagrannoch formerly belonged to the Cathedral of Dunkeld, and had been feued from the Dean and Chapter of Dunkeld by Sir Robert McNair, canon of Dunkeld and prebendary of Inchmagrannoch. From Sir Robert, Inchmagrannoch passed to John and Beatrix, and the Investment was confirmed by the Queen on 18th December 1565. It would be quite in keeping with the practice of these times for the harp to have been handed over as a ceremonial gift to mark the acquisition of the lands, and it was likely that the addition of the jewelled and enamelled portrait and royal arms of the reigning monarch would have been made at this time.

As the carving on the Queen Mary Harp suggests, the instrument was probably originally made for use in a religious context. The church at Dunkeld was well-known for its music. We find the canons described in the Dunkeld Rentals of this period. "Sir William Martyne, chaplain of St. Katherine, is respected and has musical gifts. His brother John, a young priest, simple and devout, with a mastery of music" was rector of Lude. John Martyne, John Leslie and William Scherar, chaplain, were "priests born in the city of Dunkeld, all thorough musicians and accustomed from their youth to take their part in service and rule the choir". Other priests are said to have had "knowledge of the Irish tongue" (i.e. Gaelic), and to have been "highly trained in the theory of music as well as in the art of singing". We know that the organ was used in the church, and they may possibly also have played the harp, but there is no direct evidence for this. In the Book of the Dean of Lismore, which dates from 1512-40, there is a mention, in the lists of entertainers, of a Robert Clarsair Leod (Lude), but there is no apparent link between this harper and the Dunkeld Church. He may well have been one of the MacEwen harpers who, as we have seen, are likely to have come to Lude in the second half of the 15th century. But apart from the obvious musicality of the Dunkeld Church, and the religious significance of the carved designs on the harp, there is no suggestion that a harp was in the possession of the Dunkeld abbacy before the Queen Mary Harp appears at Lude. It may then have come to the Robertsons from quite a different direction.[17]

Circumstantial though the evidence is, there is one ecclesiastical establishment that clearly did possess a clarsach at the right period, and can be shown to have the appropriate connections to Argyll, where the harp is likely to have been made, and to Lude, where it is found in 1565. A comprehensive rental of the Abbey of Lindores includes an inventory of the contents made in 1530, and among the items listed is "Ane clairchew". Lindores lies on the south bank of the Tay, just opposite, and certainly within the sphere of influence of the estate of Inchmartine on the north side of the river. This was held by the Ogilvy family who had acquired, by marriage, extensive lands in Inchmartine, Strathardle, Elcho and in Atholl, while in 1518, the Ogilvys had also gained, by means fair or foul, the lands of Lude.[18]

There are several possible reasons why a harp owned by Lindores Abbey might have been removed to Atholl. Lindores was the first of the abbeys to suffer from the zeal of the Reformation, being visited by a mob from Dundee in the autumn of 1543 — although the damage caused at this time seems to have been minor compared with a second attack on the abbey led by John Knox in 1559. The valuable contents of the building may well have been removed for safekeeping on either of these occasions, to the sister church of Dunkeld, or into the custody of the Ogilvies, as influential neighbours — who were apparently not above a bit of opportunistic acquisition when they had the chance. It is also worth commenting on the fact that the Ogilvies' lands of Inchmartine follow the old Shinagag Road which, before the advent of the modern A9, was one of the main routes into Atholl by way of Strathardle. This was the road taken by Mary, Queen of Scots, on her way to visit the Earl of Atholl in 1565, the occasion on which the harp was said to have been given to Beatrix Gardyn. Could she perhaps have received the Lindores Abbey harp at this time, to be later dispensed as a gift?

How had a clarsach reached Lindores in the first place? One possibility is through the local family of Scrymgeour, constables of Dundee and standard bearers of Scotland. They were Baillies of Lindores around 1442, and held lands from Lindores in about 1521, but were also overlords of the lands of Glassary in Argyll, and hereditary abbots, throughout the 15th century, of Kilmichael Glassary, which is close to the area where the Queen Mary Harp is thought to have been made. A John Scrymgeour of Henriston was also a signatory on the discharges by John Lamont of Kilmun to John Scrymgeour in 1434, witnessed by Eoghan Clarsach.[19]

But a striking coincidence in one of the Abbey documents suggests that it may have come from quite another donor. The Burgh of Newburgh, which was founded by Lindores and was dependent on the Abbey, had its rights and privileges renewed by the Abbot in an Abstract of Instrument dated 13th July

1457. This gives a complete list of the convent of the Abbey and the baillies and burgesses of the Burgh. All of the names are much as one would expect from that part of Lowland Scotland, with the exception of one — "Angus de Insulis", Angus of the Isles. The presence of a member of the family of the Lord of the Isles as a burgess of Newburgh at this time is as remarkable as that of a clarsach in the Abbey itself.[20] A grave-slab in Iona, dedicated to Angus, son of Angus of the Isles, shows similar intertwined split-palmette leaves to those at the foot of the pillar on the Queen Mary Harp, and is also, unusually, carved with four different beasts. Three of these beasts, a lion, a griffin and a two-footed dragon, appear on the roundels on the pillar of the harp. However, we have not yet been able to confirm the identity of the Angus of this slab.[21]

Patronage by the Lords of the Isles may have been the reason that Lindores Abbey was chosen as the place of confinement of James Douglas, when he failed in the rising against James II in 1484. He had been one of the MacDonalds' staunchest supporters — it would be appropriate that they should try to make his life sentence as comfortable as possible. He accepted retirement to a holy life, became a monk and died there in 1488. Does his presence account for the inclusion, in the same inventory, not only of the clarsach, but also of "twa pairs of thabills wt thair men" — chess boards and a set of pieces? Life at Lindores would seem to have had a certain ease and elegance which may have helped to mark the slow passage of the religious day.

Graveslab of Angus MacDonald, Iona

It is clear that these harps were rare and beautiful instruments then as now, and were certainly important and significant enough to be used as ceremonial gifts by Queen, Prince or chieftain. By piecing together the tiny scraps of evidence it may eventually be possible to trace the progress of these few surviving clarsachs, since their construction over 500 years ago.

7 COURT AND COURTIERS

The musicke then, and heavenly harmony
Of instruments accorded in a kie,
Maist musicall and delicate to get,
Sall their be heard together sweitly set:
As clarshons cleare, douce friddoning of flutes,
The viols swift and finest Venus lutes,
Ioynd with the voice of men, and breisting boyes,
Quhais measour iust sall modulat the noyse:[1]

The inauguration of Alexander III is commemorated on a contemporary seal of Scone Abbey, which was probably struck shortly after the ceremony. This took place at Scone on 13 July 1249. Officiating are the earls of Fife and Strathearn, the bishops of St. Andrews and Dunkeld, and the abbot of Scone. The King's Poet, whose duties were to recite the royal genealogy, to compose an ode, and to present the wand or sceptre of Kingship, is also portrayed. A seventh, smaller figure is depicted immediately behind the poet. He carries a triangular object at his left shoulder. Bannerman suggests that this represents the King's harper, who is likely to have assisted the poet in his inaugural duties, and to have accompanied or performed the newly composed ode. The identity of the royal harper at this date is not known. The first musician to be described as "the King of Scotland's harper" is Master Elyas, in 1278. However the Galloway-based family of Mac a' Bhreatnaich clarsach-players provided harpers to the royal court for a number of generations, and Bannerman postulates that they came from the appropriate Gaelic cultural background to accompany the "ollamh rig Alban" or poet at the ceremony at Scone.[2]

In 1290, at the wedding of of Princess Joan of England to Gilbert de Clare, a Scottish herald was present at the court of Edward I in London. He was James de Cowpen, described as "King Caupenny de Scotia, who came (to Westminster) to the feast of the aforesaid nuptials". He was paid 50s. — a considerable sum — by gift of the King, for performing his duties as a "Rex Haraldorum", a King of Heralds. These heralds were officials of the court who had responsibility for organising jousts and tournaments, and were concerned with knighthoods and blazons, and with drawing up lists of knights for muster. They were also employed on more serious military matters, as messengers or secret agents. King Caupenny may have been a Herald of Alexander III of

Scotland, and subsequently of John Balliol, who abdicated in 1296, fleeing to England to escape Robert the Bruce. From this date, when he again attended a wedding of one of the royal princesses, James de Cowpen was employed at Edward's court, where his knowledge of Scotland, its terrain and its noble families would have been of great value to the English king in his campaigns against the Bruce. There are many references to James de Cowpen in the Wardrobe Accounts, detailing payment of wages to him, and describing the livery with which he was issued. The heralds wore the king's coat-of-arms emblazoned on their tabards as a sign that they were answerable to the king himself, and paid for out of his Privy Purse. He also provided the cap, baton and cup of the Rex Haraldorum. In addition, James Cowpen received many valuable personal gifts from the king, including costly jewellery and a horse. The scribes give various different versions of his name, including Jakettus de Scotia (Jamie of Scotland), Monsire Capenny, Capigny, Capainy, Capini, Capin and Copyn. Most interesting of all is the fragment of an account book from the King's Chamber, which probably dates from between 1300-1307, and refers to him as "Roy de Copiny, *harpour*".

The heralds divided their time between knightly ceremony, military duties and, in the royal household, minstrelsy. They were expected to arrange and perform in theatrical and musical performances, and to direct and stage-manage royal events. King Caupenny was regarded as one of the elite amongst these minstrels. For entertainment at a special function he might receive a sizeable reward, the modern equivalent of which would be around £1000, as he did on the occasion of the knighting of the Prince of Wales in 1306. He also "topped the bill", at that feast, with two distinguished guest musicians from France, Philip de Cambrai and Le Roy de Champagne, for whom Caupenny had the honour of collecting the "largesse" during the festivities. Later he travelled with the Royal Household north to Lanercost, where he staged plays to amuse the queen. Perhaps taking advantage of the soothing, healing reputation of harp music, he also played to the king during his long and painful illness there. The last entry which refers to him is a payment of wages on 13th June 1307, in Carlisle. This perhaps indicates that after Edward's death, James de Cowpen returned to his home in the north. His descendents may again have found favour at the Scottish Court — in 1503 King James IV paid 40s for a saddle and harness for a "Johne de Cowpanis". Although the information which relates to King Caupenny comes to us from English sources, the esteem in which he was held, and the swift progress of his career would indicate that his musical skill was well recognised before he left Scotland, where he probably performed similar courtly duties.[3]

Another Scottish musician also played at Princess Joan's wedding. John Comyn of Badenoch, "the Black Comyn", had been exiled from Scotland for supporting his brother-in-law John Balliol's claim to the throne, and was living in England, under the watchful eye of Edward I. With him, he brought his "citharista" — probably a clarsach player rather than a harper. He is likely to have been a native Gael but, since it was common for the minstrels to be multilingual, he may have been able to perform in French as well, this being the usual language of the Court. (Edward himself is only known to have spoken English on two occasions; the first when making a rather irreverent pun on the name of the Earl Marshal, who was called Bigod; the other during a crusade in 1271, when an assassin of the Old Man of the Mountains made an attempt on his life. The struggle was heard by Edward's own harper who rushed into the tent and, though the King had by this time managed to kill his attacker, began to belabour the corpse with a wooden stool.) Whatever language Comyn's minstrel performed in, his song found favour with the King, who rewarded him with a mark.[4]

From the Court Accounts and other State Papers, we see that the "King's Harper" held a particularly prominent position in the royal household from the Norman period onwards. He may have been in charge of the less important musicians who dealt with the day-to-day entertainment of the court. Royal harpers were often particularly favoured by their masters, sometimes with grants of lands. In 1296 Edward of England restored the lands, previously held in Perth and Fife, to Elyas the king's harper.[5] Like James de Cowpen, Elyas apparently transferred his allegiance to become a servant of Edward I after the death of Alexander III, with whom he too had visited England. It was in 1303 near Sandford, just north of Largo Bay in Fife, that Edward I met five Scottish harpers, whom he rewarded for their playing. Even now, in the age of mass-communication and fast travel, to assemble five harpers, with their instruments, at short notice would not be an easy task. Such a convocation, therefore, suggests that there might have been a school of harp-playing in the area, perhaps under the tutelage of the royal harper, Elyas. Robert the Bruce, as we have mentioned, patronised several harpers and, in particular, made a grant of land to Thomas "Citharista", who appears as Provost of Rutherglen from 1328 to 1329, and again at the Coronation of David II in 1331. Perhaps he was the "minstrel of the King of Scotland" to whom the Accounts of the Abbey of Durham record a payment in 1333-34 ("Histrionibus Regis Scocie, 3s. 4d.") — they also note the purchase, at that date, of a harp for what seems like a very fair price! "In 1. Cythara emp. pro Thom. Harpour, 3s." David II himself gave land to Patrick McChruitear in Carrick, while in the Thanedom of Aberlemno, he gave the lands of Balveny and Tolecandantum (possibly now known as Tillywhandland) to "Ade Chichariste" of Forfar. The same harper may be linked with the placename "Harperakirhade" between Inverarity and Monikie, which was recorded in 1471. Another of David's favoured harpers was Nicholas Chicharist of Linlithgow, who may be connected with the "Crouderland" at The Binns.[6]

Harp and clarsach were heard at court not only in the hands of professional musicians, but were also accepted as instruments on which those of noble birth might display their musical talents. Writing in 1437, Walter Bower, who was Abbot of Inchcolm and thus had the opportunity to become familiar with courtly life, described the assassination of James I, and the character and abilities of the murdered king. His skill in the art of music was particularly noted. Bower writes "This man indeed [was a distinguished] musician, not only in singing, but also in a high standard of performance on the drum, for example, and the fiddle, on the psaltery and organ, the flute and harp, the trumpet and pipe, certainly not [just] as an enthusiastic amateur, but attaining the highest degree of mastery. Mother Nature [who is a kind of force and power grafted on to human kind by divine agency] gave him distinction of a lively kind beyond all human capacity for judgement, especially in handling the harp [... in tactu cithare ...], as if she had pre-eminently endowed with these gifts another Orpheus, the first and foremost of all lyrists who play delightfully and sweetly upon their lyres. In this he clearly displayed the innate talent of the Scot, in surpassing wonderfully even the Irish themselves in performances on the harp (liricis)". He then quotes the passage from Gerald of Wales on Welsh, Irish and Scottish instruments. Bower's fulsome compliments on the musical ability of the king probably owe much to courtly flattery, but James was known to have spent much of the eighteen years during which he was in captivity in England in study of the arts and sciences. Since he was only thirteen years old when he was captured as his father attempted to send him to safety in France, it is doubtful whether he could have acquired a great deal of this musical education before he left Scotland, so we do not know what type of harp he may have played. He is likely to have been instructed in the music that was fashionable at any of the European courts of the period. Bower's description, by using the different words "cithara" and "lyra", does seem to be attempting to make a distinction between the instrument played by the King, and those typical of the Scots and Irish — perhaps the gut-strung harp as opposed to a clarsach? However, James certainly wrote poetry in his native Scots, (as can be seen in his book "The King's Quair") and enjoyed his country's music. An evening is described at James's court after his return from exile. It sounds delightful. "Both afore soper and long aftere ynto quarter of the nyght, in which the Erle of Athetelles and Robert Stward were aboute the Kyng, where they were occupied at the playing of the chesse, at the tables; yn syngyng, and pypyng, yn harpyng and other honest solaces of grete plesaunce and disporte".[7]

During the reigns of James II and James III patronage of music remained strong, despite the turmoil of war. The Treasurer's Accounts for this period have not survived so we know only that musicians and players from Scotland and the Continent often performed at court, and that miming — which is closely dependant on music — was especially popular.

The Treasurer's Accounts are, however, extant for the reign of James IV, 1488-1513, and give us a colourful and detailed picture of the amusements and courtly life of the period. They tell of hawking and jousting amid banners painted gold, vermillion, white and viridian, of the mending of the queen's hangings of arras and scarlet; the purchasing of finely fashioned trappings for the great horses, and payment of "bridilsilver" to their grooms; of the "pirnis (pins) of gold to sew the king's sarkis with"; of swans' collars, "tua ringis saphiris" and pearls as a present for the queen from her husband. The king not only gave bounty to his family and nobles, but also showed charity to his needy subjects — to "ane ald failyeit preist" in Perth; to "the blind wif that hed hir eyne schorne"; to "Andro Craw that wes hurt"; and "to the woman that nursit ane barne" (bairn) in Stirling. We read of the court cooks and the food and supplies brought in — four hundred "haddockis", "foure stane of cheis", butter, meal and ale, wine and venison, pike and trout, plovers, moor fowls and "quyk heronis" (live herons). Sometimes special offerings of "strayberies" or "cheryis" would be presented to the king or queen and their bearers rewarded. The king amused himself at hunting with his dogs, practising his skill with the crossbow or gun, or at playing at the bowls, or at cards with his courtiers — he frequently lost money! There were often entertainments — dancers, storytellers, "gysaris" (jesters) and musicians from Italy, France, England and the Low Countries. The court was well acquainted with the European music of the times but Scottish musicians, both Highland and Lowland, were also familiar performers. The first mention of a harper is of an unnamed musician who played for the king at Linlithgow at Eastertime, 1491. Blind Harry, a singer or storyteller, and Bennat, who was probably a fiddle player, were paid on the same occasion.

Harpers, both named and unnamed, feature regularly and can be divided into two main groups — those travelling musicians or harpers attached to a particular patron, who were rewarded for a specific performance; and those musicians who were regularly employed at Court and tended to be paid at regular intervals.

An exception to this may have been the family of clarsach players named MacBhreatnaich, who make regular appearances at Court between 1491 and 1513, yet seem to have been based in Galloway. "Martyn harper clarsach" is the first to be named, playing with "toder Ersche clareschaw", and indeed these two Gaelic harpers appear together occasionally, especially in the earlier years, so we may speculate that the second musician may have been Martyn's son, John. The Exchequer Rentals tell us that Martyn MacBhreatnaich, "citharist", held the lands of Clutag and Knockann, near Wigtown, at least as far back as 1471 (before this date the Rentals do not give the names of the tenants), and they continued in his possession until 1489-90. At this date John MacBhreatnaich, "clarshioner", who was presumably his son, took over the tacks of his father's holdings, which may mark the death of Martyn. On 15th January 1506, another generation later, Rolland MacBhreatnaich received the letter of tack of Knockan, and from 1507 he makes his appearance at Court.[8]

Since "Rolland" is the Anglicised version of the Gaelic name "Lachlann", this man may be the Lachlann MacBhreatnaich or Galbraith described in the Gaelic poem by Duncan Campbell of Glenorchy. Campbell is mentioned frequently in the Treasurer's Accounts and obviously enjoyed high standing and favour at court. He probably entertained the king near Balquhidder in 1501, on which occasion a clarsach player and "tua Heland bardis" performed for the monarch. Since both Rolland and Glenorchy are thought to have been killed at Flodden in 1513, doubt has been thrown on the possibility that Glenorchy could have composed the poem for the harper. It is an elegy on his death. However, Professor William Gillies makes it clear that the poem is a satiric elegy, which would have been composed during the subject's lifetime — then, as now, it was not considered appropriate to mock the dead.

"Ma theasta, ni chuala me
leitheid Lochlainn ar leimhe
o chruthaigh Dia na daoine: ..."

(If he is no more, I have never heard of Lachlann's
like for being obnoxious)

"Ce do-ni leamh gach aoinlios?" (Who is making every court irritable?)

"Co a-ni solar gan naire?" (Who is shamelessly scavenging?)

"Ce iarras ar mhnaibh oga
coin bheaga agus neasoga"

(who is asking young ladies for little dogs and ferrets)

"Ce as firleamh i gcoitcheann?" (Who is really awful in general?)

These darts must surely have been directed at a person who was able to answer back in the tradition of satiric bardic contests! The poem also mentions that Lachlann had no heir, and indeed, after 1513, the lands of Knockann were no longer held by MacBhreatnaichs.

It is also worth noting that Clutag and Knockann may have been in their possession before 1471, the date at which records of the names of tenants begin. Like most of this area of Galloway, these estates originally belonged to the Douglas family but passed to the Crown after they were attainted in the 1450's. The Douglasses rose again to be created Earls of Morton during the 16th century. By the end of that century we find it recorded that the Regent Morton, James Douglas, had a clarsach player in his household named Galbraith — perhaps one of the hereditary MacBhreatnaich harpers, still associated with a longstanding patron.[9]

Another harper who was regularly employed at court was James Mylson, who is referred to in the Accounts and other sources simply as a "minstrell", as well as a "harper". Mylson first appears in the records in 1496. In 1497 the king awarded him all the goods of Thomas Young, a goldsmith of Perth, which had gone to the Crown "be reasoun of bastardy" (which seems to mean that the claimants to Young's fortune were not of legitimate birth, and thus could not inherit it). A goldsmith's estate was presumably especially covetable. Interestingly, though Mylson received regular wages along with the other established court musicians, some separate awards were made to him, sometimes jointly with Alexander Harper. The individual payments were made at St. Andrews, Perth and on three occasions, including the last noted payment to Mylson, at Falkland. These towns are all within a fairly small geographical area, which may fit the picture of an aging favourite, lacking the health required for sustained travel to the other royal residences.

Alexander Harper is the only court harper at whose background we can speculate, since some details about him are given in sources other than the Treasurer's Accounts. The first payment he received on 15th November 1501 was to help him purchase a horse. Alexander continues to receive money (and a second horse) up to 1508, and it is reasonable to suggest that he can be identified with the Alexander Harper who held land in Dunfermline at the beginning of the 16th century. The first tentative link occurs with a "Sandie Harper" who was part of the Dunfermline Burgh Court which sat in August 1489, and who was possibly the "Sande Harper" who received a payment from the king at Stirling in February 1498. Since "Sandy" is the familiar form of "Alexander", it is tempting to assume that this was the young Alexander. Whatever the case, an Alexander Harper is noted in the Dunfermline Burgh Court records in 1500, while another mention in 1501 makes it clear that he held property there, which lay between New Row and the Abbey Wall. Since the first note of Alexander in the Treaurer's Accounts occurred during the royal perambulations through the north-east of Scotland, he may also have had a connection with that area, and perhaps is the "Alexander Harper" who witnessed a letter of presentation to a chaplaincy made by the Earl of Sutherland on 31st August 1515. Unlike several others of the court musicians, Alexander certainly survived the disastrous events of 1513, for in 1514 the Burgh Court records the sale by Alexander and his spouse "Jonet Jaksoune" of a tenement of land inherited by Janet. It was purchased by Dean Robert Swyntoun, sacristan of Dunfermline Abey, and was not the holding in the New Row, since this is again mentioned as being Alexander's property in 1527. Over the next century local records list a number of people named Harper, and it seems probable that most of them were related to Alexander, especially since the personal names "James" (after the king) and "Janet" occur frequently. We do not know if any of his descendants also played the harp.

There are two other harpers who feature regularly in the Accounts, but something of a mystery surrounds the fate of one of them. It can be accepted that there were at least two harpers using the name of "Pate", or "Patrick".

The first of these received money for clothes in 1494, and continued to receive regular payments over subsequent years. The second "Pate Harper" — this time with the additional qualification of "Clarsach" — first occurs in 1501, and again the initial payment was for clothes. In both cases it seems that the harpers were being fitted out with the royal livery on joining the court establishment. During the following three years both "Pate Harper on the harp" and "Pate Harper on the clarsach" continue to appear together in the Accounts until 1st January 1504, often both listed in the same entry.

At this point, the picture becomes rather murky. In September 1503 a tabourner or drummer named William, who also features frequently in the Court Accounts under his "stage name" of Guilliam, was tried for the slaughter of a Patrick Harper. The Provost and Baillies of Edinburgh denounced the said William and "put him to the horn", outlawing him. Not until May 1506 did the king grant "William Broun alias Gilliam Tawbronare" a pardon for "the killing of Patrick Harpere and all other crimes". There is a peculiar anomaly between the dates of the murder in late 1503, and the payment of wages on New Year's Day 1504 to the harper who was apparently killed at least four months previously. Perhaps the wages due to Pate Harper, which were normally paid at Easter and New Year, were given instead to his heirs — though in that case one would have expected Pate to be referred to as "umquhile", or deceased. The mystery deepens when we see that Guilliam was paid on the same occasion and, indeed, received regular rewards between 1503 and July 1507. What was an apparently convicted murderer and outlaw doing at court, still entertaining the king and queen and still prospering? He was even able to employ another drummer, Ansle, who is described as "Guilliam's man". One begins to suspect that there may have been some intrigue in the royal household. If one looks at the entries which concern the harpers, "Pate Harper, clarsach" occurs on no less than ten occasions over the next ten years, twice with his son, who is not named. "Pate Harper" is only mentioned on four occasions and, strikingly, at no time after the beginning of 1504 are both "Pates" listed together. Does this mark the death of Pate Harper on the harp? It may be that, with his demise, not every scribe thought it necessary, or took the trouble, to specify that the remaining "Pate Harper" played the clarsach. (In 1513 there is an entry which records payment to "Odonelis harpar quhilk past away with him". The minstrel of an Irish prince would almost certainly have played a clarsach, but the scribe did not find it necessary to be exact about the name of the instrument.) On the other hand, could the Guilliam and Patrick, who are mentioned in the criminal records be the sons of the court minstrels? If so, one would have expected it to be mentioned that they were junior members of their families. If they were completely different persons, there would seem to have been a surfeit of William Tabronours and Pate Harpers in Edinburgh at the time![10]

Other harpers passed through the court in the "tail" of the Highland chiefs, like the clarsach players of Maclean and the Earl of Argyll in September 1506. Some churchmen also brought musicians with them, such as the Bishop of Ross's harper in 1506, and the clarsach player of the Prior of Whithorn, 1506-7. The king was often entertained by local or itinerant harpers on his travels in Linlithgow, Fowlis, Duchal, Elgin, Eliotstown and Dingwall, and by clarsach players in Dumbarton, Perth, Glenluce, Stirling, Balquhidder, Wigtown, Inchmahome and Ayr. Several of the harpers are described as being blind, though, surprisingly, no blind clarsach players are mentioned. There are also payments in 1496 and 1497 to "Johne harpar with the ane hand" — which surely gives a clue as to the kind of music he played : presumably a single melody or harmony line. The pattern, as one would expect, is that the harp appears most frequently in the Lowland and east coast areas while, on the whole, the clarsach is found in Highland locations and on the west coast. A full list of the isolated entries which feature harps or clarsach is given in Armstrong's "The Irish and Highland Harps".[11]

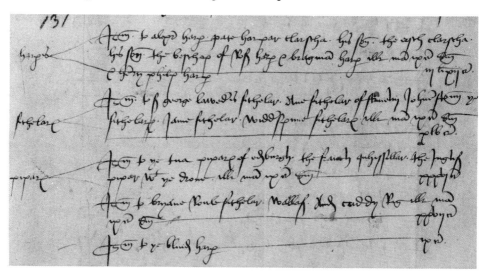

Extract from the Treasurer's Accounts, 1506 — payments to harpers

However, by taking the references in context, it is possible to make some interesting speculations about the court musicians. They are usually paid singly, but sometimes they are paid as a group, where the entry specifies that *each* was paid a certain amount, and the total is given at the end.

"February 1497 Item, that samyn day, be the kingis command to Adam Boyd, Bennet and James Mylson, menstralis, to ilk ane ixs; summa ... xxvijs".

From time to time, however, there are entries which link two or three names — in this case, paid a single fee. For example: "Item, to Adam Boyd, fithelar, and Mylsone, the harpare, xxviijs".

"Item, Bennet, fithelar, and Fowlis the harpar, xxviijs" in 1497 and "Item, to ane fithelar and ane clarschaar in Wigtown, xs" in 1506.

"Item, to Alexander, harpar, Adam Boyd, and Quhinbore, taubronar, xlijs" appears in 1507.

The fact that these musicians were paid as a group would suggest that they may have played in consort, as duos or trios. The usual combination appears to have been that of harp or clarsach with fiddle, and sometimes with a drum. Alexander, Bragman and Pate Harper (clarsach?) — three harp players — were paid together in 1507, as were "Rolland clarschaar and Pate Harper clarscha" in the same year. Martyn MacBhreatnaich and "toder Ersche clareschaw" (his son?) also seem to have played together regularly.

One name worth noting, which occurs in several entries between 1507-1512, is that of Adam Dickson. He is described most often as a lutanist, but on other occasions as a harper and as a piper — he must have been a versatile musician. This also points to the fact that the music of each instrument would have influenced, and been absorbed by the others. There are references, at various times, to musicians, especially lutanists, being sent to train on the Continent, but these include no examples of harpers or clarsach players. No music which is specifically associated with the harp or clarsach has survived in Scotland from this period up to the mid 16th century, but one can assume that there would be influence from the Continent on the gut-strung harp at least. The strong links between the clarsach and the lute in Scotland during the 17th century suggest that the treatment of the court music of the day, and probably some of the native music, would have been much the same on both instruments. This is especially likely if the harp or clarsach and lute were commonly played in consort, together, and with fiddle, viol or drum. Just such a consort is illustrated in a fine group portrait from the court of Christian IV of Denmark. It was painted in about 1618, and shows an Irish harper playing in a quartet, with bass viol, lute and flute.[12]

The cataclysmic defeat of the Scottish army at Flodden, in 1513, effectively wiped out much of the royal household. The leaders of many of the great families of Scotland lay amongst the 12,000 dead claimed by the victors. It is said that this was prophesied by a ghostly herald who, the night before the battle, read out the names of those who were to fall, from the Mercat Cross in Edinburgh. King James's body was taken to London where it lay embalmed until after the Reformation, when Queen Elizabeth's master-glazier hacked off its head to serve as a rather gruesome pot, in which he kept useful objects. In Scotland, the new King James V was a year-old infant. His mother, Margaret Tudor, was English and his cousin, John, Duke of Albany, who was the other major influence on his early life, had been brought up in France. It is not surprising, then, that when court life eventually resumed, it reflected these changes. This period proved to be a turning point for the harp at court. French and Italian minstrels were especially favoured, and the young king himself was taught to play the lute. Thomas Wood wrote in 1566 that "James the Fifth who was a musician himself ... had a singular good ear, and could sing that (which) he had never seen before, but his voice was rawky and harsh".[13] Several lutanists performed at court, but fiddle and viol found most favour with the king. References abound in the Accounts to the four musicians regularly maintained as "The King's Violers". The harp and clarsach appear only rarely. Payment was made in 1520 "to ane harper"; in 1529 "to ane Westland harper"; and "to an Ireland Clairsochter" in 1533.

This decline continued during the reign of Mary, Queen of Scots (1542-87). A single entry records a payment to "Stewvyn Tabronar and ane other harper with him" when they entertained "my Lorde Governour", the Earl of Arran in 1548. Mary was said to be an accomplished musician, who played lute and virginal, and who sang well ("for a queen", said the English Ambassador!). There is no evidence, however, that she herself played either the harp or the clarsach.

During the minority of Mary's son James, the Accounts from the Earl of Morton's regency mention two harpers who played regularly at court — John Baxter and Robert Galbraith (of the MacBhreatnaich family?) who appear to have been attached to Morton's own household. With the accession of James VI to the throne of England, the royal court moved its permanent base to London. During the later years of Elizabeth's reign, there had been a tremendous interest in the Irish wire-string harp, and its "melting and prolonged tones". Like the Scottish lords, the Irish chiefs who supported the English government often brought harpers in their retinues on their visits to Dublin and London. Harpers were also employed in the households of the Anglo-Irish nobles, and Irish harps and harpers soon became the fashion in England itself. The queen appointed Cormac MacDermott, an Irish harper, to the Royal Musick, during the last months of her reign, in 1603, and he remained at court to serve her successor, James, until MacDermott's own death in 1618. James's wife, Anne of Denmark, also retained an Irish harper between 1607 and her death in 1619, when he retired to comfortable estates in Ireland.[14]

Most of the references are to instruments or musicians of undoubted Irish origin. Some care must be used, however, since right up to the 18th century the word "Irish" was also used to denote "Erse" or Highland Scottish. Therefore where the player was a Scot, it is possible that their "Irish" instrument would have been a wire-strung Highland clarsach.

This may be the case with the king's favourite, Robert Kerr, a son of Sir Thomas Kerr of Ferniehirst, near Jedburgh, whose extraordinary story is worth recounting. This young man had the misfortune to break his leg when thrown from his horse during a tournament. He had, however, caught King James's eye (as handsome young pages often did). The king ordered him to be attended by his own doctors and visited him personally. In a meteoric rise to fortune, Kerr was soon knighted, and was loaded with honours, including the appointment of Lord High Treasurer of Scotland, and the title of Earl of Somerset. In the licentious and intrigue-ridden royal court, he became involved with Frances Howard, daughter of the Earl of Suffolk. She had been married as a child of thirteen to the equally young Earl of Essex. She now fell in love with Kerr and, to escape from her predicament, sought the aid of a well-known Doctor of the Black Arts. Whether his potions were efficacious or not, she succeeded in attracting the object of her desires, and in estranging her husband. She then sought a divorce, on such scandalous grounds that historians of the last century refused to print them. The king indicated his support of her petition, which was duly granted, and she and Kerr were married. Kerr had at this time as his secretary and confidant, Sir Thomas Overbury, who, it appears, expressed his objections to the marriage with rather more honesty than he could afford, in the company of such devious and intolerant listeners. He succeeded in offending his employer, his countess and her uncle, the Earl of Northampton. Kerr induced Overbury to refuse an appointment offered to him by the king himself, who promptly threw Overbury in the Tower to punish his disloyalty. There, the Countess of Somerset arranged for him to be given small doses of poison until at last the poor man died. The accomplice who had provided the drugs unexpectedly made a confession from his sick-bed, and the whole murderous story came out. James, whose attentions had now turned to George Villiers, Duke of Buckingham, was looking for an excuse to rid himself of his former favourite, and Kerr and his wife were committed to the Tower in their turn. The king obviously did not wish to see his own part in the sordid affair become common knowledge, and secretly arranged that Kerr would not give any embarrassing evidence at his trial, in return for clemency. So, although they were condemned for murder, both offenders were eventually granted a King's pardon.

Apart from his dramatic story, Kerr's predicament is of most interest to us because, while he was imprisoned in 1615, an inventory was made of his personal effects. In his house in Whitehall were tapestries, paintings and furnishings of great luxury, and garments including nearly fifty doublets of velvet, cloth-of-gold and silk, and embroidered cloaks and nightgowns. His musical instruments are also listed — "two Irish harps" and "a theorbo in a case". The fact that "A lute, *said to be my lord's man's*" is also included would suggest that the other instruments were Kerr's own. One or both of the harps may, given Kerr's background, have been a Scottish clarsach rather than of Irish origin. It would also have been interesting to know whether Kerr played his clarsach on the right or the left shoulder. The family of Kerr was so characteristically often left-handed that they gave the word "kerry-fisted" to the vocabulary. The Kerr castles in the Scottish Borders can be recognised because their spiral staircases often twist clockwise rather than the usual anti-clockwise, to enable their left-handed defenders to wield a sword.[15]

The court of James VI, when it moved to London, was seen as rather dowdy and unfashionable. A ballad from "Satirical Songs and Poems on Costume", published c1603, mocks the change in style of James's Scottish courtiers. They abandoned their cowhide shoes for leather, it says, their jerkins of "northern gray" for bright colours, their 12d stockings for silk, and their plain leather belts for those of embroidered velvet. This comparison seems rather unfair when we look at the courts of the earlier Stewart kings, and the description of the way in which the minstrels were dressed. A statute of James III in 1471 decreed that "na man sall wear silkes, in time coming in doublet, gowne or cloakes, exept knichtes, minstrelles and heraulds". Anyone who disobeyed was fined, and their silken garments forfeited for the use of the minstrels. Heralds were resplendent in silk and satin of scarlet and white. The yeomen of the king's chamber wore doublets of green satin from Bruges with yellow hose. Red and white bonnets are also mentioned. Black and grey velvet or fine wool were often used for most formal wear, while the household wore day-to-day clothes of russet, blue and tan colours, sometimes with hose of blue and red, or red and yellow.

On several occasions the Treasurer's Accounts list the cloth bought to make new livery for harpers, which gives us a clear picture of how they were dressed.

In 1494, when Pate Harper joined the royal establishment, he received (along with stablemen, trumpeters, falconers, a saddler, a chaplain and various others) : 13 ells of Rowan tan for their gowns; 9 ells of camlet for their doublets; 5 ells of Scottish black kersey for their hose. While in 1501, Pate Harper Clarsach was fitted out with : 3½ ells tan (it is specified that it should be of a cheaper quality than that bought for Ansle, tabrouner and Thomas Pringle and Alexander Caslaw, trumpeters); 9 quarters camlet; and 5 quarters kersey. The cloth was usually a woollen fabric, or a mixture of wool and some other fibre. Camlet was a blend of wool, silk and cotton which had a watered appearance.

The usual man's outfit during the first half of the 16th century consisted of a doublet with sleeves; breeches, called "hose" which were full and lined and tapered to below the knee. Those of the lower orders never developed the exaggerated padding affected by the wealthy towards the end of the century. Stockings and shoes were normally worn — in Scotland the leather and hide trade was one of the major industries. A gown, or sleeveless loose robe, was worn over the doublet, and persisted as the sign of certain professions, even after it was replaced in general wear by the short cloak. This was part of a "suit" for court wear, while a longer, thicker version of the cloak was worn out-of-doors.

In 1511 "Adam Dikesone, harper, for his leveray goune", received "5 ells of Rowane russet (a woollen cloth)" and "2½ ells satyne" for his doublet. He was given a similar amount in 1512, while in the same year fourteen minstrels received "ilk man for his goune, doublattis and hose ... £6.10s".

One other interesting entry in the Accounts of 1506-7 records the purchase of a leather case for a clarsach. There are very few references to cases for harps or clarsachs in any of the historical sources. They do seem to have been commonly made of leather. One poem which comes from the Book of the Dean of Lismore, and probably dates from the 1420s, comments on the disappearance of the wolf from Scotland "Giodh iomadha craiceann chon alta againn um chlairsigh's um chruit" — "Though we have many a wolf-skin as cover of clarsach and cruit".[16]

The regency and reign of James VI continues the records of the harper's clothing. John Baxter and Robert Galbraith, "his grace minstrellis", were given "ilk ane £5 to buy them clothes" in 1576-8, while in 1574 they received 3 ells of English stemming for their breeks, 5 quarters canvas for their doublets, and £3 to have the clothes made. The most detailed list occurs in February 1574 when Robert Galbraith "clairschear" was given for his winter clothing: 2 ells 2 quarters "braid Inglis claith" for his cloak; 4½ ells "gray Inglis stemmyng" (a woollen worsted cloth) for coat and breeches; 3 ounces "blak pasmentis" (decorations or braid) of silk; 5 quarters canvas for his doublet (usually a linen cloth); 1 ounce black silk (thread); 6 ells "hardin to be buffingys and stenting" (linen for padding and stiffening); 2 ells lyning; ane hatt.

It is interesting to compare this list with the clothing bought by the Thane of Cawdor in 1615 for his clarsach player, whom he was taking with him on a visit to London. Cawdor obviously wanted the appearance of his harper to do justice to his own rank. The garments are of comparable quality to those ordered for the Thane's own son, Duncan, the following year. Purchased for "the man that playis on the harp" were: 4 ells 3 quarters "Kenssir" (Kentshire) cloth for his cloak and breeks at £6.13.4 the ell; 3 ells of fustian (a cloth of cotton and flax or flax and wool, with a silky finish which was used as a substitute for velvet) for his doublet at 40s the ell; 3 quarters "Inglis stenning to be his sokis" at £3.6.8 the ell; 4 dozen buttons at 3s4d the dozen; half an ounce of silk; stinting (stiffening) for his doublet and cloak neck; 4½ ells of tweel (for lining) at 12s the ell; strings for the "breik knyis" — 3s; for the making of the cloak, doublet and breeks — £4; "Ane pikindaill" (a ruff or collar with starshaped points, which sounds much like that worn in the portrait of the Irish harper at the Danish court) — 26s8d; a hat and hat string — £4. Fitting out one's servant was an expensive business. The harper appears to have preceded his master to London by sea, around 6th July 1615. The next entry reads "Item, geifin to the clerchoman to pay for his victuall and passage to Londoun — £6.13.4d", followed by a payment to James Langlands, skipper in Leith, for some armour. The clarsach player may have accompanied Cawdor when he returned to Scotland with the Earl of Argyle on 19th August 1615.[17]

The reign of James VI, with its shift of cultural emphasis to England, marked the end of any appearance at the royal court of Scottish harp or clarsach. There had never been as many musicians employed in the Scottish royal household as there had been in England. This reflects the more modest court life of that country. Indeed, in 1583, even the roof of the Chapel Royal at Stirling Castle was only of thatch, which tended to suffer from "weitt or rane". Nevertheless, as Farmer points out, given the interest and skill of the Stewart monarchs from James I to Mary, it is likely that music at the Scottish court was of as high a standard as most royal establishments in Europe of that time.[18]

8 THE SCOTS LAIRDS

"In Musical Airt, and diver's science
As in Psaltrie, in Luit and Harp playing
Versificat in meter and dyting
In congrew verse, and to keep accidence
In sic effairis we have experience."[1]

Outside the Royal Court less evidence survives for the existence and activities of harpers in the Lowlands and East Coast areas where Scots, rather than Gaelic culture, was dominant. In Aberdeen the Burgh Records of 1398-1407 list a number of musicians, including "Andrea harper" and William harper". It is possible that these represent early surnames, but the context of the entries suggests that their professional occupations are being described. An example of this is "Meg of Abernethy, harper" who is also listed simply as "Meg of Abernethy". Another member of her family, Joh. Abernethy, gave 3d to a collection made by the inhabitants of Aberdeen, contributing towards the expenses of an embassy to England as did W. Harper in 1408.[2]

Meg of Abernethy is important because she is one of the very few women harpers in the history of the harp in Scotland, and the only one whose name is given. Women played an active part in the life of the nation, as can be seen from the frequency with which their names occur in the documents of all historical periods. However, though many harpers appear in the Court records, none of these are female. The only other known reference to a woman harper comes from the Household Book of the Dowager-Countess of Mar. The Earldom of Mar marches with the border of Moray about the area of the Abernethy Forest in the west, and included Aberdeen in the east, before the creation of the Earldom of Huntly. It was thus on the fringe of the Highlands and some of the visitors to the household reflect this influence. On March 21, 1642, the Countess paid 12s "to ane woman clairsocher who visit the house in my lord his time". It is possible that other entertainers such as "ane blind singer who sang at the time of dinner", in May 1638, or the "twa Highland singing women, at my ladys command", in September of the same year, may also have accompanied themselves on harp or clarsach, but this we are not told.[3]

The lack of historical evidence for female harpers is striking in view of the fact that in traditional song and story women appear to play the instrument as frequently as men. But since most of these legends and ballads were not 93

Detail of woman harper, Crathes castle

recorded, in the form in which we know them, until the 18th century at the earliest, it is possible that the harp playing of their heroines may be a later addition to the detail — perhaps substituted for singing. (In the still later versions of some ballads it is possible to see how the fiddle, in its turn, displaced the harp as the instrument played, for example, in "King Orfeo" or in "Binnorie".) In Ireland too, references to female harpers largely belong to myth and legend though by the end of the 18th century the names of several professional women players are known; the "Maire Dall" of Carolan's tune "Blind Mary" taught another blind woman, Rose Mooney, who appeared at the Belfast Harp Meeting of 1792. Denis Hempson, the oldest of the harpers taking part, was reputedly taught by Brigid O'Cahan, and is quoted by Bunting as saying that in former times, women of the best families were often taught to play the Irish harp. The Scottish pictorial representations in the "big houses" certainly feature women along with the harp, as in the paintings of Dean House and Crathes Castle.

From the existing scraps of evidence it would seem that very few women made their living as musicians at any time and, if they did enter the profession, it was usually as singers. In the Highland areas in particular, there was no tradition of females training in the bardic arts, although informally, song and story were an integral and important part of their lives, accompanying and lightening their daily work. It is probable that in the Lowlands, as in the Highlands, poetry was most often sung — Alexander Scot, who is most often thought of as a poet of the 16th century, is described in 1582 as "Alexander Scot, musician", and thus may have accompanied himself on lute or harp.[4] That the female entertainers who are described as singers would have performed formal poetry in Gaelic or Scots is most unlikely. The fact that professional women harpers are found in Ireland by the end of the 18th century may reflect the decline of formal bardic education due to lack of patrons and other cultural pressures, to the point where women could enter on its fringes. In other words, the status of the harper had sunk by that time to the level of an occupation considered suitable for females. Running parallel to this, however, the use of the harp by women in aristocratic households in Scotland and Ireland appears to have been more or less continuous. It was not used by them in a professional capacity but was played, along with the other instruments of the day, in wealthy and more leisured circles. Even so, it never enjoyed the widespread popularity, from 1500 on, of the lute and cittern or, subsequently, of the various keyboard instruments.

Apart from Meg, all the other Scottish harpers whose names are known to us are male. On 1st November 1462, John Hathvy, harper, of Swanston, near Edinburgh, was a witness to an instrument of resignation of land. His name is probably of English or Welsh origin but it crops up in various forms, such as Hadoway or Hathway, in Scotland from 1410 onwards. A Robert Hathway, burgess of Edinburgh, who may be a descendant of John Hathvy, was summonsed in 1550 for illegally purchasing wine in an attempt to circumvent the trade prices set by the burghs.[5]

Lord Semple, who held lands near Glasgow, employed a harper who was probably the "menstrale" that "Lord Semple had with him when he so pleased the King", during the monarch's visit to a monastery in nearby Paisley. James was apparently breaking his journey on the way to the Priory of Whithorn, and on this occasion rewarded Semple's musician with the sum of 14s. The harper's name was John Haislet. His name and occupation are given in a (very long!) list of Lord Semple's followers on 17th July 1526 when Semple and 586 of his men were granted a respite by King James, "for the tresonable slauchter of umquhile Cornelius de Mathetema, Ducheman, at oure soverane Lordis Tolbuth of Edinburgh in time of perliament in contrar his proclamation of peax". It is likely that this pardon also took into account some of the frequent attacks and skirmishing which had been going on between the Border lairds. A few months later, however, they were at it again, and Semple was summoned for "breking of lawborowis" — invading the lands of John Mure of Caldwell. A "Johne Fidlar" is also numbered amongst his servants.[6]

Lord Semple and his supporters had simply been visiting the Paisley monastery in 1504, but some religious houses gave harpers lands or accommodation, possibly in return for their musical services. This arrangement did not always go smoothly — in 1612 a harper called James Gordon who "possessis tua chalmeris, callit the bak chalmeris" of Glenluce Abbey, was told to remove himself, and a few weeks later, in a further attempt to eject the harper, his wife and he were served with a writ. The buildings of the Abbey had been occupied by Sir John Gordon of Lochinvar, in the mid 16th century, and the convent of Glenluce, under their abbot, John Hay, had great difficulty in dislodging him and his followers. The Gordons were subsequently made commendators (in effect, lay abbots) and then temporal lords of Glenluce. They remained as such, with the dispute over its occupancy obviously continuing, until the monastery was purchased by the Crown in 1619.[7]

That branch of the Gordon family had established itself in south-west Scotland, but the greater part of their lands lay in the north-east in Aberdeenshire. We do not know the names of any harpers connected with the Gordons in this area, but "Harper-ford", a place-name which dates from before 1775, is found near Gordon Castle. In Castle Huntly, another Gordon seat, the family arms are carved on an armorial over the fireplace. As was the custom, the monarch's arms were also portrayed. The fireplace dates from 1606, shortly after the Union of the Crowns, so the Royal Arms include a harp, representing Ireland. Most of the harps which figure in heraldic devices tend to be rather fanciful hybrids which show a good deal of artistic elaboration, such as the harps on the plasterwork wall frieze at The Binns, near Linlithgow, or at Castle Menzies at Weem. The harp in Castle Huntly, however, is such an accurate and well-executed clarsach that the sculptor was obviously copying an instrument with which he was familiar.[8]

An equally fine clarsach is depicted behind a carved figure representing one of the Liberal Arts in the walled garden at Edzell Castle. This splendid and elaborate garden was created in 1604 by Sir David Lindsay, Lord Edzell. He travelled widely on the Continent as a young man, and the influence of the international contacts that he made at that time continued in his later commercial ventures and in his scholarship and artistic tastes. Delightful sculptures, illustrating the Planetary Deities, the Arts and the Cardinal Virtues, decorate panels round the walls of his garden. They show German, Italian and French inspiration and, in the case of the Planets, are copied direct from contemporary continental engravings, a series of illustrations made in 1528-9 by the Nuremberg Kleinmeister who is generally identified as a pupil of Dürer. The Seven Liberal Arts are elegantly executed on the south wall. An inscription, which reads "Musica", arches over a lady who has regrettably lost her head, but the fine carving of the lute that she plays has survived undamaged, and in the background are a viol, another lute or theorbo, and an unmistakeably homegrown clarsach.

"Musica" — garden at Edzell Castle   *Hill House*

Further south, near Dunfermline, we find a sculptural record of what appears to be a gut-strung harp. William Monteith of Randieford came from the Falkirk area, but married into a family named Bruce and thus subsequently obtained lands in Fife. In 1623 he built the House of Hill and over one of the windows placed a portrait of himself playing the harp. The instrument shown is a floor-standing, lightly built harp, with a curved fore-pillar and arched neck which are reminiscent of the "Renaissance" harps of the preceding centuries. Monteith sits on a stool to play it, with the harp resting on his right shoulder. The detail of his clothing is still clear enough to see that he is wearing a coat which comes down below his hips, and a large stiff ruff which frames his face.[9]

Musicians were employed by civic bodies, as well as by the aristocracy. In 1549, the Edinburgh Hammermen, one of the town guilds, recorded payment to "viollaris, harperis, pypparis, fidlaris and uther menstralis". A century later, harpers were still wandering the streets of Edinburgh — even on a Sunday! On 21st August 1649, the Kirk Session of Canongate-Holyrood delivered judgement on several of its wayward congregation:

"Prophane of the Sabbath — Compeared Jon mcmath barbour Jon Rae tailler Robert coppersmith James Laing wright Ralph Potts Harper all delaitted be the visitor of Leith for prophanation of the Lordis day in waigeing and going astray in the time of divine servie qlk they could not deny. The session hath scharpelie rebuiked them not be be found in the lyke umle — seveir censure and publict satisfactioun". Although "Potts" is not a particularly Scottish surname, it is found in several of the Border towns from the 16th century onwards, while a George Pott was made a burgess of Edinburgh in 1694. Ralph Potts buried a son, William, in Greyfriars Kirkyard, Edinburgh, in 1661, and died himself in the same year.[10]

A clear picture of the status of a harper in the Lowland burghs can be gathered from three testaments, registered between 3rd March 1597-8 and 24th May 1614. The first was made by Robert Mcmillan, a harper from Glasgow, who died in September 1597. It gives an inventory of his personal gear. His estate, including various debts still owed to him, amounted to about £517 13s 4d. He had deposited £40 worth of gold and silver in the hands of one of the Edinburgh goldsmiths. He also left several bequests, including two gold rings to William Douglas, servant to the Laird of Drumlanrig, "ane stand bed wt the bed and furnising thereof togedder wt ane hundred punts to T. Broun"; and articles of clothing to other beneficiaries. But the most significant is the entry "Item he leuves to Andro Callum ane buird (a table) sex stuillis ane chyre wt his clairscheocht".[11]

The will of an Andro Callum has also survived since his death in 1611. Again, his personal possessions are listed in great detail, including furniture and soft furnishings ("ane blue" and "ane green mat covering" and "ane fedder bed"), kitchen utensils and dishes, brassware (tua great brasin chandlerie" and "ane basson of brass", and "tua tyn chalmer potis price thairof xxs"), and weapons, including a pistol. There is, however, no mention of Robert Mcmillan's clarsach. Is this the same man who benefitted from Mcmillan's will? This is confirmed by a third testament, that of Jeane Laird, who died in 1613, and is described as the "relict of Andro Callum menstraler indweller in Ed the tyme of hir decease". As well as the widow's part of one third of her husband's gear which had been left to her as was the custom, she had also inherited two outstanding debts which had been owed to him and which still had not been repaid by the time of Jeane Laird's own death three years later. This reference neatly links Jeane Laird and Andro Callum, and is confirmed by an obligation for a money transaction which was noted in the Register of Deeds on 17th June 1601 between John Leyis, elder, merchant of Edinburgh, and Andro Callum in Edinburgh and his wife Jeane Laird. As well as this, Jeane's own description of her husband as a "menstraler" makes it clear that this was the musician to whom Mcmillan had left his instrument. What became of the clarsach is less certain. Since a third of the estate would also go automatically to any children, it is possible that the instrument had already passed to one of their offspring. The O... Callum yr and George Callum yr mentioned in the testament may indeed be their sons, but we know for certain that Andro and Jeane had at least one son. The Edinburgh Register of

Apprentices records that "William Callum, son to Andra Callum minstraler", was apprenticed to Alexander Mossman, locksmith, on 15th August 1595. It seems that William did not follow his father's footsteps in taking up a musical career so the clarsach may have been disposed of after Andro's death. It should also be remembered that the inventory of the deceased's goods, and the registering of the testament was done for tax purposes, so the fewer items of value that appeared on it, the less tax their heirs might have to pay. The sums of money involved in the wills are considerable, in view of the fact that the fortune of a laird of modest but comfortable means would amount to about £100 at this period. Clearly, these musicians were wealthy and, to judge from their personal possessions, led a life of some luxury.[12]

Other scattered references to harpers in the Lowlands occur throughout the 17th century. The Household Book of Archbishop Sharpe records a payment in 1664 "to a harper at his graces direction — £2 8s". James Sharpe was born in Banff in 1618, and led an eventful life, becoming minister of Crail in 1649. In 1660 he went to London to represent the Presbyterian dissenters but secretly changed sides and emerged as a supporter of the restoration of episcopacy, and was himself consecrated as Archbishop of St. Andrews and Primate of Scotland. His harsh treatment of the Covenanters earned him many enemies and, after surviving an attempt on his life in 1668, he was brutally murdered on Magus Muir near St. Andrews in 1679. The fee to the harper was therefore paid during his rule as the most powerful churchman in Scotland at a particularly troubled time in its history.[13]

More peacefully, the Campbells of Cawdor, while they should probably be counted as a Highland family, often made trips to the south. Cawdor employed a clarsach player of his own, as mentioned in the previous chapter, but he also patronised the local musicians. In Glasgow on Friday, 1st October 1591 his accounts record "giffen to the Lawland harper — 6s. 8d". This seems to have been the standard rate for musicians at the time, and similar sums were paid to a lutanist and the town piper. This is the last known specific reference to a "Lowland" harper. In 1682 a subsequent Laird of Cawdor also favoured harp music. The Chamberlain's book of Accounts of the current family expenses notes "To a harper £1.8s". While, on a visit to Edinburgh, a night out consisted of "Coach to Abbeyhill ... Dinner at David Robertsons ... wyne ..." and to finish the evening "a harper, paid 14s." On another occasion the Laird enjoyed "Dinner at Crombies with Glengarry ... Wyne after dinner" and paid "To a harper — 10s".[14]

It is likely that the records would have mentioned if these harpers had been Irish musicians. However, we do know that Irish harpers were employed from time to time in the aristocratic households of Scotland, either on a permanent basis, or as they travelled round the "big houses". During the 1680's the Duke and Duchess of Hamilton employed a resident harper rejoicing in the very Irish name of Jago McFlaherty. He not only played the Irish harp for them, but was also apparently involved in the musical education of the daughters of the house, and in caring for the other musical instruments at Brodick Castle, on Arran, or at their other estates near Glasgow. In 1682 he was sent on a trip to Edinburgh to buy replacement strings for the Hamiltons' virginals.[15]

An intriguing letter dating from 15th August 1627 refers again to an Irish harper. It was addressed by Lord Ogilvy to the Earl of Nithsdale. Ogilvy had sent a company of soldiers for a regiment being raised by the Earl to fight in Germany. Especially recommended to Nithsdale were several musicians. "Thair is of this number a clarchocher, ane Irishman, borne of good parantage, quha pleyes verie weill, and I know zour Lordship will not live him the worse that he is off zour awin religion. I pray zour Lordship cause ws him weill and if ze think it necessar that he stey with zow for ane certain tyme, qwhill his captaine be reddie to tak voyage to Germanie, he will be reddie to serve zour Lordship otherwayes he will attend his capitaine."

It is possible that the description of the talented Irish musician may fit the best known of the Irish harpers who travelled round Scotland at this period — Ruairi Dall O'Cathain.[16]

9 IRISH INTERPLAY

"Bot quhen ressoun and perfyte sapience
playis the harpe of eloquens ...
Than seisses of our hert the wicket will
Fra fawart language than the tong is still."[1]

The voyage across the Irish Sea was often made by the harpers of both Scotland and Ireland. Most of the Irish musicians were welcome and successful guests of the Scottish chieftains — but there were exceptions.

In about 1490 Angus Og, son of John of the Isles, was in Inverness after military expeditions to Athol, Arran and Lochaber which had secured some of the MacDonald lands. He had fallen foul of a daughter of Rory Dubh MacLeod, whom he dispossessed of lands in Lewis and had also gained the enmity of one of the Mackenzie chiefs. These two plotted Angus's death. There was an Irish harper in Inverness at the time known as Art O' Carby, or Diarmaid O' Cairbre, who is said to have come from Co. Monaghan. He fell madly in love with Mackenzie's daughter and her father promised him the girl if he would murder Angus Og. O' Cairbre is said to have composed the following song while fortifying himself with alcohol to commit the deed :

"Tanmin do dhia a mharchruch neich crichd Bhalbhrichd
Gu bheil tanmin an cansiort mata puinsuin an Gallfit."

— meaning that the rider of the dappled horse (in other words, Macdonald) was in danger of his life if there was poison in his long knife which he called "Gallfit". Macdonald went to bed, attended by John Cameron, Locheil's brother, and the poet MacMhuirich. The harper crept into his chamber when all were asleep and cut the throat of Angus Og. He was immediately captured, and the plot discovered when jewels which belonged to Mackenzie and MacLeod's daughter were found on his person. The harper apparently refused to implicate them, though he is said to have been drawn after horses till his limbs were torn assunder. His head was hung from a pole by a withy passed through the throat. It was the subject of a poem by the Dean of Knoydart, whom Derick Thomson identifies as John MacMhuirich, the bard who accompanied the party of Angus Og. Addressing the harper's severed head, he says:

101

"A chinn Diarmaid Ui Chairbre,
giodh lor th 'airgne agus t' uaille,
cha mhor liom mead do dhocra
ge 'taoi i gcrochadh re cuaille ...

Do milleadh leat ri Ile,
fear imirt fhiona is airgid,
'ga dta an trilis ur iarnaidh,
a chinn Diarmaid Ui Chairbre ..."

(Thou head of Diarmaid O' Cairbre, though great enough are thy spoils and thy
pride, not too great I deem the amount of thy distress though thou hangest from
a stake ...
   By thee was destroyed the king of Islay, a man who dealt wine and silver;
whose locks were fresh and crisp, thou head of Diarmaid O' Cairbre ...)[2]

This episode passed into the oral tradition and surfaces later in the History
of Scotland of Hector Boece as the assassination of a Pictish king, and in a
slightly different version as the attempted murder of one of the MacLeods of
Lewis. An Irish harper named Mac O Charmaig was said to have been a guest
of MacLeod when he fell in love with the daughter of his host. Planning to
abduct the lady, he lulled the household to sleep with an enchanting tune called
"Deuchainn-ghleusda Mhic O Charmaig", and was about to murder MacLeod
when the lady's brother appeared in time to prevent him from striking the fatal
blow. The treachery of this harper towards the MacLeods was one of the
insults flung at Rory Dall Morison, harper to Iain Breac MacLeod in the 17th
century by Clanranald's poet, Donald MacMhuirich. In a poetic flyting
between the two men, one of MacMhuirich's verses reads :

"Cha bu chuilean de'n t-seorsa
as am bu choir a bhith 'g earbsa,
gun fios nach cinneadh fo mheuraibh
Deuchainn-ghleusda Mhic O Charmaig.

(A whelp of that breed ought not to be trusted as there's no knowing but there
might sound forth under his fingers "The Tuning-trial of Mac O Charmaig").

The tale was sufficiently firmly established in the folk-memory for the
allusion to be immediately understood by the object of this slur, even though
the story itself may be apocryphal.[3]
   Of all the Irish harpers who visited Scotland over the centuries, Ruairi Dall
O' Cathain is undoubtedly best known. This is in part due to the unfortunate
confusion between O'Cathain and the similarly named Scottish harper,

Ruaidhri Dall Morison, which led several writers to suggest that they were one and the same person. This is patently untrue, since O'Cathain died around 1650, some years before the birth of Morison whose life is described in chapter 11. Several of the known harp tunes, however, are traditionally ascribed simply to "Rory Dall", with no other clues as to their provenance.

Ruairi Dall (Blind Rory) O'Cathain was born sometime in the late 16th century. In the Memoirs of Arthur O'Neill (one of the ten harpers who took part in the Belfast Harp Festival of 1792) we are told that Ruairi Dall was of noble birth and held extensive estates in the North of Ireland, including the towns of Coleraine, Garvagh, Limavady and Kilrea. O'Neill says that, as befitted his rank, O'Cathain always travelled in Scotland with an appropriate retinue of servants. Colm O'Baoill, however, in his study of Irish Harpers in Scotland, points out that this information is not supported by the known historical background of the O'Cathains. The last chief of the main line was Domhnall Ballach, who died in 1628, and whose brother Ruairi (which is indeed a common name in that family) was killed by the English in 1601. Domhnall Ballach's son, also called Ruairi, was executed in 1615. It would thus appear that, contrary to Arthur O'Neill's statement, Ruairi Dall was not heir to the chieftainship of the Ui Chathain.

O'Baoill points to a different version of his origins, which is given in "Dalriada : or North Antrim" by William Adams, published by "The Coleraine Chronicle" in 1906. This reads "The last inhabitant of Dunseverick was Gilladuff O'Cathain, a very respectable gentleman, but unfortunately joined the insurrection of 1641 under Sir Phelim O'Neill of Tyrone, as was already stated. Gilladuff had two sons, Torlough, who was hanged with his father in Carrickfergus, and Rory Dall (or Blind Rory) who escaped to the Highlands, and is said to have changed his name to Morrison. He was a great musician — he could play on both harp and bagpipes. He was much respected by the Highland gentry, and was called 'Rory the Irish Harper'". This account probably derives from local oral tradition and, though it contains obvious inaccuracies, some details can be confirmed. The O Cathains held lands within the sphere of influence of the MacDonnell's of Antrim. An Giolla Dubh O'Cathain and his son Toirrdhealbhach Og took part, with the Scottish mercenary Alasdair Mac Cholla Chiotaich MacDonnell (who had married a member of their family), in the rising of 1641. Both father and son were executed. Another son, Manus, served as one of Alasdair Mac Cholla's leaders in Scotland, and was hanged there after their defeat at Philiphaugh. There may have been yet another son who was also called An Giolla Dubh. From the known dates, one can certainly suggest that Adam's identification of Ruairi Dall as a member of this branch of the O'Cathain family, and as a son of the elder Giolla Dubh, is feasible. In March 1611 An Giolla Dubh O'Cathain and Toirrdhealbhach O'Cathain took part in a lease of land in North Antrim. If, at this date, one of An Giolla Dubh's sons was old enough to enter into a legal transaction, O'Baoill concludes, his brother may well have been of an age to travel as a musician to Scotland.[4]

In 1615 Colla Ciotach, the father of Alasdair, captured a ship belonging to Henry Robinson of Londonderry, and pressed some of the sailors into service for the return voyage to Islay. Among these sailors was Robert Williamson, who described how they then travelled to Canna and were entertained by MacDonald of Clanranald. He says "There they went ashore and feasted and drancke with there friends and chieflie with Mc Callan, O Cathan his wife, her husband then being in Scotland". Ronald Black suggests that the "O Cathan" mentioned is Ruairi Dall O'Cathain (the other chiefs of that name all being in prison at that time). Ruairi appears to have travelled to the mainland while his wife remained in Canna as the guest of Clanranald (Mac 'ic Ailean). Given the long-standing family relationship and military alliance between the Macdonalds and O Cathans, it would not be surprising if they were treated as honoured friends on their arrival in Scotland. This may indeed mark Ruairi's first visit to that country.

Whether he ever returned to Ireland, we do not know — though some of the tunes that he played certainly entered the repertoire of the Irish harpers. The news of Alasdair Mac Cholla's death in 1647, at the battle of Cnoc na nDos in Ireland, is said to have been brought to Scotland by a harper who landed at Portpatrick in Galloway, and told the sad news to the Gaelic poet, Iain Lom. Iain Lom himself had served as a guide to Alasdair before his victory at Inverlochy, and as a bard on that occasion. It is possible that this harper might have been Ruairi Dall O'Cathain, though by this date he would have been of advanced years.[5]

Ruairi Dall appears to have spent much of his life in Scotland. O'Neill's "Memoirs" give us a detailed account of one episode in his career. "Amongst other visits in the style of an Irish chieftain he paid one to a Lady Eglintoun, and she (not knowing his rank) in a peremptory manner demanded a tune, which he declined as he only came to play to amuse her, and in an irritable manner left the house. However, when she was informed of his consequence, she eagerly sought to contrive a reconciliation and made an apology, and the result was that he composed a tune for her ladyship, the handsome tune of "Da mihi manum" ("Give me your hand") for which his fame reached through Scotland and came to the ears of the Gunpowder Plot prophet James the First of England (then the sixth of Scotland). O'Keane delighted him so very much that the crabbit monarch walked towards him and laid his hand upon his shoulder as a token of his approbation, which one of the courtiers then present observed to Roger. "What!" says O'Kean, somewhat nettled "A greater man than ever James was laid his hand on my shoulder". "Who is that?" says the King "O Neill, my liege", says he, standing up".[6]

This story was also related by Denis O Hempsey, the oldest of the harpers who appeared at the Belfast meeting in 1792. While the details are probably fanciful embroidery, some historical facts suggest that it is at least founded in truth. The family history of the Eglintons recounts how Alexander Seton (1588-1661) succeeded to the Earldom of Eglinton in 1612, and changed his name to Montgomerie. He married the daughter of the Earl of Linlithgow, Lady Anne Levingstoun (d. 1632). Eglinton's title was disputed by King James until 1615, at which date he gave his approval, and the family developed a very friendly relationship with their monarch.

Colm O Baoill points out that the Capuchin Annual (Dublin 1970) cites this reconciliation as the event commemorated by the composition of the melody "Da Mihi Manum" by O Cathain.[7] After he succeeded to the English throne in 1603, James made only one visit to Scotland, in 1617. At this time he was entertained at the Eglinton family home in Glasgow. It would seem reasonable to suggest that it might have been on this occasion that O'Cathain encountered the King and made the tune for Lady Anne. We know that she too had musical interests and probably played the virginals herself since she paid 53s 4d, in 1617, to have virginals brought from Callander to Eglintoun in Ayrshire. The facts, however, suggest that the story may be connected with an other branch of the Eglinton family, rather than the senior line. The Montgomeries of Braidstone, who were frequently referred to as 'Eglinton' in Northern Ireland, possessed large parts of the O Neill lands in Ulster, partly through the influence of George Montgomery, younger brother of Hugh, 6th laird of Braidstone. Dr. George Montgomery had taken part in the secret negotiations with Elizabeth I, to make James VI her heir, and James had subsequently created him Bishop of Derry and Clogher, and given him substantial church possessions in the same area.[8]

Hugh of Braidstone led a very colourful life. He had a longstanding feud with the son of the Earl of Glencairn and, while in King James's service, followed him to Holland. There they challenged each other to a duel, and Braidstone was thrown in prison, in danger of having his hand cut off as a punishment. He persuaded his sergeant, Robert Montgomery, to pay court to the daughter of his jailor, the Provost Marshall. This the sergeant accomplished so effectively that in a few days he had won the girl's consent to marry him. The Montgomerie manuscript tells us : "The Laird (as the design was laid) had the daughter and his sergeant into his room, and there privately contracted or espoused them together by mutual promises of conjugall fidelity to each other, joining their hands, and making them alternately repeat (after him) the matrimonial vow used in Scotland, they exchanging one to the other the halves of a piece of gold which he had broken and given to them to that purpose". During subsequent celebrations with the Marshall and his household, the Laird, with the newly-wed couple, slipped out and took ship for Scotland.

Braidstone used his own experiences in furthering his ambitions in Ireland. Con O Neill of Clanneboys was at this time a prisoner at Carrickfergus.

Braidstone organised an escape in return for a promise that he would take possession of half of O Neill's lands. He employed a cadet of his family, Thomas Montgomery, to make love to the Town Marshall's daughter, and gained her parents' approval to their wedding. In the relaxed and festive atmosphere, Con was smuggled on board a ship to Scotland, where he was entertained for a time at Braidstone. The story was told to the compiler of the manuscript by the Marshall's daughter herself, a girl named Annas Dobbin. Braidstone took O Neill to London, where his brother George was at that time James VI's Chaplain, and arranged for an audience with the King. Con was graciously received at court, pardoned and allowed to *kiss the King's hand*. James granted Braidstone's petition that the lands should be planted with British Protestants, and that tenants of Irish extraction should not be granted fees. Although the Montgomeries' plans were not entirely successful, and some of the territory they coveted was given by the King to other Scottish lords such as the Hamiltons, they were still established in Ulster as substantial and powerful landowners.[9]

The O' Cathain's had a close relationship with the O Neills, as principal vassal-chiefs of the Earls of Tyrone, and it is quite likely that Ruairi Dall O' Cathain would have performed for the most powerful landowners in his own area. Indeed, a Richard O' Cahain (the Anglicised form of Ruairi) was involved as witness to a land transaction in 1607, part of the convoluted dealings between Hugh Montgomery of Braidstone and Con O Neill.[10] This episode then brings together all the chief protagonists of the story of "Da Mihi Manum", and considering that the earlier part of Arthur O'Neill's account of Ruairi Dall's life is unreliable, it might well provide a better scenario for the composition of the tune. The Latin title is unusual. It appears first in the Wemyss manuscript of 1644, and the Balcarres manuscript of 1692. The English or Gaelic translations were not given until Bunting's 1840 edition. Interestingly, in 1645 the 6th Earl of Eglinton, campaigning in Ireland, received a bundle of lute-strings from Sir John Seton in London (a distant relative of his). It is possible that tunes played by Ruairi Dall returned to Ireland in this way.[11]

John Gunn, in his "Historical Enquiry respecting the Performance on the Harp in the Highlands", tells of another event in Ruairi's life. Gunn says that about the year 1650 Ruaidhri Dall Morison, accompanying the Marquis of Huntly, visited Robertson of Lude. To celebrate the event, he composed a tune called "Suipeir Tighearna Leoid" or "Lude's Supper". Since Morison was not born until around 1656, it is clearly impossible for him to have been there. However O'Cathain, in his last years, might have made such a visit. He is thought to have died shortly after 1650. The connection with the Marquis of Huntly must also be in doubt since George Gordon, the second Marquis, was outlawed for his support of Charles I, was arrested in 1648 and executed in 1649, after which his estates were held by Argyll until 1660. It may well be that Gunn's date is inaccurate, especially since O'Cathain appears to have been in Scotland from around 1615 onwards. A connection between the harper and Huntly may have been suggested by Gunn due to the title of the tune "Port Gordon", which is also sometimes attributed to Ruairi Dall. Gordon is the Huntly family name, but there is another possible link with the Robertsons of Lude, which we will examine later in our study of the tunes.[12]

O'Cathain may well have been at Lude much earlier than 1650. William Tytler of Woodhouselee, writing at the end of the 18th century, says "The last of these strolling harpers was Rory or Roderick Dall, who about fifty years ago, was well-known and much caressed by the Highland gentry, whose houses he frequented. His chief residence was about Blair in Athole and Dunkeld. He was esteemed a good composer and a fine performer on the harp, to which he sung in a pathetic manner. Many of his songs are preserved in that country" (i.e. in Atholl). Indeed, the important collections of Scottish music which contain old harp tunes, and which were published in Tytler's lifetime were the work of Perthshire musicians Daniel Dow and John Bowie. While the date that Tytler gives is clearly erroneous, and would fit neither O'Cathain nor Morison, there is a strong possibility that the rest of his statement may be true, and, while Morison may have made short visits to Perthshire, O'Cathain spent much of his time in the Atholl area.

This possibility is strengthened by a comment made by Arthur O'Neill, which seems till now to have gone unremarked but may be of particular significance. He says that O'Cathain travelled to Scotland "*where there were great harpers*". O'Neill was not a man to dispense praise lightly, dismissing as he does, much of the harping of his contemporaries as mere "tol-lol". It is also noteworthy that O' Cathain chose to go to central Scotland and not to the West Coast or Islands, where the MacDonnells, to whom the O Cathains were so closely related, had their sphere of influence.[13]

There was without doubt a striking concentration of harpers in Perthshire in the 17th century. If one adds to this the obvious attraction for a harper of seeing the two early clarsachs at Lude, it seems very possible that Ruairi Dall O'Cathain might have settled in Atholl. There was certainly a great deal of harping going on there, before his arrival and after his demise. O'Cathain is likely to have have travelled widely in Scotland, and is said in O'Neill's "Memoirs" to have died "in a nobleman's house, where he left his harp and a silver key to tune it". The nobleman was Sir James MacDonald of Sleat, on the Island of Skye, who died in 1678. The fate of the key, at least, is known in part and is recounted later in this book.[14]

The O Connellan brothers were harpers from Co. Sligo who are said to have visited Scotland in the late 17th century. There are some contradictions between the two accounts of their lives which have come down to us. James Hardiman says that Thomas O Connellan was born early in the 17th century, was the composer of more than 700 airs, and died in Co. Limerick before 1700, after which his brother Lawrence travelled to Scotland, taking with him some

of Thomas's tunes. Two of them became popular there as "The Battle of
Killiekrankie" and "Lochaber No More". This claim was repeated by some
of the harpers at the Belfast Festival. But according to Arthur O'Neill, Thomas
himself crossed the Irish Sea ... "He made himself conspicious in Scotland by
means of the tune of 'Lochaber' which he plastered upon the Scotch as one
of his own compositions, whereas it is well known it was composed by Myles
O'Reilly of Killinkere, in the County Cavan, under the name of "Limerick's
Lamentation". However Conlan arrived to City honours in Edinburgh, chiefly
by means of that tune among others. I heard they made him a bailie or
burgomaster in Edinburgh, where he died". O'Neill's "Memoirs" also mention
a brother, but give his name as William and make no suggestion that he ever
went to Scotland.

Colm O'Baoill points to one piece of evidence which may confirm O'Neill's
account as being more accurate. In the Edinburgh Council Record of Jan. 11.
1717 "the Council appointed the Dean of Guild and his Council to admitt and
receave Thomas Occulay harper" and two others to be "burgesses in Common
forme". O'Baoill speculates that the otherwise unknown surname 'Occulay' is
a scribal attempt at the Irish 'O Connellan'. Under normal circumstances, any
person wishing to set up in business in the city would apply to the Dean of
Guild for admission as a burgess and, if successful, would have his name
entered on the Register of Burgesses. Since Thomas Occulay, harper, did not
go through this process, but was made a burgess by an act of the Town Council,
it almost certainly means that he was awarded this status as an honour,
presumably for his professional skill as a musician. The date 1717 would also
tie in with O'Neill's story.

There is no evidence that O Connellan visited any other part of Scotland.
Of the other tunes in Bunting's collection, five of which are ascribed to
Thomas, two to William, and two to both brothers, none have titles which show
any Scottish connection. It seems likely that, as held by the accepted tradition
amongst Bunting's contemporary harpers, he did most of his composing before
he went to Scotland. Bunting gives the dates of some of the O Connellan tunes
which appear in his collection as around 1660 and 1670.

O Sullivan examined the supposed origins of the tune 'Lochaber No More'
or 'Limerick's Lamentation' which is frequently linked with Connellan's
name. Most of the harpers, who were Bunting's informants in Belfast,
attributed the tune to Myles O Reilly of Co. Cavan, born c. 1635. The earliest
instrumental versions appear in Scottish manuscripts — the Leyden Manuscript written for lyra-viol c. 1692, under the title 'King James' March to
Ireland'; and the Atkinson Manuscript (1694) entitled 'King James' March to
Dublin'. An untitled version of the same melody is included in the Skene
Fiddle Manuscript (c. 1712). In each case, the tune is in 3/4 time, making it
likely that the title is purely commemorative, though in any case, organised
marching to a 4/4 or 6/8 beat was not used by Scottish soldiers until after this

period. The historical event to which it refers is apparently the military expedition of James II from Kinsale to Dublin in March 1689. During the same campaign ocurred the siege and capitulation of Limerick in 1691, with which the two Irish titles for the tune are linked — 'Limerick's Lamentation' and 'Sarsfield's Lamentation' (after the commander of the Irish forces in Limerick).

The earliest recorded association of these titles with the tune occurs in Daniel Wright's 'Aria Di Camera', published about 1725. The Scottish information in this book was largely provided by a Mr. Alex Urquhart of Edinburgh. The Irish airs were apparently communicated to Wright by "Mr. Dermt. O'Connor, of Limerick". O'Connor was a scribe employed in London in 1720 by Maurice O'Connor, a successful Irish lawyer, to copy manuscripts of Irish poetry. A variant of the tune similar to that in Wright's 'Aria Di Camera' is found in the Wighton Collection of English, Irish, Scottish and Welsh Airs published, in Alfred Moffat's opinion, "not later than 1735" in which it is called 'Irish Lamentation', while a version described as "a much mutilated setting" was published under the title 'Reeves Maggot' in Playford's "Dancing Master" in 1703. The melody was mistakenly linked with the words of a poem "Since Coelia's my foe" which was printed in a book by Thomas Duffet in 1676 where they were headed "Songs to the Irish tune". The tune in question, however, is a completely different one, which was printed along with this poem in Playford's book of "Choice Ayres, Songs and Dialogues to sing to the Theorbo-Lute or Bass-Viol", also in 1676. The first time the melody 'Limerick's Lamentation' was associated with these words was in "The Lover's Opera", published in 1730.

The poet Allan Ramsay wrote the words "Farewell to Lochaber and farewell my Jean" which give the tune its commonly known Scottish title. The poem was first published in his "Tea Table Miscellany" in 1724 though the tune was not actually printed alongside them until Thomson's "Orpheus Caledonius" in 1733. The title 'Lochaber' thus apparently dates from no earlier than 1724. Variants of the melody as a song tune, however, seem to have been current in Scotland for some time before this date. Robert Burns commented on the tune which he collected for the ballad 'Lord Ronald, my son' that: "This air, a very favourite one in Ayrshire, is evidently the original of 'Lochaber'". James Dick, in his "Songs of Robert Burns", makes the point that the single strain construction of the 'Lord Ronald' melody would indeed tend to confirm Burn's theory that it is of an earlier date than the double strain 'King James' March' tunes. Highland vocal versions of a typically pentatonic structure, of which the well known song "Crodh Chailein" is one, were apparently widespread throughout Scotland during the 18th century to an extent which makes it unlikely that they were derived from an Irish tune imported only around 1700.[15]

The other melody "Killiekrankie", which is often attributed to O

Connellan, also has a very mixed musical pedigree. It is associated to many other tunes which go back to at least the early 17th century. In England it relates to "The Clean Contrary Way", "Gilderoy" and "The Miller of Dee" which appear in collections for bass viol, viol and virginals, and were also sung. In Ireland it is also related to "The Star of the County Down"; and the Gaelic song "Gleanntan Araighlin Aobhinn". In the Scottish Atkinson Manuscript of 1694/5 it features as "The Irish Gillycranky". As a composition of the O Connellans', it is sometimes referred to as "Planxty Davis". This title seems to have been attached to the tune by mistake, and probably instead belongs to a tune to which Carolan wrote words — "The Two William Davises". The name "Killiekrankie" refers to the battle fought in Perthshire in 1689 between Highland forces led by Claverhouse in support of James II, and the army of William III, under Major-General Mackay.[16]

Both these tunes, therefore, seem to have existed in the song tradition prior to their appearance as instrumental pieces, when they may well have been played by the O Connellans, Myles O'Reilly and other harpers. Yet another harper, on record in North East parish, Edinburgh, in a "list of papists" of March 1709, is "Daniel Melvile harper", along with "Helen Melvil his spouse", who are described as being "from Ireland". They do not appear in similar lists of 1704 or 1711, and so may have resided in Edinburgh for only a short time. The couple may well have travelled elsewhere in Scotland, since the Seaforth Papers of c. 1700-1710 mention payment of wages of £01-01-06 to "Mr Meluing the harper". "Melvin" is a common North East version of the name "Melville", and so this may be identified as the same musician. The name is rare in Ireland, mainly found in Ulster, and is of Norman origin. It is likely, therefore, that Daniel Melvile came from a Scots "planter" family, or had simply been on a visit to Ireland. In either case, he too would have helped to disseminate the current repertoire of Scottish and Irish harp music.[17] There was clearly a pool of tunes which were common to Scotland and Ireland, and were used by musicians from both countries. Other examples of melodies claimed as harp tunes which occur on both sides of the Irish Sea are "Mary Scott", found in several of the Scottish collections, which was entitled "Planxty Scott" in Ireland, and "The Fairy Queen", a composition sometimes attributed to Carolan, but which is probably an adaptation of an older melody. Carolan, indeed, often used Scottish tunes, quite openly, as he did with "When she cam ben, she bobbit" and "Cock up your beaver", as themes on which to base a series of variations. Some Scottish airs, like "The Lass of Patie's Mill" (Carolan's Cap) were on other occasions adapted, re-titled and attributed to him as original compositions. It was a common practice of the times (and still occurs today!) and a natural progression of music traditionally handed down by word of mouth.[18]

10 HIGHLAND HARPERS

"Ma's bard, fo'n uir, fo'n uir,
Ma's clarsair, do'n dun, do'n dun".
(If bard, under ground, under ground (with him),
If harper, to the castle, to the castle).[1]

Many of the great Highland families employed harpers. Indeed, from the early records which survive from the 15th century, and probably for some time before that, until the mid-17th century, it is clear that a harper would have been an accepted member in any household of rank. In these Gaelic-speaking areas of the north and west, the instrument used would undoubtedly have been the wire-strung clarsach.

One of these noble households would have been at Kildrummy Castle in Strathdon, the 13th century castle of the Earls of Mar. This was held by Alexander Stewart, the Wolf of Badenoch, fourth son of Robert II. His son, also Alexander Stewart, who lived from c. 1375-1435, apparently employed a harper named Duncan — "Duncannum Clarseough". This man must have been of some standing, since after the fall from power of his patron, in 1438, the Crown awarded him lands at Wester Cloveth, near Kildrummy, to support him in the poor straits in which he now found himself. The King, after all, was also a Stewart, and a close relative of Mar.[2]

An early history of the MacRae family, written originally by Mr. John Macra, minister of Dingwall, who died in 1704, and transcribed by Farquhar MacRae of Inverinate in 1786, mentions the name of "An Cruiteire Buidhe". Macra writes "We are informed that Colin the son of Colin Fitzgerald, about the year 1283, came from Ireland to Ross-shire with sixty warriors of the clans MacRae and Mackenzie. A number of them remained in Kintail; and among them was a MacRae celebrated for his proficiency in Music. He was called in consequence of being either yellow-haired or dun-skinned 'An Cruiteire Buidhe', i.e. the yellow or dun musician, and was engaged by the Laird of Kintail to be family harper in Castle-donan. He had a house built for him at Dornie with grazings attached at a place known to this day as 'Lag Innis a' chruiteir' ". If the date given by Macrae is correct, this musician may have played either the 'cruit' or the 'clarsach'. The story seems to have some basis in fact since descendants of this man, known as 'Clann a' chruitear', were later found in the area. But some details of the account are inaccurate — the Colin 111

Fitzgerald mentioned is an Anglo–Irish ancestor invented, probably by the Earl of Cromarty in an attempt to give his pedigree a Norman link. In fact, the Mackenzies descend from a common ancestor shared with the Mathesons, one Gilleoin of the Aird, who was of Gaelic descent. In view of this, 'An Cruiteire Buidhe' and his descendants may possibly be linked to another tale of a harper called MacRae or MacRath — the name literally means 'Son of Fortune'.[3]

After his defeat by Hector Roy Mackenzie at Tobar nan Ceann (The Well of the Heads, so called from the number of Munros slain there that day), Sir William Munro of Fowlis returned dispirited to his home. There he found a visiting harper, who attempted to cheer him with the advice that all men must face the changing fortunes of war, and that his defeat had not been due to lack of personal courage or leadership, but to the inexperience of his own followers. His attention caught, Fowlis asked the harper's name and on hearing it said "You surely must have been fortunate, as your name imports, and I am sure that you have been more so than I have been this day, but it is fitting to take your advice, MacRath". The harper, trained as he was to wit and extemporary verse, answered:

> "Eachann le sheachd fichead fear,
> Agus thusa le d' ochd ciad
> Se MacRath a mharbh na daoine
> Air bathais Cnoc-Faireal".

> (Hector, with his seven score men,
> And you with your 800,
> He is the 'Fortunate One' to have slain your men
> At the battle-front of Knock-Farrel.)

The battle to which he referred was that of Druim-a-Chait, or of the Cat Ridge, which took place in 1501. Sir William's fortunes revived and, marrying the daughter of MacLean of Duart, he remained an influential member of Highland aristocracy.[4]

The harpers of the MacDonald Lords of the Isles were the MacGhille Sheanaich family. They were thought to have been of Irish origin, and have been linked with an entry in the Annals of Ulster, recording the death from plague at Tuaim da Ghulann of 'Amlaim MacShenaigh accomplished emperor of melody in 1371'. However, recent research suggests that the family were indigenous to Kintyre, and derived their name locally from the church dedicated to St. Sennan at Kilmashennan. There were close links between Kintyre and the North of Ireland, and if 'Amlaim' were of the same family, these connections may explain his Irish name, and the existance of one or two other intrusive Irish names in the MacGhille Sheanaich pedigree. The first recorded appearance of the family in a Scottish context is probably that of a

'Duncan McOhanak' who witnessed a notarial instrument at Finlaggan, the palace of the Lords of the Isles, on 14 June 1456.[5]

After the forfeiture of the Lords of the Isles at the end of the 15th century, the Crown records and the Campbell papers contain the earliest written documentation of the activities of the MacGhille Sheanaichs. The changing fortunes of this family of harpers can be followed through the Rental Rolls of the next two centuries. The Exchequer Rental of 1505 shows that 'Muriach McMaschenach cithariste' held the four merkland of Brunerican, Amod, Dalsmeran, Lag na Damh and Innean Coig Cailleiche in south Kintyre. Four merklands were a sizeable holding, but compared with the eight merkland held by 'Johannes McMurech Albany', the Kintyre representative of the MacMhuirich bardic family, it provides a good example of the relative status of harper and poet in Gaelic society. At this time the lands of Lephenstrath and half of Lyel passed from the hands of Gillecallum McMurrich, one of the bardic family, to the possession of 'Gillecallam McCosenach', and remained with this branch of their family until late in the 18th century.

Gillecallum, described as 'gillcollm Mcoschenock in Kyntyr', appears, along with other members of his family, in the name-list of musicians included in the Book of the Dean of Lismore compiled around 1512-1540. "Muireach cithariste", as befits the head of his kindred, is listed simply as 'mcoschennak a brounerre. At what date he died is not clear, since the Exchequer Rolls of 1541 describe the holder of Brunerican only as 'McIlschanoch', while Lyel and Lephenstrath were held by 'Iboy McIlschannoch' and Pubil and Integy by 'Donaldo McIlshannoch'.

The Dean's list names Muireach's son as 'Aodh Riabhach' but in the Argyll transcripts for 1543 the name of the next tenant of Brunerican appears to read 'Ache Mcosennok' — perhaps a misinterpretation of Aodh. The full entry, remitting his rental by command of the King, reads : "Brouneregyn, Drumhyrenicke, Dalsmeryll, Lagnadurif, Innerkneiekalliche, Amoit iiij lib viij's money, iiij bolts malt, vj stonis mele v stons cheis, ane multone, ane weddir, gewin and remittit to ye said Ache be ye command of the Kingis hieness order his handwrit and signet".

This 1543 Rental also lists an Ache McOsennok — possibly the same man — as paying full rent at Mauchrebeg, while other family lands were in the possession of 'Duncan McGillcallum VcOsennock' and 'McMolane Mcosennak'. The next list, in 1596, mentions 'Murdoch McCochennoch' at Lyel and Lephenstrath and also gives the name of the senior member of the family holding Brunerican — Duncan McIllsenoch. He was still in possession in 1605. By 1619, however, his lands were no longer held rent-free, and the tenant addressed only as 'McOssenok' paid a rental of £106.13.4d, while Murrachie Maceanry VcOssenok paid rental of £57 for Lephanstrath.

Three more members of the family appear at this time : Hew, holding Mucklock at a rental of £25; Muriacke oig, holding Achenaslisaig at £20; and

Gillecallum, holding part of Knockreachmoir. Hew was the father of Malcom McO'senog, minister of Kilchievan c. 1630, who died sometime between 24 April 1639 and 10 October 1640. "Minister McOschennok" and Gilles, his brother, jointly held Glak, Strone and Mucklock in 1636, and it is probably the minister who as 'Malcolme M'Osenog' appears on a list of Kintyre tenants who each subscribed 4 merks to Lord Lorne at Kinlochkilcherane on 17th October 1636. The minister signed his own name, but the only other member of the family included in the list was 'Murioch oig McOsennog', who appears to be among those who could not write their name.

"Murriock oig the harper takisman thereof idem in will" held the lands of 'Brunerican, Amod, Auchenaslaisaig, Lagnadaive, Inincokaleoch and Dalsmuriall' in 1636. The holding, however, is now described as only 2 merkland. The Argyll rentals of 1625 and 1627 (twice) contain the entries "Allowit to murrioch Mcshennocken harper during my Lordis will the maills of Auchinlessen xxlib", indicating that for some of this period at least part of the harper's rental was remitted, perhaps as compensation for this major reduction in his lands.

The disruption of 1647, and in particular the seige of Dunaverty Castle, from which neighbouring Brunerican could not have escaped involvement, must have led to considerable devastation in that area. Only 'Moriah in Lemnastra, leased lands past 5 years', 'Duncan in Kepregan posessed from 1651' and a 'Duncan in Amod' are recorded in the rental of 1653. It is from this period that the family seems to have lost the original Harper's Lands of Brunerican, and probably their status as professional musicians. They now turned to other occupations or became just ordinary agricultural tenants. Indeed, by about 1671 only one of the family 'Malcolm McOsenog' was in possession of a tack, that of Lephenstrath, and even that land was not as it once was. "This room was 2 merkland, but being spoiled by the water is sett at the extent of a 20 shilling land, as to Public Burdens only". The "2 markland of Bruneriken sett to Ralstoune for 21 years from 1669 at £90" had passed out of MacGhille Sheanaich hands, while their other ancient holdings were in the possession of Campbells, MacCumbrays and Hendries.

It is clear that since the days when Muriach Cithariste appeared on record in 1505, the MacGhille Sheanaich family had undergone major changes in their function as musicians and in their economic standing. Following the forfeiture of John, Lord of the Isles in 1493, his lands were taken under the Crown, and administered initially by the Earl of Argyll. Often overshadowed by the antagonism created towards the end of the 16th century when the Campbells moved to fill the power-vacuum left by the loss of the Lordship, the early Campbell administration was conducted with sympathy towards the MacDonalds and their former tenants. Macdonnell of Dunniveg and the Glens, and Argyll, who were related by marriage, were in fact said to have worked well together.

The MacMhuirich poets, however, may not have been entirely happy with this situation. Their 8 merkland holding was still in the possession of John MacMhuirich and his son Cathal in 1543, but some time between then and 1596 the MacMhuirich poets moved from Kintyre to serve the MacDonalds of Clanranald. Although descendants of the family remained in Kintyre, and probably include the 18th century musician and poet William McMurchy, the mainstream of the bardic tradition had moved north.

Yet the MacGhille Sheanaich harpers stayed in Kintyre. What role did they now have? Since at least one member of the family was still able to function as a harper around 1620-36, the instrumental skills had clearly been passed on. At this time when Murrioch oig, though with a reduced land holding, is clearly described as a musician, it is probably noteworthy that 'MacMarqueis', a member of another bardic family who held the 3 merklands of Laggan nearby, has the description 'poet' appended to his name.

It would seem that the link between poet and harper in that part of the Gaelic world remained alive into the first half of the 17th century, but this does not necessarily mean that all was well. It is probably significant that it is during the period of the departure of the MacMhuirichs that the MacGhille Sheanaich family began to move into other professions. 'Gillechreist Mcoshenag ye dempster in Kyntire' is recorded between 1610-1636, while Malcolm McOsenog the minister witnessed a charter by Andro Bishop of Lismore in 1622. On August 24th, 1583, at the town of Ayr, George Hamilton, one of the burgesses of Ayr, undertook to pay George Gibson the sum of "Fourscoir fifteen merkis for the price of one tun of wine received from Gibson by Duncan Leyche M' Illshnnocht in Kintyre". Duncan, along with his son, also Duncan, undertook to reimburse the said George Hamilton. From the description "Leyche" it would seem that the MacGhille Sheanaichs had also turned to the practice of medicine.

This father and son are probably the 'Duncan' and 'Duncan Mor' MacGhille Sheanaich who are listed in the 1596 Kintyre inventory as holding, among other lands, the merkland of Brunerican. Another of the tenants in possession of two merklands is one 'Rannald M'Alaster Herper'. It would seem that, if medicine was practiced by more than one generation of MacGhille Sheanaichs, it was given up before 1636 when Kintyre was being covered by Duncan, one of the MacLachlan medical family, who held five merklands. The appearance of the harper Ranald M'Alaster raises the question as to whether any of the contemporary MacGhille Sheanaichs were practising as professional harpers.

An explanation may perhaps be found with the widow 'Aine McOshennok' who is on record as holding Lephenstrath in 1636. The most probable route for her to have obtained Lephenstrath would have been through her father — unfortunately her late husband's name is not recorded. It is possible that she was the wife of Ranald McAlester, a member of another local family. To have trained as a harper at that time and place, he would almost certainly have been a product of the MacGhille Sheanaichs, one of Gaeldom's principal harping families. At a time when the male representatives of this family seem to have been diversifying into other fields, when the demand for a harper's services, which closely related to that of the poets, had run into the doldrums, the continuity of tradition which led to 'Murrioch oig the harper' may temporarily have diverted via the daughter of the line, or her husband.

The period of decline in the MacGhille Sheanaichs' status continued into the 18th century. Apart from the holders of Lephenstrath, all the other members of the family appear as small subtenants, sometimes on holdings formerly possessed by their forebears. One of these smallholders, Neil MacGhille Sheanaich, part holder of 'Penlachlin', very close to Kilmahennachan where the family originated, died in 1731 leaving his widow Ann Heymann in possession.[6]

Other important patrons of both poets and harpers were the Lamont family whose name is so closely linked with the existing early clarsachs. In their family papers is found the name of Eugenio Clarsach of Kilmun in 1434 — the earliest mention of a MacEwen harper. Another reference from the same period may be that in the Exchequer Rolls of 1456 to 'Archibaldo Lowman, lutatori' — Archibald Lamont, player on the lute. Since it is unlikely that the lute itself would have been used in the Highlands at this date, the name is most probably a mistranslation of 'clarsach'.[7]

The skills of harping were probably handed down through the MacEwen family in an unbroken line, but some members had other functions as well. In 1461–62 the names are recorded of Donald the poet, Eugen (Ewen) the clerk, and Donald, son of the poet. A document of 1530 witnessed by Dowgall Harper was also signed by Robert Robertson of Struan indicating yet another contact between the Lamonts' harpers and the Robertson family at this period. Dowgall's son appears a generation later, in 1560, as Dougal Harperson.

The 'Finlay roy harper' who witnessed a Lamont document in 1568-69 has sometimes been identified as 'Fionnladh am bard ruadh' in the lists of entertainers of the Book of the Dean of Lismore but that 'Fionnladh' is apparently the bard who was attached to Eoin of Clan Gregor. Since Eoin died in 1519, it would seem unlikely that the two 'Finlays' could be the same person, unless he were very long-lived.[8]

Mention of the last Lamont harper may be found in 1661 when proceedings were instigated against Archibald, Marquis of Argyll, for a horrific massacre of Lamont clansmen which took place in 1646. This act was in retaliation for a treacherous attack by the Lamonts, who had invaded Campbell territory as allies of Alasdair Mac Cholla Chiotaich and his Antrim Macdonnells, in support of the Royalist cause, and 'for the ruin of the name of Campbell'. Dougal, Sir James Lamont's harper, was among those who attacked Baron MacGibbon of Glendaruel, and seized a boat-load of thirteen cattle which he was transporting to the Lowlands on Argyll's behalf. Next, the Lamonts laid seige to the Tower of Kilmun which belonged to a Campbell boy at that time in Sir James' own guardianship. They accepted the surrender of the defenders of Kilmun on promise of quarter, but subsequently executed the whole garrison 'except one who was in a hot fever'. The Campbells took the first opportunity to avenge their men and beseiged the Lamont castles of Towart and Ascog. Eventually Sir James Lamont surrendered Towart but first carefully negotiated a written agreement with his enemies to allow himself, his soldiers and the women and children with them to go free. He then persuaded Ascog Castle to surrender. No doubt remembering the Lamonts' own perfidy, the Campbells promptly threw Sir James into the dungeon of Dunstaffnage, where he remained a prisoner for five years, during which time he was not permitted even to change his clothes. He fared better than his clanspeople however. For eight days the Lamonts were imprisoned while their lands were burned and pillaged. Many Lamont women and children were murdered at this time. A boy of fifteen, who hid 'under ane brae', described the fate of the rest. The Campbells took them by boat to Dunoon and there in the churchyard 'they most cruelly murthered, without assyse or order of law, by shotts, by durks, by cutting of their throats, as they doe with beasts, above ane hundreth, and lastly they hanged on one tree thirty and six at one tyme of the cheifs and special gentlemen of that name, and before they were half hanged they cutt them downe and threw them in by dozens in pitts prepared for the same; and many of them striving to ryse upon their feet were violently holden downe untill that by throwing the earth in great quantity upon them they were stifled to death'. Among these 'special gentlemen' perished 'Dougal Harper alias Mackalaster, servant to the said Sir James Lamond'. This 'dule tree' on which the Lamonts were hanged was said to have soon withered and died, while for years afterwards a red, blood-like substance seeped from its roots — a fact sworn to in a Declaration of 1661 by the Minister of Dunoon and the Provost of Rothesay, and attested to by one of the burgesses.[9]

The Campbells of Argyll themselves had their own harpers in the MacVicar family. 'Brayne' or Brian MacVicar 'Cytharista' (harper) to the Earl appears as a witness in Rental Rolls on 11 June 1549. He is almost certainly the 'Braane M^c a vicar' included in the lists of the Book of the Dean of Lismore. Later in the 16th century the story is told of a confrontation between the Earl of Argyll and Lord Huntly of Gordon. Argyll apparently employed a witch in his household whom he consulted to divine the outcome of his actions when important decisions had to be made. The witch told Argyll that if he fought with Huntly at that time, his harp would sound in Buchan — Gordon territory — and that his pipes would play in Strathbogie. Argyll took this to mean that he would hold his victory celebrations in the Gordon lands, and launched his attack on Huntly at the battle of Balrinnes. But he had misinterpreted the witch's prophecy. The day was won by the Gordons who, amongst their other prisoners, took captive both Argyll's harper and his piper.[10]

The Campbell pipers were the MacKellars, and a letter, dated 17 August 1802, from Patrick MacVicar in Edinburgh to James Ferrier, Argyll's Receiver General, relates family traditions about these musicians. At this time the MacVicars' harp would appear to have been still extant … 'The Mackellars of Glenshira on the one hand, like the McVicars in Glenarray on the other, were looked upon by the noble family of Argyll as a kind of Life Guard almost within cry. MacKellar was the family's chief musician in ancient times, and I have seen myself in my grandfather McKellar's house the remains of a Keeste Clarsach and Bolg Layd, i.e. the Harp and Case with the Quiver and Case. The ford of Auchlarsain, i.e. the Harper's ford in Sheera, between Stucksgarden and Kilblaan, has been pointed out to me, where sat on each side of the River the two musicians of Stucksgarden and Kilblaan playing in concert. Their ancient tales and achievements in support of the Noble Family are little inferior than those of Ossian for Fingal'.[11]

The Campbells of Breadalbane also patronised a branch of the MacEwen poets, based at Kilchoan, north of Kilmelfort. They may have employed a resident harper, or perhaps a member of the family played the instrument, since their Accounts for February 1658, among a list of items purchased, show a payment for 'Harpstrings' of 12.00s. The Breadalbane home was frequently visited by musicians. In September 1662 they welcomed 'the pyper and his man' … 'with Glenlyon's fiddler and his man' for 'some part of the week'. Lady Weem and her family were regular guests. She was the wife of the chief of clan Menzies, and the Menzies harper, who resided at Logierait in Perthshire, may well have accompanied them. Also in 1662 we find the first contemporary reference to one of the boys who, it was said, used to carry the harper's instrument for them when travelling. Visitors to the Breadalbane household between 11-18 October include 'the Harper and his man two dayes'.[12]

The Breadalbane accounts kept a detailed record of all the food and drink consumed by the household and their guests. We can speculate as to what the harper and his man would have been offered, though we do not have a specific menu for the two days that they were in residence! The figures in brackets refer to the total amount of each commodity consumed during the year 1662-63. Porridge, bannocks and breads would have been the staple diet, made from oatmeal (113 bolls), malt (67 bolls 2 firlets) and flour (6 bolls 2 pekis). Claret wine (14 gallons 3 quarts), white wine (9 gallons) and sack (1 pyrit) were drunk. Large amounts of meat were eaten including beef (502 pieces or joints), marts (23) and veals (15); mutton (121 wethers), lamb (9) and goat (9 kids); pork (3 'swyne') and bacon hams (8). The harper would certainly have been offered the herrings which till recent times were daily fare on the West Coast and Islands — the Breadalbane household consumed an astonishing 5190 'gray' or fresh herrings in 1662 as well as 700 'red herringis' or kippers, 222 salmon and 42 'kilin' (dried or smoked) fish. Butter (27 stone 4 pound), 'great cheiss' (21 'cabuckis' — whole cheeses) and 'small cheis' (69 stone 2ps) were often eaten.

Poultry was common — 455 fowls and capons, and 29 geese — while 'Rabbats', venison and capercailzie were brought from the wild from time to time. Meat and fish would often have been preserved in salt (10 bolls 1 peck) which was an important feature in their diet. The Breadalbanes' noble guests frequently contributed a few sheep or cattle towards the feeding of their men, but the harper would no doubt have sung for his supper![13]

Towards the end of the 17th century musical activity in the Campbells' home seems to have declined. Inventories of items which were stored in a 'loft above brewhouse' list, in 1682, 'on harpsicord in a case and on empte case'. Whether it really is a harpsichord which is meant, or whether it is a misnaming of a harp, we cannot be sure but a second inventory of 1684 includes 'on old harp, and on old Clossmans sadle'. Perhaps this was the harp brought to Breadalbane by Monyvaird's man on 3rd June 1672.[14]

Among the harpers who travelled around Scotland, Campbell of Auchinbreck was famed as a generous patron, and his home in Argyll as one where they would receive a welcome. In 1582, the name of the Auchinbreck family's bard, MacAllester, is recorded in the Black Book of Taymouth. The Campbells of Auchinbreck were influential in war and politics. Duncan Campbell of Auchinbreck took charge of the Campbell troops if Argyll himself were to be absent and was killed by Alastair MacCholla when Argyll fled at the battle of Inverlochy in 1645.[15]

The lands held by the Auchinbreck lairds at Kilmichael and Glassary were also of importance as a centre of religious significance. A bell-shrine, said to have been that of St. Moluag, a Pictish saint of the 6th century, was found near the chapel of Kilmichael Glassary. This bell, the story goes, St. Moluag miraculously made with a fire kindled from rushes after a smith had refused to make one for him on the excuse that he had no coal. The shrines often had their own hereditary custodians, known by the name of "Deoir" or Dewar. These families were usually said to have been descended from the saints themselves, or were cadet branches of the landowners who had endowed the church. A family of MacIndeors were responsible for the Bell of St. Fillan, and were associated with the Glenorchy branch of the Clan Campbell. One of these "Donald Pypar McYndoir Pypar" signed a bond of man-rent at Strathfillan in 1561 to take Colin Campbell of Glenorchy as his adopted son. These MacIndeors appear, under Campbell patronage, to have spread west along Loch Aweside into Glassary. However, the Kilmichael-Glassary Bellshrine may have had its own separate line of "Deoirs".[16] Certainly a "Lucas Mackilmichael Deor alias McIndeor" was granted life rent on the property of Kilchoan by Donald Campbell of Duntroon on 18th May 1609.[17]

The harper of Sir Duncan Campbell of Auchinbreck at the end of the 17th century was Duncan MacIndeor, who appears to have been connected to the Kilchoan family. He died at Upper Fincharn in the Parish of Glassary where, according to his inventory, he was residing at the time, although it is evident that he also had a home in Edinburgh. He left a wife, Christian Campbell, and daughters, Mary, Katherine and Jean. A gap in the inventory, left for another name, may have been for a fourth child who was also seriously ill at that time, or Christian may again have been pregnant. Duncan's brother Neill was named as overseer of the children in the event of their mother's remarriage.

At the time of Duncan's death, Neill was also living at Upper Fincharn, along with a Donald MacIndeor, his wife, Margaret Campbell, and Donald's mother, Mary Beith. Neill does not appear among Auchinbreck's seven tenants in Over Fincharn, listed in a writ for unpaid feus and teinds, brought by Charles Maitland, the brother of the Duke of Lauderdale on 27th February 1672. At this time Auchinbreck was badly in debt. The list does include a Duncan and a John MacIndeor — the former is probably the harper; the latter, who died in September 1688, was the husband of Mary Beith and father of Donald. Interestingly, a family of MacCruitears also appears, though the name in this case is probably an old one. Both MacCruitears and MacIndeors feature again in name lists which were compiled in 1685, naming those rebels involved in an attempted rising by Argyll against the Crown. Both Duncan and Neill are included in this, although associated with a different parish. Neill's stock was declared forfeit for his part in the rebellion. A list of Fencible men, made with a view to raising troops in 1692, again shows the names of Neill and Donald MacIndeor amongst four names at Over Fincharn, but the only Duncan MacIndeor mentioned falls under Kilmartin Parish, with no indication where in the Parish he was living. Since Duncan the harper certainly owned a dwelling house in Edinburgh, it seems likely that he travelled around a great deal more than did the other members of his family. The harper may himself also have acted as a dempster at the justiciary court which roved around Argyll in the late 17th century.

On 11th December 1695 a decree records that "Chrystiane Campbell relict (widow) of Duncan MacEndeor harper" indweller in Edinburgh is decerned to pay ... Campbell, surgeon in Edinburgh the sume of £15.10sh." The debt was incurred for medical treatment to Duncan and the children. Duncan's inventory lists all those owing him money at the time of his death, and among these were his brother Neill at Over Fincharn and Robert MacIndeor of Kilchoan. Others included Alexander Lambie, Auchinbreck's gardener, Colin McLauchlan, brother to Craiginterve, and two members of the College in Edinburgh. Debts owed by Duncan included two small sums to his brother Neill, others to Robert MacIndeor of Kilchoan, Donald younger and Mary Beith of Fincharn, Donald MacCullum, factor to the estate of Lauderdale, John Campbell of Glassary (for a firlot of meal), and five people, all residents of Edinburgh. Duncan's debts together with servant fees and funeral charges, amounted to £121.1.8d. His assets, comprising of six great cows, two two-year-olds, ten goats, and his household plenishing in Edinburgh, together with monies owed to him, amounted to £1337.6.8d, which left a movable estate of £1215.5s.

This was a large sum compared with inventories left by his contemporaries about Fincharn and Kilchoan, who also tended to have more stock but held fewer bonds. As a professional harper, Duncan would not have derived his living solely from the land. Therefore to assess his financial position, we can compare his status with what little is known about the economic status of the other harpers about the end of the 17th century. Of three who exist as more than just names, Alexander Menzies, harper in Ballinearn, near where the River Tay meets the Tummel, was the nearest in wealth to Duncan, according to his testament and inventory, recorded on 20th December 1705, and a sasine recorded posthumously on 29th July 1706. The testament, dated 13 August 1713, of "Robert Robertson, alias Clarcer, sometime in Straloch", barely covered his liabilities, while "John Robertson alias Clarsair" at Poldornie (?), who received a commission as one of the poor men of the parish of Blair Atholl in 1709, was presumably in reduced circumstances at the time. Auchinbreck's harper appears to have been an affluent member of his profession, although it is possible that he and Alexander Menzies represented the end of an old order, and that by 1700 the status of the professional harper was undergoing a rapid decline.

Of Duncan's musical connections, it is only possible to speculate. He would, no doubt, have entertained Sir Duncan Campbell of Auchinbreck and his wife, Lady Harriet Lindsay, at nearby Carnasserie Castle, which was their home prior to Auchinbreck's involvement in Argyll's abortive rising of 1685, during which the castle was destroyed. Lady Harriet was the daughter of the Earl of Balcarres, so the harper was probably familiar with the type of material contained in the Balcarres Lute manuscript which was compiled in 1694. The manuscript contains several versions of the harp airs of Port Atholl and Port Gordon, and it is possible that, while living in Edinburgh would have brought Duncan into contact with the prevailing musical tastes of the Lowland aristocracy, his presence there would have added to the popularity of these harp tunes. The Auchinbrecks' interest in harping continued into the next generation. Sir Duncan Campbell's son James married the daughter of Iain Breac MacLeod of Dunvegan, Janet, who was certainly interested in music, having been taught to play the virginals in Edinburgh around 1695. Through his wife's family connections, the Auchinbrecks may well have been visited by her father's harper, Ruaidhri Dall Morison — there is no doubt that, well into the next century, their home gave a warm welcome to any harper travelling through the area.[18]

Duncan MacIndeor may also have played in Edinburgh for the Laird of Cawdor, head of another branch of the Campbell clan whose relationship with harpers was of longstanding. John Campbell, Bishop of the Isles, was a second son of the house of Cawdor. He left a bequest in his will, dated October 1585

: "I laiff to David McFeye harper, by his hundreth pundis I aucht hym, with the feye sax lib." "Jo. B. of Ihyles". John Campbell's predecessor was Bishop Carswell, who was not an enthusiastic supporter of Gaelic culture, complaining in the dedication of his catechism that the Highlanders paid more attention to pagan tales and the idle songs of Fin MacCumhaill and Goll MacMoirne than to the Word of God! Bishop Campbell seems to have had a different taste in music.[19]

The harper of Campbell of Cawdor at the beginning of the 17th century has already been mentioned in chapter 8. By the mid 17th century Adam Smith, servitor to Cawdor, is described in a Fraser manuscript history as being able to play several instruments. "Edam Smith master of the musicains in Murray for virginall, harp and organ, was Calders domestick". Smith must have played for the Frasers at Lovat nearby where, around 1640, we are told that the Master of Lovat "had a wonderful fancy for musick variety of which he still had by him the harp, virginels, base and trible viol in consort". This account comes from a history of the Fraser family written by James Fraser who lived from 1634-1709. He also mentions that "Mr. John Houston, the minister of Wardlaw and his sone Mr. Thomas, were great musitians, vocall and instrumentall, who frequently attended, besids James Tarras and David Cerr, both domesticks". Cerr was Lovat's own musician and, like Adam Smith, probably played a variety of instruments, performing the classical music of the day as well as traditional music.[20]

Moving further north-east, a contemporary account of the death of a harper named Donald McKean is quoted in a Sutherland family history. On 13th February 1602 a party of travellers, including the Earl of Sutherland's harper, were caught in a great snow storm. Those who refrained from drinking the usque-baugh (whisky) "which happened by chance to be there" survived. The less abstemious members, including the harper, did not.[21]

The death of another harper was commemorated by the Carn a' Chlarsair, the Harper's Cairn, in Ross-shire. This cairn of stones was built either in the grounds of the present-day schoolhouse or where the Tarradale Inn now stands. During the 16th century small water mills were being introduced to the Highlands. One of these belonged to the Laird of Tarradale. He quarrelled with one of the Mackenzies of Ord, "Iain Dubh a' Ghuibhais" or Black John of the Fir, who took a band of men to destroy the Laird's mill. As they returned from this raid, they unfortunately met a travelling harper and, fearing that he might raise the alarm, they murdered him on the spot. The field nearby is known as Achadh a' Chlarsair.[22]

Mackenzie of Applecross also often entertained itinerant harpers. He is said to have rewarded the harper of the Earl of Antrim, on a visit to Scotland, with a handful of gold and a handful of silver. On his return to Ireland, the harper was asked where he received most generosity and answered "The right hand of the Laird of Applecross"; and when questioned as to the next most liberal patron, replied "The left hand of the Laird of Applecross". The best known of the Earl of Antrim's harpers was Cornelius Lyons (fl. c. 1700) but the musician in this story must have been his predecessor since the episode is said to have taken place in the early 17th century. There is no evidence that Mackenzie of Applecross employed a harper himself, though we do know that he maintained a piper.[23]

The Laird of Grant certainly included a personal harper in his household, who probably accompanied him on his visits to the Lowlands. One of these was to Edinburgh in 1620 when the expenses of Sir John Grant record payment to "Mulleachan the clairscher at the lairdis command and deliverit be himself xxxs." By 1638, however, the Laird was writing to his agent in Ayr to ask why the "clairscher" had failed to return from there. The agent, John Donaldson, explained that there had been a drunken fight between the harper and a violer named John Hay which had left the violer "very ill hurt in the head, where out there is two bones come, and it is in doubt if he will ever be well". The clarsach player was "hurt in the hand; where he is or how he may be, I can not learn, for I have not been very curious to ask". One might speculate that the relative extent of their injuries would be consistent with the two assailants striking each other with their respective instruments![24]

During the 17th century, and probably before that time, the various septs of the MacLeans in the Western Isles were often associated with harping. According to a manuscript history of the clan, the Laird of Coll, John Garbh Maclean "was a wise and pious man, a great lover of musick and very hospitable. Captain Witters, Governor of Duart Castle during Cromwell's usurpation, said of him that he much resembled K. David, being a great reader of the holy scriptures and a good player on the harp, he was very temperate as appears from his refusing to wisit a friend of his in the Isle of Sky, who promised to give up the evidence of a considerable Debt he had against his Family if he would come but for one night to his house and make merry with him. Coll's friends urged him to go but he told them he would not be drunk once for any consideration, which he saw he could not miss to be, or disoblige his friend if he ... this piety and temperence he shewed thro the whole course of his life. He was first married to Florence daughter to Sir Dugal Campbell of Achnambreck and Lady Mary Erskine the Earl of Mar's daughter". This history was written by Dr. Hector MacLean of Grulin (1703-1784), whose interest in his family history had begun in his early twenties. His view of the Laird of Coll may have been overly favourable, when one contrasts it with the apparent experience of Florence, John Garbh's first wife. She was the daughter of Auchinbreck by his wife Mary, the sister of Thomas Erskine, first Earl of Kellie, a family well-known for its interest in music. Florence married John Garbh, her second cousin once removed, sometime before February 1620, and bore him three sons and five daughters. Their youngest son was killed at Inverkeithing in 1651 in support of the Royalist cause. In 1655 the barony of

Coll was appraised for John Garbh's debts and was granted to George Campbell, Sheriff Clerk of Argyll, but after the Restoration, the sasine of estate was obtained by Sir Norman MacLeod of Bernera — the friend whose invitation to take drink, Coll had refused.[25]

Florence Campbell, Lady Coll, is said to have gone mad after the battle of Inverlochy in 1645 where her brother, Sir Duncan Campbell of Auchinbreck, was captured and executed by Alasdair Mac Cholla. Fifteen hundred of his Campbell men were also said to have been slaughtered in the rout, and the fighting force of Clan Campbell was effectively wiped out for a generation. Amongst their butchers were a number of her MacLean relatives. In her grief, Florence Campbell composed a bitter lament "Tuireadh le Fionnaghal Chaimbeul, Baintighearna a Chola".[26] Perhaps this expression of her feelings served to increase hostility towards her from her husband's family. An account by a descendant of the Auchinbreck line tells us that "One of the ladies of Auchinbreck was married to MacLean of Coll, but for what cause I know not was obnoxious to him and to the Clan", who apparently threatened her life. However, some of the MacLeans "more mercifully inclined than the rest had her securely conveyed out of the house to a boat they had in waiting. They arrived with her in Knapdale I believe, as the nearest place where some of her relations were. Of course she never returned to Coll nor dared the men who rescued her, they were of the name of MacLean but they have since been known by a particular patronymic". Unfortunately we are not told what this alias was. The poor lady must have been dead by 1649 when her widower remarried. He certainly appears to have been skilled in harping, and was said to have composed a number of harp tunes including "Caoineadh Rioghail" (The Royal Lament) on the execution of Charles I. Variants of this tune are found in several of the early manuscripts and printed collections. The other tune attributed to John Garbh — "An Tom Murrain" (The Hillock of Bent-Grass) — appears to have been lost. Lachlann, the grandson of John Garbh, was also a patron of musicians. A poem composed on his death by drowning in 1687, says: "You were never miserly with precious things, and harpers paid you court ...

> Cha robh thu taisgeil air seid,
> 'S thug luchd teud an aire dhuit"[27]

On the island of Mull another cluster of harpers were associated with the MacLeans of Duart. Here the earliest records begin in 1674 when the rental of the estate was taken over by the Duke of Argyll's bailiff. The Rental Roll reads : "Under Phanmoir (Fanmore) possest be the harper and pretends kyndnes thereto for his service, and pays nothing ... 1d (1 pennyland)". This area of Mull, according to William Matheson, was known as Fanmore nan Clarsairean, and that family of harpers were called "MacNeill nan Cailleach" or MacNeill of the Old Woman. The name apparently comes from further up the west coast. Another family of MacNeills lived not far away in Ballygowan. They were smiths and armourers and while the name of "Patrick McNeile Smith" is found in a list dated 1716 which recorded all males on MacLean lands, their weapons and whether they had taken part in the recent Jacobite rising, by this time there are no McNeill musicians at Fanmore. The harpers had presumably moved, or more probably, the profession had died out in their family.[28]

Fanmore was part of the Duart estate but was relatively distant from the castle itself — the MacLeans' pipers lived much closer, within four or five miles of their patron. It is significant, however, that one of the important bardic families, the O Muirgheasans, who were originally of Irish descent, had a branch on Mull who served the MacLeans. Their lands were at Penmore at the top of Mull. The MacNeill harpers' lands were much closer to those of the bards than they were to Duart. Again, as in Kintyre, we find an association between harper and bard. It is perhaps also worth noting the place-name "Glac an Fhidleir" (the Fiddler's Holding) which also occurs near Fanmore.[29]

A lament by the poet Eachann Bacach, composed in 1649 on the death of Sir Lachlann MacLean of Duart, describes for us the scene in his castle:

> "'N am na faire bhith glasadh
> Biodh a' chlarsach ga creachadh:
> Cha bhiodh ceol innt 'an tasgaidh
> Ach na meoir ga thoirt aiste
> Gun leon laimhe gun laige,
> Gus 'm bu mhiannach leibh cadal gu foill.

(As dawn began to lighten the harp would be exploited: no music would remain stored in it, but the fingers would draw it out painlessly and untiringly, till at last you desired to sleep awhile.)"[30]

Several of the other minor MacLean chiefs in Mull employed musicians. "An Account of the Depredations Committed on the Clan Campbell and their followers during the years 1685 and 1686" was an attempt to obtain restitution after an abortive rebellion at that time, when Atholl and his followers, including the MacLeans of Mull, had raided Argyll's lands. Among the list of goods which were stolen is "Item, from John Roy McIaertich, in Ardinstuir, be the harper's son in Mull, Lochbuyes servant, ane horse", worth £40.00.[31]

There must have been many harpers in the Highlands of the 16th and 17th centuries. In a number of castles of the north-east, the fire-places or lintels are carved with mermaids playing harps. They are delightfully executed, in a similar style to each other, but different enough in detail to make it clear that they were not slavishly copied, one from the other. The harps are usually

Urquhart

Cawdor

realistically depicted. The mermaid was linked with the harp in folk-tale, but it is not clear why several families should have chosen this motif to decorate their great houses. The mermaids are found at Urquhart on the Black Isle, which dates from 1651, and from about 1670 at the Campbell castle of Cawdor. They can also be seen, dated 1679, at Kilcoy Castle, on the Black Isle, which was held by the Mackenzies. This stands very near a castle above Conon Bridge, called Kinkell Clarsach to distinguish it from another Kinkell in the same area. At Kilravock Castle, the mermaid carving is dated 1662 and commemorates the wedding of Hugh Rose to Margaret Innes. Indeed, the coat-of-arms of the Roses still bears a harp as its crest. It is likely that the sculptures all mark marriages amongst these notable families.[32]

Gaelic poems and songs too, show that harpers were found in many noblemen's houses. The MacDonald poet Iain Lom includes some of the best descriptions in his compositions. He says of Lachlan MacKinnon of Strath:

"Dhomh-sa b'aithne do bheus:
'N am dol fodha do'n ghrein
Chluinnte faram nan teud mu d'chluais ...

(I was familiar with your way: at the time of the setting of the sun, within your hearing there sounded the clear notes of harp-strings ...")

One of the MacDonald chiefs, either Alasdair nan Cleas, or Ranald Og of Keppoch, is described as receiving rewards for his loyalty from King James around 1620:

"Thug is cruit fo theudan
Agus cead a seinn 'na sheomar ...

(He has done this, and also given (you) a stringed harp and permission to play it in his chamber.)"

While in the castle of Duntulm, stronghold of Domhnall Gorm Og MacDonald, we are told:

"Bidh cruit agus clarsaich
'S mna uchd-aillidh
'N tur nan taileasg gearr ...

(There will be violins (?) and harps and fair-bosomed women in the tower of short chess-boards.)"

And again, how Sir Donald MacDonald of Sleat's galley would sail:

"Gu Dun-tuilm nam fear fallain,
Far an greadhnach luchd ealaidh
Gabhail failte le caithream
As na clarsaiche glana
Do mhnaoi oig nan teud banala binn.

(Bound for Duntulm, home of the robust men, where minstrels are in high glee, singing a welcome with loud strains from the shining harps in honour of the young bride whose voice is modest and sweet.)"

Sir Donald married Margaret Douglas, daughter of the 3rd Earl of Morton in 1662.

Perhaps the most evocative description of the music of the clarsach comes again from Iain Lom, in his "Lament for the Marquis of Huntly", which dates from 1647, and conjures up the atmosphere of warmth and cultured elegance in the chief's household:

> "Bu ro mhaith b'aithne dhomh t'aighear
> 'N am dhuit gabhail gu d'sheomar:
> Bhiodh foirinn air tailisg
> Is da chlarsaich an comhstri,
> Gus am freagradh am balla
> Do mhac-talla nan organ,
> Fion dearg Spaineach 'ga losgadh
> 'N cuid a dh'obair nan orcheard.

(Very familiar was I with your festive ways when you proceeded to your chamber: chess-men were placed on chess-board while two harps vied with each other until the wall answered to the echo of the organs (?), and red Spanish wine shone brightly in the handiwork of goldsmiths.)"[33]

11 RORY DALL MORISON & HIS CONTEMPORARIES

Bha mi latha 'm Blabheinn	*I was one day in Dunvegan*
mar ri Iain saidhbhir na Hearadh	*with bountiful John of Harris*
an comunn na clarsaich	*among devotees of the harp*
far am biodh luchd dan 'ga leantail:	*where poets kept pace with its music*
gun deanainn fhin is Ruaidhri	*Roderick and I would compose*
duaṇagan beaga de rannaibh	*rimes of a few verses,*
's gheibhmid deocha brioghmhor	*and I would receive potent drinks*
b'fhearr leam na miadachd de bhannach.	*that I preferred to a sizeable bannock.[1]*

While the fortunes of the Highland harpers were on the wane from the mid 17th century onwards, one harper stands out in song, story and folk-memory. This is Ruaidhri Dall MacMhuirich — Rory or Roderick Morison, the Blind Harper of Dunvegan. That his fame should so persist is due no doubt to the fact that he was one of the last professional harpers, and that he was an outstanding performer who combined musical and poetic talents. In the past several historians have made the error of confusing or combining the identities of Ruairi Dall O'Cathain and Ruaidhri Dall Morison. Far more information has survived on the life of the Scottish harper, however, and Rev. William Matheson's learned, fascinating and exhaustive study of Morison's life and background has clearly traced the pattern of his career from his birth, around 1656, to his death in 1713 or 1714.

Rory Dall was the eldest son of John Morison, a tacksman of Bragar on the Island of Lewis. John was a well-to-do farmer, holding a sixteen-pennyland, one of the largest agricultural units in the area. The Morison family were descended from Allan, last of the twelve hereditary Breitheamhan, or judges. John was a man of standing in the community, and of some talent also — he is reputed to have played the fiddle and to have been able to extemporise in verse. He had five sons and one daughter.

Two of his sons, Angus and John, entered the church, a calling which Rory too intended to follow, but, while at school in Inverness, he fell ill with smallpox and was blinded. After this blow to his prospects, he decided to pursue a musical career. Alexander Morison, in his account of Rory Dall's life, published in "The Costume of the Clans" in 1845, says that at this point Rory went to Ireland to learn to play the harp. John Mackenzie, however, writes that Morison could already play several instruments but that he excelled upon the 129 harp, and that his visit to Ireland was made in order to fraternise with other players. Whatever the case, his father declared that it had cost him more to make Rory a harper than to make his two brothers ministers of the church!

According to Mackenzie, on his return from Ireland Morison "called at every baronial residence on his way". From clues in his own poetry, it would seem that Rory Dall's early travels in Scotland were, in fact, much less of a triumphal progress. He appears to have joined a band of travelling musicians. Matheson suggests that, as a man of breeding and education, he found it difficult to be accepted by those who were not his equal in these respects. In his song "Creach na Ciadaoin" (Wednesday's Bereavement), Morison says —

> 'Cha bu mhise chuis fharmaid -
> ghabh mi tearbadh o' n treud sin
> far an robh mi am mheanbhghair
> an toiseach aimsir mo cheitein"

> "I am no object of envy.
> In my early youth
> I gladly separated from that band in which
> I was a butt of sly laughter".

The separation occurred during a sojourn in Edinburgh — probably in order to visit the harper's brother, Angus, who had transferred his theological studies from King's College, Aberdeen, where he had been between 1679-80, to Edinburgh University where he remained until 1683. It was on this occasion that Rory encountered Iain Breac MacLeod. Iain Breac, as chief of the Clan MacLeod, had travelled in the summer of 1681 to pay court to James, Duke of York, who was in residence at Holyrood Palace between October 1680 and March 1682, representing his brother, Charles II as Commissioner in Scotland. Morison's meeting with MacLeod was fortuitous and established a relationship between patron and poet which lasted for the following decade.

Rory Dall moved to Dunvegan and became a tenant at Claggan, a sizeable holding, for which he paid 80 merks in rent. A song by the Mull bard John Maclean sends greetings to Skye, and says:

> "'s an teach mor tha ro chaitcheann, na biodh moran d'ur stad ann, 'n uair a theid sibh do 'n Chlaigeann gu faice sibh Ruaidhri".

> "and the big house, too much thronged by all and sundry, do not stop for long there, when you go to Claggan, so that you may see Roderick."

The agricultural work at Claggan would have been done mainly by Morison's subtenants because of his disability and because of his social standing. He was both tacksman and harper — music was accepted as a profession suitable for a gentleman. Ramsay of Ochtertyre writes "He was born a gentleman and lived on that footing in the family". Thus Rory Dall did not hold his lands rent free from MacLeod as appears to have been the case with some other members of the large household at Dunvegan.[2]

Iain Breac was one of the last Highland chiefs to maintain a household in the old style. The Jacobite Risings and the all-consuming spread of Anglicization were to mark the end of a way of life which had changed little for centuries. As well as the harper, MacLeod employed a bard, a piper and a fool. The bards were the O' Muiregheasains, one of whom, named Donnchadh, was paid 20 merks in 1706 as a fee for composing an elegy to the late chief, Norman MacLeod.[3] Their pipers were the famed MacCrimmons, represented at this time by Patrick Og MacCrimmon. This family held ancestral lands in Skye, and established a college of piping which flourished at this period.[4] Neither they nor the O' Muiregheasains appear in the Dunvegan rent-rolls so it would seem that they held their lands rent-free in return for their services. MacLeod's fool or jester was one Norman MacAndy. Accounts also record payment to a "violer", apparently a Lowlander named James Glass, and the purchase of a plaid for him in 1683-84. "Glass" (or grey) may have described the colour of the fiddler's hair, since his name is also listed as "alias Monro".[5]

The MacLeod home in the days of Iain Breac was clearly full of music and poetry. The Blind Harper's songs draw a picture of feasting and merriment in cultured companionship — how the young men of the clan would sit over wine and meat, listening to tales of the heroic deeds of the ancestors of their chief, and passing sun-wise the drinking-horns, or scallop-shells of whisky. Early in the morning to rouse the household, or before the meal, the pipes would strike up in the hands of the great Patrick Og MacCrimmon, while later the softer, soothing notes of the clarsach would charm the ear.

> "An am eirigh gu moch
> ann an teaghlach gun sproc, gun ghruaim,
> chluinnte gleadhraich nan dos,
> is an ceil' air a cois o'n t-suain;
> an trath ghabhadh i lan,
> is i chuireadh os aird na fhuair
> le meoir chionalta ghniomhach
> dhrithleannach dhionach luath."

"At the time of rising early, in a household incapable of gloom or low spirits, the roar of the drones could be heard, and their partner astir from sleep. When it (their partner) had taken its fill, it would not fail to proclaim all it had got, aided by a caressing, active finger, dancing, deft and nimble".

"An trath chuirte 'na tamh i
le furtachd 'na fardaich fein,
dhomh-sa b'fhurasd' a radh
gum bu chuireideach gair nan teud,
le h-iomairt dha-lamh
cur am binnis do chach an ceill:
righ, bu shiublach ri m' chluais
an luthadh le luasgan mheur."

"When it (the bagpipe) was relieved and laid to rest in its own quarters, I could readily relate how beguiling was the sound of harp-strings, impressing all with their sweetness, under the play of two hands. Ah me! how fluent was the quick measure played close to my ear by swiftly moving fingers."

Other entertainments were also enjoyed:

"Gheibte fleasgaich gun ghrain
cur ri macnas gun sgrath, gun fhuath,
is mnai fhionna 'n fhuilt reidh
cur an grinnis an ceill le stuaim;
an deidh ceilearadh beoil
dannsa oileanach ordail suas,
le fear bogha 'nan coir
chumail modha ri por an cluas."

"Young men whom none could disdain might be seen engaged in dalliance, without distaste or aversion, and fair, smooth-tressed women displaying their charms with modesty. After voices had been lifted up in song, they took the floor for dancing, accomplished and precise, with one who wielded a bow near at hand to make the measure sound in their ears."

Although the harper here speaks with apparent appreciation of its music, he is reputed to have regarded the fiddle with animosity. A line in a poem composed by Duncan Macrae of Inverinate alludes to this dislike when, describing Morison, he says: "'s e 'g eudach ri mac Dheors" — "Jealous as he is of George's son" (George's son or George's daughter was a poetic name used to describe the fiddle). Matheson also quotes the tradition that, on hearing a fiddler playing music normally performed on the harp, he said :

"Masa ceol fidileireachd
tha gu leor siod dheth".

"If fiddling is music, that is enough of it".

Interestingly, another story related in Matheson's book tells us of Rev. Angus Morison, the harper's brother, who was also given to extemporising in verse, and apparently had a rather wicked tongue. At a wedding he is supposed to have said of the bride to the bridegroom:

> "Ge salach i 's ge rapach i,
> 's ge dubh lachdunn riabhach i,
> 's e do chuid-s' an drasd i."

"Dirty and untidy as she is, and black, sallow and grizzled as she is, she is yours now."

To which the bridegroom replied "Mas e sin mar a tha i, tha gu leor agam dhith" — "If that's how she is, I've had enough of her", and refused to continue the ceremony.

Perhaps the harper was alluding to this family story when he made his unfavourable comment on the fiddle — the instrument is often referred to in song and poetry as its player's "second wife". Since his father, too, is said to have been a fiddler, it seems unlikely that he would have had a deep inherent dislike of the instrument itself. But it may well be, since the fiddle was gaining in popularity at this period, while the clarsach and the old bardic style of music was on the wane, that his jealousy was aroused on a professional level. For this reason the harp tune entitled "Fuath nam Fidhleirean" (The Fiddler's Contempt) has often been associated with Ruaidhri Morison, but we will discuss this in our chapter on the music of the harp. Whatever his feelings towards the fiddle, there is no doubt that the MacLeod castle at Dunvegan would have created a suitable climate for musical interchange between harp, pipes and fiddle, and it is due to the adoption of its music by the other instruments that some of the harp tunes have survived.

Morison's stay at the castle — "far 'm biodh tathaich nan duan, iomadh mathas gun chruas, gun chas", (a song-haunted place abounding in good things, given without stint or question) — was to come to its end in 1688. MacLeod ordered him to remove himself to Glenelg, on the mainland. The reasons for this apparent exile are not clear, but Matheson suggests that it may have been connected with the political situation at the time. Pressure was being brought to bear on the major chiefs to declare themselves as supporters of James VII, or of the Government of William of Orange. Iain Breac was apparently treading a delicate line, attempting to remain uncommitted to either side. The Blind Harper, however, was a vociferous and outspoken Jacobite, as can be seen in his song "Oran mu Oifigich Araid' (A Song About Certain Officers). :

"Ach 'n uair thig Righ Seumas
's a dh'eighear e 'na choir,
cait am bi na h-eucoraich
a threig e d' an ceart deoin,
's a bha gu saidhbhir feudalach
ag eirigh air an stor,.
'n uair thar iad sast is eiginn
air iad fein thobhairt a leon?

"When King James comes and is proclaimed in his inheritance, where will the wrongdoers be who deliberately forsook him, and who were rich and well-provided, rising in the world on the strength of their possessions, once they obtained purchase and the applied power to extricate themselves from distress?".

It must have been a political embarrassment to Iain Breac to have his own harper publicly voicing such sentiments.

The farm at Totamor was apparently given to him rent-free, which may have been intended as some compensation for his enforced removal. Still, Morison found his new situation isolated and not a little insecure. There were frequent raids in the area by the cattle-reivers who roamed the mountains of Lochaber. The Harper appealed to them in a song called "A' Cheud Di-luain de'n Raithe" (The First Monday of the Quarter) to take pity on a blind man and to leave him in peace. He then describes their prowess as warriors and hunters, and as brave and honourable men. The flattery apparently had the intended effect and he suffered none of their depredations.

In 1693 Iain Breac MacLeod died. The Harper's songs tell of his sense of shock and loss, and his longing for the days that have now gone forever :

"An deidh fhalach 'na aonar,
bidh e daonnan an uaigneas —
sgeul mun gearanach daoine,
mnai caointeach nan luathbhos,
is iad ag comhstrith ri cheile —
ceol gun eibhneas, seachd truaighe:
leum mo chridhe 'na spealtadh
mu 'n chaismeachd 'n uair chualas.

"Hidden (in the grave) all along, he will ever be in solitude : the thought of it makes men moan, while weeping women, beating their palms together without rest, seek to outdo one another — it is unjoyful music, sevenfold misery. My heart burst in fragments to hear the sound of the (funeral) march."

Morison's relationship with the new chief, Roderick, had none of the warmth of the friendship and patronage of Iain Breac. His heir was often absent fron Skye, and did not take seriously the responsibilities of his position, indulging often in reckless spending. He seems, however, to have been a likeable character — his tutor, Martin Martin, described him as "the kindest friend I had on earth". Even Rory Dall addresses him in "Oran do MhacLeoid Dhun Bheagain" (A Song to MacLeod of Dunvegan) as "my joy, my inspiration and my disquiet". Despite this composition, which goes on to castigate him for his errant ways, and for failing to uphold the great traditions of his father, MacLeod seems to have taken no retaliatory action against the Harper. The O' Muiregheasain poets and the MacCrimmons were still maintained at Dunvegan so it may well be that the rift was due simply to the incompatibility of two different personalities.

Morison found a new patron in John MacLeod of Talisker, a man well known for his hospitality and liberality. Many poets and musicians visited him, including the bard John MacLean of Mull, and also John Mackay (Am Piobaire Dall), piper to the Lairds of Gairloch, who had studied with Patrick MacCrimmon in Skye. He too was a poet, who mentioned Rory Dall in his compositions — sometimes quoting a phrase or two of his friend's own lines:

> "Tha mise chuideachd an drasd,
> mar fhuaim tuinne ri traigh,
> far 'm bu chuireideach gair theud dhomh,
>
> aig an rioghain gun sgod,
> nighean Taighteir Mhic Leoid,
> riamh nach d'fhuaras mu'n or gleidhteach —
>
> "I am the guest just now
> like the sound of a wave on the shore,
> where beguiling to me were the tones of harp strings,
>
> of the lady without blemish,
> daughter of the Tutor of MacLeod,
> who was never found to be a hoarder of gold."

The lady to whom he refers is Christian, daughter-in-law of John MacLeod of Talisker. Mackay also describes a hunting party, which took place in the Reay country, in the north-east Highlands, during the last decade of the 17th century. "Cumha Choire an Easa (The Lament for the Corry of the Waterfall) takes the form of a dialogue between the poet and the Corry of the title. Recalling the event, it says:

"Bu lionmhor de mhaithean na h-Eireann
thigeadh gu m' reidhlean le h-ealaidh;
sheinneadh Ruaidhri Dall dhomh failte,
bhiodh MacAoidh 's a chairdean mar ris".

"Many of the nobles of Ireland
would come to my green sward in merry mood;
Blind Rory would play a salute to me,
Mackay and his friends would be with him".

John Mackay apparently suggests that on this occasion the Harper played a tune "Failte Choire an Easa". It cannot be simply a coincidence that a variant of the piobaireachd "Cumha Craobh nan Teud" (The Lament for the Harp Tree) is entitled "Corrienessan's Salute". It is probable that it was a version of this melody which was performed by Rory Dall.

This period of Morison's life would seem to have had its share of friendship and conviviality, and his prowess as a harper and poet was still highly regarded. When, in about 1700, John MacLeod of Talisker died, the Harper faced, for the second time, the loss of a patron and friend. An elegy for MacLeod composed by Lachlann Mackinnon says :

"Gum b' ionndrainn do luchd-theud thu,
do dh' fheumaich is do bhardaibh,
gum b' ionndrainn do na h-uile duin'
a buineadh bhith am pairt riut;
gum b' ionndrainn mhor do Ruaidhri thu,
ged 's aoighidh math aig uaislean e;
call caraid an am cruadail thu
do dh'uaislean Earra-ghaidheal".

"You were mourned by harpers
by the needy and by bards
you were mourned by everyone
who in the course of business had dealings with you;
You were greatly mourned by Roderick,
although he is well found as a guest of gentle-folk;
(your death meant) the loss of a friend in need
for the gentle-folk of Argyll".

The Harper left his lands in Glenelg and is said to have gone to live with his father-in-law in Lochaber. He had married, presumably around 1690, Catherine, daughter of John Stewart, a factor, of Lochaber. They had at least one son, James, who by 1723 had established himself as a merchant in Stornoway. Rory Dall, as Mackinnon's poem suggests, seems to have travelled around a good deal at this time. Alexander Morison says that he made occasional excursions to the houses of the chieftains in the Highlands and Isles, and corroborating this, John Mackenzie writes that "he indeed occasionally visited gentlemen's houses, but he was always under special invitation". It seems that he may, as this poem suggests, have been a guest of Mackenzie of Coul and Applecross :

> "Teaghlach na Cuile 's na Comraich
> 's dluth ri d' shloinneadh chairdean,
> teaghlach fiughantach na h-Alba
> fhuair an t-ainm 's an t-aite;
> gach ard uaisle 's cliu bu dual duibh
> anns an duan-s' chan airmhear:
> gach ni tha bhuaith' de 'r cliu ri luaidh
> 's e chunntadh suas an Clarsair".

> "The family of Coul and Applecross
> is close in your reckoning of kinsfolk
> the most hospitable family in Scotland,
> who won that fame and place;
> the high nobility and renown that you inherited
> cannot be related in this song;
> whatever it lacks in proclaiming your fame —
> it is the Harper who could sum it up."

A note identifies the "Clarsair" as the Blind Harper — but the reference also no doubt alludes to the earlier Mackenzies' liberality to the Irish harper of the Earl of Antrim. It would not be surprising if Morison were to go to Coul since it was in that parish, at Contin, that his brother Angus was now minister. We have seen that he travelled to the north-east, and there are also clues that he may well have made at least one trip to Perthshire. Indeed, given the signs that the Atholl area may have had a reputation as a centre of harping, it would perhaps have been unusual if he had not gone there at some point in his life.

Morison seems to have been led, on at least some of his travels, by his wife, but may also, as was the custom, have employed a lad to carry his clarsach. A far from flattering picture of the couple is given by Duncan Macrae of Inverinate in his sarcastic reply to one of the Harper's Jacobite poems:

> "Is ged bha Catriona urrasach
> 's Mac Mhuirich bha 'na lorg,
> mo bheachd-s', giodh e as ullamh
> air ni chumadh le chuid ord —

bhon thubhradh Gille-micheil rium,
cuim' 'n islich mi mo ghloir? —
an donas grot a bhuidhinn iad
nach d' chuireadh leo 'san stop.

"And although Catherine was self-assured, and Morison who trailed after her: to my mind, though he is readiest at fashioning something with his hammers — (i.e. playing the harp) — since I have been called Gilli-michell, why should I lower my voice? — devil the groat have they earned but has been spent by them on drink" ...

"Ach 's ro-mhath chulaidh shugraidh
fear a dhuisligean 's a dhoigh,
ged a chuir e culaibh
ri mhnaoi-phuisde dh 'fhag e breoit';
nach airidh nis air sgiursadh e,
nam biodh giuistinnean f'a choir? —
is e sior chleachdadh siursaidheachd
bho b'ise 's uire ceol."

"Very good as a merry fellow is one of his wiles and ways, though he has turned his back on his wedded wife, leaving her in broken health. Does he not now deserve to be whipped, if justices were within reach of him, as he persists in his whoring because the other's music is more delectable".

The "other woman" in this case is of course the harp, so it would seem that Catherine did not always accompany her husband on his wanderings. Though these verses show the scurrilous exaggeration which typifies this type of poem, there is, no doubt, some truth in them. Morison, in his own compositions, declares himself very willing to accept a drink.

It is said that Rory Dall returned to Lewis and that he died there. A stone in the old cemetery at Eye is sometimes pointed out as marking his grave. This, however, is probably a case of mistaken identity. It appears that in fact he went back to Skye at some time around 1713, when the accounts of the factor, John MacLeod of Contullich, record the purchase of a plaid for "blind Roderick". Whether he was at Dunvegan during his last illness, we do not know, though John Mackenzie writes that enquiries were made after his health by the household at the castle, and that after his death, his body was taken there for burial. The exact date of his demise is not known, but a letter, written by his brother Angus, sometime before 1st August 1714, uses the phrase "if poor Rorie were alive". He must therefore have died during that or the previous year.

Ruaidhri Morison does not seem to have been a composer of instrumental music — none of the existing harp tunes can be definitely attributed to him.

He was, however, skilled at fitting music, either old or new melodies, to his own poetry, and is also likely to have included solo harp tunes in his repertoire. Some of the songs of the Blind Harper have survived and have passed into the general oral tradition. Though they must have altered in the transition from formal bardic composition to folk-song, and sustained the changes that are to be expected over three hundred years, they show that he was a master of his craft when composing in the amhran metre, whether the subject is eulogy, elegy, or the sarcasm of the "aoir" or flyting. What is striking about his work is that he steps outside the formalised expression of admiration or grief, and gives us an insight into his personal emotions. We can follow his admiration of his patron, and his pleasure at being taken up by MacLeod. We can enjoy his sly, ribald flirting with the ladies of the household in "The Harp Key Fair" where the lost harp key is used as a phallic symbol. We can agree with his own admission that he is ill-advised so loudly to proclaim his dangerous political sentiments in "Oran mu Oifigich Araid" and sympathise with his isolation in Glenelg, growing an unkempt beard — out of sight, out of mind. His tongue can be ascerbic or even coarse, but he could also use it with dignity and delicacy, and there is no doubt that the outpouring of sadness at the loss of his friends is heartfelt, and goes beyond the usual scope of the carefully crafted bardic compositions. He comes over as a strong character, not entirely likeable, but capable of wit, humour and great loyalty — perhaps this strong personality is the reason that he is remembered in anecdote and proverb. Seven of his major compositions are given in full with scholarly translations in Matheson's book.[6]

Contemporary with Ruaidhri Morison was another blind harper, Lachlann Dall. Alexander and Donald Stewart give his name as "Lachlan Mac Ionmhuinn, an Clarsair" so he may well have been a MacKinnon. He has sometimes been identified as the poet Lachlan Mac Thearlaich Oig (MacFhionghuin) but this is rejected by both O Baoill and Matheson who point out that the poet was a fiddler but did not play the harp and that, since his verses mention that he carried a gun, he does not appear to have lost his sight.[7] Lachlann Dall is described in a beautiful lament composed by the poetess Sileas na Ceapaich, daughter of Gilleasbuig, chief of the MacDonalds of Keppoch. She was born around 1660 and married Alexander Gordon of Camdell some time before 1685. She spent most of her life at Camdell and in Urlarmore House, Banffshire, near the modern village of Tomintoul, and later at Beldorney Castle, a few miles south-west of Huntly. They had five sons and probably three daughters. Sileas's poems were composed in the older bardic syllabic metres, or in the newer stressed metres which were becoming widespread in Scotland in the 17th century. They were without doubt intended to be sung, some of them being based on the metre and tune of popular songs. The subjects of her poems range from political comment — she was an ardent Jacobite — to laments for friends and heroes lost in the Rising, poems dedicated to her own family describing the loss of bereavement or separation, and religious poems, most of which were composed after she suffered a serious and debilitating illness. On a lighter note, she offers advice on courtship to young girls, describing her own youth as "frolicsome". Rightly or wrongly, Sileas gained a reputation as a woman whose behaviour was somewhat loose. She was not the only female poet to suffer from such a slur, and it may have been a reaction to the fact that she had the temerity to trespass — by composing syllabic verse — on what had been a purely male preserve. Her relationship with Lachlann Dall seems to have been warm and affectionate, both delighting in song and music over many years.

Cumha Lachlainn Doill

Slan a chaoidh le ceol na clarsaich
Ona ghlac am bas thu, Lachlainn;
Cha bhidh mi tuille 'gat iargain,
Ni mo dh'iarras mi chaoidh t' fhaicinn;
Fhuair mi mo chleachdadh ri d' cheol-sa
'Nuair a bha mi og 's mi 'm phaisdean,
'S ged a thainig mi 'n taobh tuath uat
Thigeadh tu air chuairt do m' fhardaich.

(Farewell forever to the music of the harp, since
death has taken you, Lachlann; no more shall
I bewail your absence, nor ever seek to see you.
I became accustomed to your music when I was a young
child, and though I came north from you, you used to
come visiting my house.)

Gheibhinn sgeula uat gu cinnteach
Air gach aon ni bh' anns an aite;
Gheibhinn sgeul air MacMhic Ailein,
'S air na dh'fharraidinn de m' chairdibh;

(I would be sure to get news from you about
everything in the place; I would get news of
Mac Mhic Ailein, and all those of my friends
I would ask about ...)

'Nuair a ghlacadh tu do cheile
'S a bhiodh tu 'ga gleusadh lamh rium,
Cha mhath a thuigte le h-umaidh
Do chuir chiuil 's mo ghabhail dhan-sa;

Bu bhinn do mheoir air a cliathaich
'Nuair a dh'iarrain Cumha 'n Easbuig,
Cumha Ni Mhic Raghnaill lamh ris,
Cumha Mairi 's Cumha Ghilleasbuig.

(When you took your loved one and were tuning
it beside me, a fool would not have understood
very well your making of music or my reciting
of poems. [This line is translated by Professor
W. Gillies as "your accompanying my singing of
verses".] Your fingers were sweet on its side
when I would ask for Cumha 'n Easbuig, Cumha Ni
Mhic Raghnaill as well, Cumha Mairi and Cumha
Ghilleasbuig.)

Cha chluinn mi chaoidh Socair Dhana,
Cumha na Failte na Oran,
Nach tig na deoir o mo shuilean
Le trom-thuirse o nach beo thu;
Ged a bha iad dall do shuilean,
Cha bu dall an cuis no dha thu:
Cha bu dall do bheul ri sugradh,
'S cha bu dall air luths do lamh thu.

(I shall never hear Socair Dhana, Cumha
or Failte or Oran, but the tears will come
from my eyes in deep sadness that you are no
longer alive. Though your eyes were blind,
you were not blind in one or two matters:
your lips were not blind in sporting, and you
were not blind in the nimbleness of your hands.)

'S truagh leam do chlarsach 'ga rusgadh,
'S truagh leam gach cuis mar a thachair;
'S duilich leam nach tig thu 'n taobh so,
'S gun mo dhuil bhith chaoidh ri t' fhaicinn;
Iarram air Dia bhith riut iochdmhor
'S do leigeil am miosg nan Aingeal;
O bha do thlachd 's a' cheol 's an t-saoghal,
Ceol am miosg nan naomh dha t' anam.

(I am grieved that your harp is laid bare (?); I am
grieved at the way it all happened; I am saddened
that you will never come to this part and that I can

never expect to see you. I beseech God to be
merciful to you and to admit you among the angels:
since your delight on earth was in music, may your
soul have music among the saints.)

Cha d'iarr thu phorsan 's a' bheatha
Ach na gheibheadh tu o uaislean,
'G imeachd le sugradh 's le aighear
'Nuair bhiodh tu caitheamh do dhuaise;
Ciod an sta dhomh bhith 'gad chaoidh-se
'N deidh gach saoidh a rinn ar fagail?
'S ge bu toigh leam e ri m' oige,
Slan a chaoidh le ceol na clarsaich.

(You asked no portion in life but what you got
from noblemen, going about in playfulness and
joy when spending your reward. What use for me
to mourn you, after all the heroes who have left
us? And although I loved you in my youth, farewell
forever to the music of the harp.)

This graceful and moving tribute tells us much about the function of the
harper. Lachlann travelled widely throughout the Highlands, from Skye to
Argyll in the west, over through Glencoe and up to Sileas's own home in
Banffshire in the north-east. Passing on the gossip and news of "every dwelling
in every village" was an enjoyable and important part of his visits. He seems
to have had no settled base of his own but to have journeyed from patron to
patron, living off their bounty during a career which must have spanned some
fifty years.

The music mentioned by Sileas covers four important forms of verse : Dan,
Cumha, Failte and Oran (Cumha and Failte being types of Oran), and the
suggestion is that the harper would have accompanied her singing on some
occasions. She also lists four specific titles of tunes "Cumha an Easbuig" may
be the "Cumh Easbuig Earraghaal" found in Daniel Dow's collection. The
Angus Fraser manuscript and the MacFarlane manuscript also contain tunes
called "Easbuig Earraghaidheal" and "Cumh Easpuic Erra-ghaoidheal".
"Cumha Mairi" may have been a version of "Cumha Mairi Nighean Alasdair
Ruadh", now played as a piobaireachd. It was said to have been composed by
Padruig Og MacCrimmon around 1705 on the death of his friend the Skye
poetess. The tune may have appealed to Sileas both for its melody and for its
subject. "Cumha Ghilleasbuig" is probably the poem composed for the death
of Sileas's father in 1684 by Iain Lom, but no tune is known for it, or for Cumha
Ni Mhic Raghnaill, which is given in error as the title of a poem in
Macpherson's "Duanaire".

Sileas also composed a short poem about the music of the harp. Some scholars have interpreted this as meaning that she herself played the instrument, but that it was made difficult for her to do so by the reactionary attitude to Gaelic culture of her son James, and by her financial situation. This seems, however, to be reading more into the poem than is warranted. The other suggestion is that Lachlann's death may have reawakened the longing that she had been in a position to retain him in her household. Whatever the case, her words provide a fitting epitaph for a valued friend.[8]

Rory Morison and Lachlann Dall for much of their lives seem to have led an apparently wandering existence. Though they were certainly held in obvious respect, they were to a large degree dependent for security on the fortunes of their patrons.

In contrast, Alexander Menzies, in Perthshire, was a remarkably affluent musician, to the extent that he was able to lend considerable sums of money to lairds in his own area. Menzies, described in his testament as a "harper in Ballinearn", was of a local family.[9] His brother Thomas held land at Rotmell, further south down the Tay, opposite Easter Dalguise, while his sister Janet and a James Menzies (Janet's husband or son, or possibly another brother) were at Duntyme. The Faskally Papers of 1698 make it clear that Donald Robertson of Killiechangie had badly mismanaged his financial situation, and was deeply in debt to a number of creditors. Robertson of Faskally attempted to sort out the mess in which Killiechangie found himself. Both men were cadets of Robertson of Struan, though they were not closely related. Included in the list of debts was £1066 owing to "Menzies, Harper". On 23rd June 1698 Killiechangie was given precept of sasine "of anual rent of £60 upliftable from the mylntoun of Dalkabon, In favour of Alex Menzie Harper in Killiechangie" by heritable Bond granted by Donald Robertson of Killiechangie on a loan of £1000. The previous Martinmas, a bond preceded the above for the "sowm of £1000" at "an rent of Three score pounds". Menzies signed the document himself, and so was apparently literate. A few years later, on 15th October 1703(5?), an inventory of "such writs as affected the lands of Dalcabon acquyred be Alex. Robertson of Ffaskeillie from Donald Robertson of Killiechangie" lists "Item ane heritable bond granted be Killiechangie to Alex Menzies harper for the sume of Ane thousand pounds bearing infestment in the lands of mylnearn dated 25th June 1698". Menzies had apparently held "wadset" of the lands of Moulinearn or Milton of Dalcapon, which means that he was holding Killiechangie's property as security for the loan, and in the meantime, drew the rents and income from the land until such time as it was redeemed by the borrower.

Robertson still had not repaid the debt by the time of the harper's death. This must have occurred prior to 20th December 1705 when his inventory and testament was drawn up. This also tells us that "there was owing to the said defunct at the tyme of his decease, The somme of One Thousand pounds scots money and the somme of One Hundred and fifty pounds of expense contained in a bond granted be Charles Steward of Ballequhan to the said defunct dated the third day of February 1702". It should be noted that the inventories do not tell the full story of the deceased's possessions. They usually deal with the part of his estate which requires action — usually debts owed to him or by him, and with moveable goods which may be disposed of. It is clear, however, that Alexander Menzies was a wealthy man, worth well in excess of £2000, that music was his profession, and that he was brought up and lived in the heartland of harping.[10]

12 THE ATHOLL CONNECTION

Mhic an fhir a Srath h-Ardail,
Bhiodh na baird ort a' tathaich
'S a bheireadh greis air a' clarsaich
'S air an taileasg gu h-aighear
Is a sheinneadh an fhidheall
Chuireadh fiughair fo mhnathaibh.

Son of him of Strath Ardle
whom the bards frequented
and who would be a while at the clarsach
and cheerfully at the backgammon
and who would play the fiddle
making women expect the dance.[1]

The Atholl area of Perthshire was, without doubt, a focal point for the clarsach. It may, indeed, have been the main centre of harping activity in Scotland over a long period of time. Perthshire itself had immense significance throughout early Scottish history. The meeting and inter-mingling of Pictish and Dalriadic or Scotto-Gaelic cultures can be traced there from the 8th century onwards, while later it was the crossroads between Lowland Scot and Highland Gael. At Scone was the Stone of Destiny on which the Scottish kings were crowned, and the nearby town of Perth was, for a time, effectively the capital of the Dalriadic Scots. The Tay valley has continued to mark the southern limit of the Highlands. Over the centuries Perthshire has in many ways been regarded as the heart of Scotland.

One place-name in particular in this area catches our attention. A Gaelic poem includes the lines "'S Domhnull Ballach nan garbh-chrioch, Rinn *Tigh nan Teud* aig Leth Alba 'n a chrich". (Donald Ballach of the Rough Bounds who made a boundary of the *House of Strings* at the halfway point of Scotland.) If the name "Tigh nan Teud" does indeed go back as far as this poem implies, then it must be at least contemporary with Donall Ballach, who lived c. 1413-1480.[2]

This concept of the centre of Scotland is alluded to by a number of Gaelic poets : Iain Lom (c. 1625-post 1707); Mairi Nighean Alasdair Ruadh (c. 1615-1707) and John MacCodrum (c. 1693-1779) all used variants of the phrase "a house and a half of Scotland". The expression is quite old and has parallels in Ireland, but in the Scottish examples, which are all linked with the claims of Clan Donald, Dr. J. MacInnes has suggested that the formula may have a special significance. The concept of a sacred place is known the world over and is usually associated with the sacred site of kingship. Yet "Tigh nan Teud" lies outside the territory of the MacDonald Lordship of the Isles, and is in the heart of the ancient Picto-Scottish Kingdom. Dr. MacInnes interprets this to suggest that the Gaels, represented and headed by the Clan Donald, were prepared to share Scotland with the Gall (non-Gaels), provided that their right to the whole was acknowledged. Otherwise they would lay claim to the whole of "Alba" — and that this might explain the intentions of Donald, Lord of the Isles, during the events leading up to the Battle of Harlaw in 1411.[3]

The site of the place-name "Tigh nan Teud" (The House of Strings) lies a few miles north of Pitlochry, at the southern entrance to the Pass of Killiekrankie above where the road to Kinlochrannoch bridges the River Garry. On maps prior to 1867, the name appears as "Balephuirt", literally the farm township of the Ferry, or "Ferrytown". Ferries were places where travellers converged and were required to wait, and Change Houses or Inns frequently appear at such places. (The name also features in early rent-rolls as "Seomar" — or "Chalmer nan Teid" (The Room or Chamber of Strings). It is well attested in Scotland how musicians were drawn to these locations by the prospect of the custom that a captive audience implied.[4]

A legend of how the house derived its name was related by Seton Gordon. He says that, in 1564, Queen Mary passed through Moulin on her way to Blair Castle to take part in a deer drive in Glen Tilt. When the Queen reached the ferryman's house, she rested and, inspired by the beauty of the view, called for her harp on which to praise it. But the rough journey along the hill road had been disastrous for some of the harp strings and the local harper was a proud man when he was sent for to repair the damage. From that incident the house where the royal harp was re-strung was named "Tigh nan Teud", and the harp was then presented to Miss Robertson of Lude as a recognition of her sweet playing and charming personality.[5]

It is a nice tale but perhaps that is all as it is confounded by numerous problems. Mary, Queen of Scots, was indeed musical, but the contemporary evidence suggests that playing the harp was not among her accomplishments. Her association with one of the Lude harps arose when her royal arms and portrait were included when decoration was added, during her reign, to an instrument that was already around a hundred years old. The story of Queen Mary's trip to Atholl is true, but her journey did not take her past "Tigh nan Teud". She followed what was then the main route into Atholl when she left Perth, going first to the Abbey at Coupar Angus where she stayed a few days, and then took the old road via Strathardle, Kirkmichael and Shinagag.[6]

Tigh nan Teud, however, does seem to have had a direct link with harpers which lasted into the 18th century. The first documentary evidence occurs in the Faskally Papers. An old cadet family of the Robertsons of Struan, in 1504, Robertson of Faskally held lands comprised of 'Calvine, Callybruar, Pettagowan, Pitteldonich, Kenordochie, Kindrochat, the whole lands of Faskally and the lands of Dysert'. The last of the line, George Robertson of Faskally (whose mother was the daughter of Robertson of Lude) moved his home from Faskally to his estate of Dysert. A breakdown of the lands of Dysert in 1757 shows that they included Baleveil, Balintuim, Corrichallun, Balmanach, Ledghrein and *Tighnateid*, all in the parish of Moulin. Among Faskally's tenants in a roll of 1700 were at (Ba)llitein : "John mctoss yr miller, John Mctoss his son, and John Robertson alias Clarsair". While further down are "Colin Ross yr and Walter Ross his sone", against what seems to read [?] emar [?] teid. The letters obscured by the binding are probably (So) emar (na) teid, since in 1704 there was an action raised between Collin Ross in Ballfourt, sometime in Chalmernateid and Alexander Robertson of Faskally over ten pounds Scots for the comprizing of the biggings of Chalmernateid. At this date the tenancy seems to have changed and in 1707 we find record of a complaint by Elspeth Robertson, spouse to John Robertson in Chalmernateid, against two other women, that they did with no offence strike her causing "a great quantitie of blood at my mouth and no/se".[7]

John Robertson can be identified with the appearance in the Atholl papers of June 24, 1709, of a commission to "John Rotson alias Clarsair at Poldornie to be one of our poormen in the parish of Blair Atholl allocating for him Two bolls of meall payable by Urrard and 4 lib Scots of money payable by the possessor of Rie 'n Chapell yearly". (Poldornie is probably a mis-reading for Toldornie or Toldournie, subject of a longstanding march dispute between Lude and Atholl during the 18th century.) The same harper is found again in a list of Rests owing to Faskally preceding Martinmas 1716 which includes "rests be malcolm Stewart in chamernateid for two years rent of corechallone £22" and "rests be John Clarser sometyme in chalmernateid now in Bellefourt £28-15." John Robertson was still living nearby — perhaps no more than a few hundred yards away — though he no longer held Chalmernateid itself. The existence of Tigh (or Chalmer) nan Teud may represent the "Harper's Land" of the Robertsons of Faskally, and would indicate that they are likely to have retained their own harpers over a number of generations. 8

Robertson of Struan also employed a harper in his household and an interesting story is told about their relationship with one clarsach player. A close Goverment surveillance was kept on the activities of this family, who were known to have strong Jacobite sympathies. Alexander Robertson of Struan died in 1688, and in 1700 his widow, Mariota Baillie, who had been his second wife, was required to seek security for the good behaviour of Duncan, Struan's second son. She is said to have forgotten her position of responsibility to the clan to the extent that she made a degrading marriage with her late husband's harper. Duncan and some of his followers apparently harrassed her and her tenants until she had recourse to law, while young Struan, in exile with James II in France, is said to have been so offended that he vowed that he would never wed, and indeed died unmarried and without an heir. This reaction to an unsuitable match seems rather extreme — one might suggest that the story became associated with Alexander Struan to account for his single, childless, state. The harper, however, seems to have been a genuine historical figure whose children were known as "Clann a' Chlarsair" and may also have played the instrument.[9]

It may be that one of these children was George Clarsair. He is listed as one of Struan's tenants at Innervack on the south side of the Garry at Baluain. He is described as "wanting a gun" (i.e. has no weapon) in a list compiled in 1705 to ascertain how many potential fighting men were in the area. The date would make him too old to be the son of Mariota and a harper, but perhaps the story has become attached to the wrong generation of Robertsons. The grandfather of Alexander and Duncan, also Alexander Robertson of Struan, who died in 1636, had ten years earlier married a lady named Margaret Graham, daughter of Graham of Inchbrakie. It is possible that she is the widow who so incensed the family by marrying her spouse's harper — more than this, her father's name was George, a name which does not appear before this time in the Struan family. George Clarsair, therefore, who lived in the right place at the right time, may be her son.[10]

Included in a similar list of tenants in 1706 is "Duncan Clarsair — servant, wants a gun". He appears under Pitcastle, Balgowan and Pitgir, all belonging to Alexander Robertson of Tenandrie. This holding lies next to Moulinearn, or Milton of Dalcapon, where Alexander Menzies was based. Robertson of Tenandrie was a cadet of Faskally. None of these harpers appear to have been particularly warlike — yet another "James Robertson, alias Clarsair" is again listed in 1705 as "wanting arms" at Clunemore in Strathgroy.

A delightful love song by the poet Alexander MacDonald, possibly written in Perthshire which he visited c1738-39, describes "Mairi Shugaideach" (Lively Mary) and her suitors. Could James have been one of them?

> "'S gil' thu na'n gruth, 's deirg' thu na'n fhuil
> 'S binn' thu na guth clarsaich.
> Dhuilt thu Iarl Unndrum a Eirinn,
> 'S phos thu Seumas clarsair".

> (You are whiter than curds, redder than blood
> Sweeter than the sound of the harp
> You rejected Ireland's Earl of Antrim,
> And married James the harper.)[11]

The most powerful magnates in Perthshire were the Earls of Atholl, and they too were patrons of the harp. A "Harper and Servant to the Earl of Athole" was buried at the old Abbey of Scone in 1639. His tombstone is said to have named him as Alastair Reid. He would have served John Murray, who died in 1642, the son of the Earl of Tullibardine, and the first Murray Earl of Atholl. Alastair Reid is sometimes claimed as a member of the Robertson family. It is quite likely that he was of the branch descended from the Robertsons of Lude, and based at Straloch. This settlement lies on the old Pictish road which runs from Atholl, eastwards to where the Lindsay Castle of Edzell — again strongly associated with harping — stands at the Glens of Clova.[12]

The testament of another harper who had lived in Straloch, dates from 13 August 1713. He was "Robert Robertson alias Clarcer". The testament and inventory of his estate was drawn up by his laird, Leonard Robertson of Straloch, who had himself declared executive dative to the deceased musician. Since at the time of his death, Robert owed him £120 Scots, as the remains of £200 Scots, for the price of nine horses bought from Robertson of Straloch, Leonard had made it his business to tidy up the estate and to call in a number of debts owing to the harper in order to pay himself. These were small sums which had been lent to local men in Carrick, Birkinhills, Kirkmichael, Pittcarmick and Auchincappel, and amounted to £160.13.4. While not in the same league as Alexander Menzies, Robert Robertson seems to have been comfortably provided for — perhaps he was no longer "on the road" as a musician, but had settled down to trade in horses, or to run a change house or stable on one of the main roads.[13]

Yet another member of the Robertson family who performed on the clarsach was Charles Robertson of Auchleeks. He was said to have been so skillful that he was known as "Charlich nan Jead" (Tearlach nan Teud) or Charles of the Strings. The Auchleeks' line, according to tradition, descends from a son of James Robertson, the younger son of Alexander Robertson of Struan who died in 1505. Auchleeks is in Glen Errochty, about five miles due west of Calvine and Struan. It is bounded by the slopes of a hill called "An Teampan", but this name probably refers to its saddle-like configuration rather than an instrument. In October 1617 a discharge is recorded "by Charles Robertson of Auchleiks to Alexander Robertsounne of Inchemagranock of debts due by him except for 1000 merks". While in 1628 debts due by Auchleeks and John Robertson of Inver, Lude's uncle, to Robert Nasmith in Clune, were assigned instead to Alexander Robertson of Lude. Charles must have died before 1649 when his son, Duncan, and his widow, Beatrice, are listed in a rent roll of the Earldom of Atholl. The widow, Beatrice Robertson, was the grand-daughter of John Tarlachson and Beatrice Gardyne, and the aunt of the then Alexander Robertson of Lude.[14]

Lude itself was undoubtedly a centre of harping. Robert Clarsair Leod, who is mentioned in the Book of the Dean of Lismore, is recorded as living at Lude between 1512–40, as is Donal Meill, a harper in Atholl. The McEwen harpers (of whom Robert may be one) were still active in the following century. "John McEvin" lived there around 1670 and may well have taught the harp to the son of his Laird. John Robertson of Lude (1667–1731) inherited the estate from his father, Alexander, in 1674, and appears to have been the last Laird of Lude to play the clarsach himself. Whether his father, Alexander, could play we do not know, but in any case, he would have had little opportunity to pass on his knowledge to his young son before his early death. It is likely, therefore, that John was instructed by one of the professional harpers in the area. John Robertson died in 1731 but his widow, who was a sister of John Farquharson of Invercauld, lived long enough to enthusiastically entertain Prince Charles Edward Stuart at Lude in 1745, where he gaily danced reels and strathspeys. The elderly Lady Lude was said to have been so excited that she behaved "like a light giglet" and that she was "so elevate while she was about the Young Pretender that she looked like a person whose head had gone wrong".[15]

It is clear that in Central Perthshire in the late 17th century there were professional harpers at Struan, Lude and Faskally, as well as Alexander Menzies at Logierait. Besides these four fully employed musicians, there were a number of other clarsach players in the same district, and this appears to continue a tradition which had existed there for some hundreds of years. This is by far the most striking concentration of harpers in any one area of Scotland. Given this, and the presence of the two very old instruments at Lude — the "Queen Mary" and Lamont harps — it is not surprising that well-travelled harpers such as Ruairi Dall O'Cathain and Rory Dall Morison should gravitate to Atholl as though pulled by a magnet. O'Cathain, indeed, is said to have settled there. O Neill's comment that O Cathain went to Scotland "where there were great harpers" may have been a more specific reference to the Atholl area than has been recognised.

Is there a particular reason for this focus of activity? Perthshire has always been a rich and fertile area, with an abundance of productive farmland, forests and hills as famed for their game as the rivers are for their salmon and their freshwater pearls. The Celtic Earls of Atholl, were descended from the mixed Pictish-Dalriadic line of Kenneth MacAlpin. The Earldom passed through a number of families before it was acquired by the Murrays of Tullibardine in 1629. This was a family whose roots were originally Flemish and Lowland Scottish, who had amassed a considerable fortune in lands and gear — over 200,000 acres in Atholl itself. They were thus able to continue a tradition which may already have existed in the area, of patronage of the arts. A number of placenames suggest a long historical connection with the bardic arts. Donald Meek suggests that Perthshire apparently supported an active school of poets and ballad-makers which may be traced in the ascription of the ballad of Ailein mac Ruaidhri in the Book of the Dean of Lismore. This collection, indeed demonstrates — most clearly in its Scots-based orthography — the interplay between Gaelic and Scots culture in Perthshire in the early 16th century.[16] This mingling of the races and cultural traditions seems to have had a stimulating effect on the music, song and poetry produced there. It would not be surprising, given the evidence in other areas, to find that harping flourished in close association with the performance of bardic poetry and balladry. But as the influence of the trained poets waned, the clarsach appears to have developed its own repertoire of instrumental music. This is likely to have been encouraged by the incursion of the European music which was current in the Lowlands, and which was, by the 16th century, being played in aristocratic households on the fringes of the Highlands. It was most often played on lute or virginals, and these instruments, in their turn, have preserved some of the earliest fragments of harp tunes to have survived.[17]

Atholl was specifically mentioned in his book of 1691, by Robert Kirk (1644-92), Minister of Balquhidder and Aberfoyle. "Finally Irishmen, our Northern-Scottish and our Athole men are so much addicted to, and delighted with Harps and Musick, as if, like King Saul, they were possessed with a Forrein Spirit, only with this difference, that Musick did put Saul's pley-fellow asleep, but roused and awakened our men, vanquishing their own Spirits at Pleasure, as if they were impotent of its Powers, and unable to command it; for wee have seen some poor Beggars of them, chattering their Teeth for Cold, that how soon they saw the Fire and heard the Harp, leapt thorow the House like Goats and Satyrs."[18]

That the fiddle was assuming some of the functions of the harp which had previously been associated with the old bardic order may be seen in a letter dated 1693 from a student from Strathspey to his Professor at King's College, Aberdee. Among the Highland customs that he describes, he says: "There were likewise 9 or 10 sometimes 11 or 12 women to travel together, who as they came to anie house two and two together sang one of those songs these 'philies' had made, they had ordinarlie a violer with them who played on his fidle as they sang, when they had done singing, then they danced, these were named 'avranich', i.e. singers".[19]

It is significant that many of the important collections of music which include compositions for the harp were made in Perthshire or were assembled by musicians with a Perthshire background. Daniel Dow and John Bowie are typical of these early collectors. Both had a particular interest in fiddle music, and it is the fiddle which fell heir to much of the early harp music. Indeed, the line of inheritance may well be direct. The most famous Perthshire fiddle player was, without doubt, Niel Gow, whose mother's maiden name was apparently MacEwen. This, as well as the fact that we do not know where Gow received much of his musical training, and that he subsequently became fiddle player to the Duke of Atholl, suggests that there were strong musical links within his family — perhaps a connection with the McEwen harpers who had been established as hereditary musicians in that area for 300 years. Certainly,

Gow's own compositions demonstrate stylistic similarities with the earlier Ports. Tunes such as his "Lamentation for James Moray of Abercairney", for example, bear close comparison with "The Duke of Lennox Port" or "Port Preist". The two main families of fiddle players in the Atholl area were the Gows and the McGlashans. Their musical influence on each other, as well as relationships by blood and by marriage, no doubt helped to create a distinctive style of Perthshire music.[20]

13 FADING ECHOES

"Dheanadh Eoghan clarsaichean (Eoghan would make harps
Nan cuireadh cacha ceol annt". If others would put music in them)[1]

The 18th century saw the continued decline of the clarsach in the Highlands. There must be little doubt that the disappearance of patronage for professional harpers was linked with the waning fortunes of a number of the great Highland families who were involved in the Jacobite Risings, and the consequent social reorganisation. But even before this time it is clear that use of the instrument was decreasing, and this was likely to be due as much to change in musical fashion as to political pressure. Still, it continued to be played by a small number of harpers, both amateur and professional.

It seems to have been relatively common for musicians to be able to perform on more than one instrument. One such was Ranald MacAilean Og of Cross on the Island of Eigg, who lived from around 1662 until 1741. According to a history of the Clan Donald, he was said to have been a good performer on the harp and fiddle, but he is best known as a piper — some outstanding piobaireachd music is attributed to him, including "The Red Speckled Bull", "The Vaunting" and "The Finger Lock". (Scott, however, related a story which associates the last tune with Calum MacRaibeart, the son of an Irish armourer who had been brought, along with his brother David, a harper, to Muckairn by the Earl of Cawdor.) There are many colourful stories about Ranald MacAilean Og, who was a man of extraordinary physical strength: that he could stop a mill-wheel turning at full speed; that he overcame the spectre of a headless woman which was terrorising the district of Morar and Arisaig; and that he was called upon to hold down the dying chief of Clanranald, Evil Donald, (Domhnall Dona Mac 'ic Ailean) when the Devil, with whom Donald had made a pact, came to claim his soul. Ranald was said to have been on good terms with the local witches, though he took no part in their rites, and they warned him that they had foreseen impending danger for him, thus enabling him to escape from a drowning accident on the river Lochy in which nine others died. On a more prosaic note, in his old age he became blind and bedridden and, if he thought himself neglected by his relatives, would talk mildly to them until they came within reach, when he would hit them a terrible smack around the head![2]

Another versatile musician was Alexander Grant, of the family of the Grants 153 of Shewglie, who were descended from a son of John Grant, the second of Corriemony. Alexander, the second of that name, was born around 1675, since he is described in a petition to the Duke of Newcastle in 1746 as being near 70 years old. Alexander was married twice, first to Margaret, daughter of John Chisholm of Comer & Strathglass, and then to Isabel, daughter of John Grant of Glenmoriston. Shewglie was credited with 14 sons and 6 daughters, one of whom, Janet, married Cameron of Clunes, and was the composer of a song on the Lochiel of the '45. Shewglie's connections were strongly Jacobite — he composed a number of poems, among which was a welcome to Prince Charlie in 1745. The opening lines are recorded as "Do bheatha Thearlaich Stiubhart, Do bheatha do ar duthaich" (Welcome, Charles Stewart, welcome to our country.) However, Shewglie, perhaps due to his advancing years, did not himself take part in the Rising. Indeed, in a letter from John Grant, Factor of Urquhart, to Ludovick Grant of Grant on 12th September 1745 the Factor reported that Corrimony had raised his tenants; "Shewglie had prevailed with him to return home at this time, but Corrimony said he would follow his own inclinations. That last night two of Shewglie's sons with a dozen young fellows had gone to join the Highland Army, but that Shewglie swore they went against his inclinations". Nevertheless, Grant of Grant had him seized and imprisoned in Inverness as a rebel, along with James Grant, his eldest son, and the Rev. Mr. John Grant.

From there they were transferred to London. In the petition to the Duke of Newcastle, they claimed that "they were peacefully at home during the rebellion, had assisted Grant of Grant by persuading 84 rebels in Urquhart to surrender at Inverness and were greatly surprised when Grant claimed they were in correspondence with these in arms and as such made prisoners by him. They had undergone great hardship in prison and Alexander was very ill of a malignant fever, they had been released from Tilbury Fort to a more comfortable confinement in a messenger's custody ... Alexander was a creditor by mortgage for a very large sum to Grant of Grant, guilty of no crime save that of having large demands against him". Ludovick Grant, on hearing of the petition, wrote to the Duke of Newcastle defending his actions, and claimed that Shewglie had been instrumental in delivering a letter from the Young Pretender to Ludovick's father. Shewglie died of fever on 29th July 1746, and his son and the minister were subsequently permitted to return to their homes.[3]

Shewglie has variously been described as a player of violin and pipes, violin and harp, and harp and fiddle. A tune in the Angus Fraser manuscript is entitled "Shewglie's Harp", though whether he was the composer of this melody we do not know. He is said to have been the author of a poem "Mairi Nighean Dheorsa", addressed to his violin, but the Gaelic words of this poem seem to have been lost. It is especially regrettable since the poem might have thrown considerable light on the attitude towards the harp in the early part of the 18th century. It appears to have been a poetic flyting or quarrel between

Shewglie's three instruments — harp, pipes and fiddle. Their owner was called upon to decide the contest, and gives an appreciation of the qualities of each instrument. We glean these details from Simon Fraser's collection of music in which he gives an air entitled "Mairi Nighean Dheorsa" and in English "Grant of Sheuglie's contest betwixt his Violin, Pipe and Harp". Fraser writes that it was acquired by his grandfather from a successor of the composer. The notes give some brief translation of the verses. "In addressing a verse to his pipe, he observes 'how it would delight him, on hearing the sound of war, to listen to her notes, in striking up the gathering, to rally round the chief, on a frosty spring morning, whilst the hard earth reverberated all her notes, so as to be heard by the most distant person interested'. To the harp he says 'The pleasure which thy tones afford are doubled, whilst accompanying a sweet female voice, or around the festive board, inspired by love or wine, I reach beyond my ordinary capacity, and feel the pleasure of pleasing'. But to his violin, which he calls by the literal name of the air "Mary, George's Daughter", and seems to have been his favourite, though held cheap by other combatants, he says — 'I love thee, for the sake of those who do — the sprightly youth and bonny lasses — all of whom declare, that, at a wedding, dance or ball, thou with thy bass in attendance, can have no competitor — thy music having the effect of electricity on those who listen to it' — and on thus receiving their due share of praise, their reconciliation is convivially celebrated".[4]

A tune also entitled "Mairi Nighean Deorsa" was published in Daniel Dow's collection, but appears to be quite different from that in Simon Fraser's. The same name for a violin was used by the poet Alasdair Og Mac Fir Ardnabighe for his song to the fiddle, which in two collections, begins "Gun b'ait leam 'bhi lamh-ruit, A Mhairi nigh'n Deorsa". Colm O Baoill identifies these as being the same poem, with minor divergencies, as that which appears in three sources, including an existing section of the MacNicol manuscript. This again begins "O ceud mile failte, Do Mhairi ni'n Deorsa". He suggests that, since these do not appear to fit either of the tunes, we may have to look elsewhere for Shewglie's original text. Interestingly, he also notes that in a manuscript collected around 1810 by Edward Bunting, the well-known Armagh-born collector of harp music, we find Dow's melody, without a bass line, with the note that it was "Copie(s?) out of old printed Book". The exchange of Irish and Scottish tunes is yet evident.[5]

Irish harpers were still making the established tour of Scotland. Denis O Hampsey, or Hempson, was, according to Bunting, born in Co. Derry in 1695. He told his life story to the Rev. George Sampson, and it was subsequently published by Bunting. O'Hampsey was blinded by smallpox at the age of three, and from the age of twelve studied the harp with various teachers, including Brighid Ni Chathain. O'Hampsey's harp, known as the Downhill Harp, is still in existence. It was made in 1702 and purchased for him, second-hand, by some benefactors. With this instrument he travelled to Scotland where he visited some of the families who were known for their interest in the harp. Rev. Sampson relates the story of his meeting with Sir James Campbell of Auchnambreac. Apparently the harper "learned that this gentleman had spent a great deal, and was living upon so much per week for an allowance. Hampson through delicacy would not call, but some of the domestics were sent after him. On coming into the castle, Sir James Campbell asked him why he had not called, adding 'Sir, there was never a harper, but yourself that passed the door of my father's house'." Tactfully, O'Hampsey said that he thought Auchnambreac was not at home. Campbell made him welcome, and was praised for his personal elegance by the harper.

O'Hampsey appears to have been in Scotland some time between 1715 and 1719. He told Sampson that he had played for "the Laird of Strone", who must have been Alexander Robertson of Struan. O'Hampsey's visit must therefore have taken place either before 1716 or after 1725, since between those dates, Struan was in exile in France. O'Hampsey spoke of the Laird's liberality — especially with the drink — on the occasion of a large grouse-shooting party.

He is indeed likely to have gone to Lude at some point. He says that on his travels he met only one laird who had a harp "and that was a very small one, played formerly by the laird's father". O'Hampsey was asked to re-string the harp and to play it, which so delighted the laird that he was asked to return to teach the harp to the laird's three year-old son, when the child was old enough. Regrettably, O'Hampsey never did return. The laird is almost certainly one of the Robertsons of Lude, though it is odd that O'Hampsey did not mention that there were two harps in the house. Bunting suggests that the "small" harp that he strung was the Queen Mary Harp, which seems a reasonable supposition. However, the dates that Bunting gives for O'Hampsey's visit do not quite tally with the known history of the Lude family. If O'Hampsey were in Scotland between 1713 and 1724 the laird he met would have been John Robertson, who died in 1729. But this John Robertson is said by Gunn to have played the harp himself — the last Robertson chief to do so. O'Baoill suggests that this, and the fact that it would be unlikely for a chief who succeeded to the title in 1673 to have fathered a son in the 1720's, points to the possibility that O'Hampsey, dictating his life story at the supposed age of 110, may have mistaken the dates. As O'Baoill points out, the son of this John Robertson, also John, who died in about 1758, fits the harper's account perfectly. In this case, O'Hampsey's possible encounter with Struan would probably have taken place after Robertson's return from exile in 1725.

O'Hampsey made more than one trip to Scotland, returning in 1745, when he apparently played for Prince Charles. Sampson writes: "being at Edinburgh when Charley the Pretender was there, he was called into the great hall to play; at first he was alone, afterwards four fiddles joined ... I asked him if he heard the Pretender speak; he replied, I only heard him ask 'Is Sylvan there?' On which someone answered 'He is not here, please your Royal Highness, but he shall be sent for.' He meant to say Sullivan, continued Hempson, but that was the way he called the name". John William O'Sullivan, the Prince's Adjutant-General, is known to have stated that Charles took no time off for entertainment in Edinburgh, but O'Hampsey's account has convincing detail about it.

There were several other Irishmen in the Prince's retinue. O'Hampsey says that he was presented to Charles by "Colonel Kelly of Roscommon and Sir Thomas Sheridan". Sheridan was one of the "Seven Men of Moidart" who landed with the Prince in 1745. O'Baoill suggests that Kelly may be Parson George Kelly, who also accompanied them at this time, though he does not appear to have held military rank, nor is it known from what part of Ireland he came. If the identification is correct, however, O'Hampsey's performance for Prince Charles can be dated fairly exactly to between 17th September 1745 and 26th September when Parson Kelly was sent back to France. Charles may have appreciated O'Hampsey's music, for Sampson writes, "He says that Captain Macdonald, when in Ireland, came to see him, and that he told the Captain that Charley's cockade was in his father's house" — perhaps a personal favour from the Prince?

O'Hampsey gave no further details of this trip to Scotland and, so far as we know, it was his last. He returned to Ireland where, at the age of 86, he married a lame woman and they had a daughter. In his advanced years he appeared at the Belfast Assembly of 1792, the oldest of the harpers, and the only one out of the ten performers who still played in the old style, using the finger nails on wire strings. He died at the age of 112 in 1807.[6]

It may be that what had become a less fashionable style of playing still found an interested audience in the Highlands of Scotland. Certainly, another Irish harper, who played with this finger nail technique, also visited the area. Echlin O'Cathain was born in 1729 in Coleraine, Co. Derry, old O'Cathain territory. He was taught the harp by Cornelius Lyons, harper to the Earl of Antrim, and a well known composer and arranger of many tunes, some of which were played by his pupil. Despite being afflicted with blindness, Echlin travelled widely throughout Europe: in Holland, Flanders, France and Spain. Bunting and O'Neill say that he played for the "Pretender" in Rome, but since O'Cathain himself does not mention such an incident in the biography which he dictated to Duncan Campbell, brother of Campbell of Inverneill in Knapdale, in 1779, it seems likely that they are confusing his exploits with those of O'Hampsey. O'Neill does tell us that "O'Cathain was strong, tall and athletic, and absolutely beat the post in expedition from Madrid to Bilbao, where after staying some time he embarked for Ireland, after which I frequently met him". O'Cathain had played for the King of Spain, but that being an "irreclaimable drunkard", he had fallen out of favour. Campbell says that his drinking habits did not affect his excellent harping, and that even when drunk he could play delightfully — Echlin apparently rated himself the fifth best player in Ireland. Gunn, however, says that he was sometimes punished for his rude behaviour by having his nails cut off![7]

O'Cathain is said by Bunting to have spent much of his time in Scotland in the Atholl area, but this seems to be a misinterpretation of Tytler's statement that Ruaidhri Dall Morison stayed in that area. Both writers appear to be confusing the two O'Cathains and the two Blind Rorys. Echlin certainly frequented the West Coast of Scotland. On 9th September 1751 the burgh records of Inverary note that "Mr. Echlin O'Kaine Harper from Coulrain in the County of Derry, Ireland, was among those admitted Burgesses, Freemen and Guild Bretheren of Inverary. Echlin would have been around 22 years of age at this time, considerably younger than his compatriot, Thomas O'Connellan, when it would appear he was made a Burgess of Edinburgh in 1717.[8]

In 1773 James Boswell, touring Scotland with Dr. Samuel Johnson, was told by Hugh MacLean of Coll that O'Cathain had performed for Alexander, Lord MacDonald in Sleat on Skye. Lord MacDonald was in financial straits at this time, though he still appreciated good music — he was himself a fine fiddler. Boswell writes: "Coll told us that O'Kane, the famous Irish harper, was once at that gentleman's house. He could not find it in his heart, but gave him a key for a harp, which was finely ornamented with gold and silver and with a precious stone, and was worth 80 or 100 guineas. He did not know the value of it; and when he came to know it, he would fain have had it back; but O'Kane took care that he should not." JOHNSON "They exaggerate the value ..."

Arthur O'Neill had also heard that tale, though he did not know the name of the laird who had given Echlin the key. He also says that it was in this nobleman's house that Ruairi O'Cathain had died, that his harp and tuning-key had been left there, and that the laird had given Echlin the key because he bore the same surname. In contradiction, we have a letter written, in 1785, in reply to Boswell's account, by Lord MacDonald himself. "O'Kane, the drunken blind harper ... having slurred over some tunes for a week at my house under the inordinate influence of Bacchus, was dismissed with two guineas in his pocket, and a key which he valued more than 100 guineas made of common agate. His reason for putting so extraordinary a value upon it was because he said it belonged to Roderick O'Kane, a famous harper in King Charles II's time, being apprehensive of losing what he deemed a precious relic during his drunken vagaries, I am informed he deposited it afterwards in the hands of a relation of mine, who I am confident would restore it to me if I thought it of importance to claim it". O'Baoill points out that the suggestion that the key belonged to Ruairi Dall came from Echlin himself; that Lord MacDonald does not link his name with it; nor is there a mention of a harp left in his house. It would seem that this historical colour may have been Echlin's own fanciful invention. O'Neill tells us that in Edinburgh, Echlin sold the key and drank the money.[9]

Unlike his teacher, Lyons, O'Cathain was not a composer, but frequently adapted both old tunes and the European music of the day for his own instrument. His fine playing of Corelli concerti was commented on to Gunn at Cambridge by a violinist named Manini.

Echlin was in Argyllshire in 1779, when Duncan Campbell took down his memoirs, and may have made subsequent visits to Scotland, perhaps up until 1790, since Gunn, writing in 1807, states that he was "within the last 20 years for some time in the Highlands". At this period the controversy surrounding the authenticity of the epic Gaelic poetry published by James MacPherson was still in full spate. The Committee of the Highland Society of Scotland commissioned an enquiry into the nature and provenance of the Poems of Ossian published in 1805. One of the individuals questioned was Hugh MacDonald of the island of South Uist — probably the Hugh MacDonald of Kilpheder whose testimony, published in a German work of 1808, was in answer to the question "Whether Ossian was known to have accompanied himself with musical instruments?" Hugh MacDonald replied "People say that Ossian accompanied his songs with the harp. I was acquainted with O Kain, an old harper who sang to harp accompaniment; he maintained it was the Gaelic or Irish harp; I myself do not believe it was our national instrument. I am not sure about it since I never took a great deal of interest in the instrumental side of it". The description of "an old harper" suggests that the occasion on which MacDonald heard O'Cathain play took place towards the end of the harper's life. Whether he returned to Ireland at this time, we do not know, but since he did not appear at the Belfast Assembly in 1792, we can reasonably assume that he may have died by this date.[10]

MacDonald's reference to Echlin's performance is interesting since it is the only one which mentions that he accompanied his own singing. There is no evidence that O'Hampsey did so. Two fascinating letters dated 1791 from J.A. Campbell to Lachlan MacTavish of Dunardry also mention O'Cathain. He writes on 3rd January ... "Dear Sir, I am favoured with your letter of the 30th Ult. regarding O Kains musick and have since receipt of your letter been making search for them among my collection of musick. I find that the best of them have been plundred from me and the Books they were in, by Mss. Casamaijor and Addison But shall write them both to send me down copies of them — Such as I have remaining here shall be made and sent to you — when the others come from London they shall be sent also ..."

Campbell writes further, on 20th January 1791 ... "I have been at the greatest pains to Collect O Kains true Irish Airs which I was fortunate enough to obtain from him while he was in good humour which by the bye was seldom the Case. The bases to the tunes now sent you herewith were made by Miss Shean who had a very delicate taste for musick and happened to be Governess to my Children at St. John's while O Kain was with me. As a proof of her Genius, when she played the tunes over to the Harper upon the Forte-Piano, he could not resist Swearing, She was a damn'd Clever *Bitch*, for she had just produced his own Basses, just as they were handed down by the famous Carline — the Correllie of the Irish Harpers — I could not entrust any person with the transcribing of the Tunes, of course did them all myself — there may be several incorrections in the way I pricked them off from our Unruly Harper which can be easily rectifyed by yourself or any proficient in the pricking off musick — all I can assure you of is, that the tunes are genuine, indeed they bear the true marks of their being so — If I can fall in with any more you may depend upon having them sent — but I think you are now furnished with those that O Kain himself considered the best of his Collection ..."

These letters raise the distinct possibility that a transcription of O'Cathain's music may yet be extant. It would be particularly significant, in that it would pre-date Bunting's 1792 collection, that it was taken down by a collector who clearly considered the accuracy and genuine quality of the written music to be of great importance and, most interesting of all, that these versions were approved by O'Cathain himself as a literal transcription of his own playing. He does not sound like a character who would have minced words on any subject! We can hope that these unique papers may yet come to light.[11]

Part of O'Cathain's repertoire has survived in an important Scottish manuscript collection. The tunes are mainly of Irish interest, though a number of them are described as "Originally Scottish Highland, improved (or adapted) for the harp by Carolan" or "by Lyons", or "by O Kain". This manuscript was compiled by the MacLean Clephane sisters of Torloisk in Mull. The estate of Torloisk is in the parish of Kilninian and Kilmore in the north of the island. Torloisk House stands in wooded grounds on the north side of Loch Tuath, and faces south towards Gometra, Ulva and the Treshnish Islands. The oldest part of the house is said to date back to 1660 but the existing house was mostly rebuilt in the Scots Baronial style from 1860. The estate has been associated with the Clan MacLean for a considerable time. The first of the Torloisk line was Lachlan Og, a younger son of Sir Hector Mor MacLean of Duart who died in 1596 at the battle of Gruinart in Islay. The MacLeans of Torloisk descended in the male line to Lachlan, who was a merchant seaman, sailing between London and Jamaica. He married Margaret, daughter of Richard Smith of Fife, and they had a daughter, Marianne, to whom Lachlan left the estate on his death in 1799. Marianne married Major-General William MacLean Douglas Clephane of Carslogie in Fife, and bore three daughters: Margaret, Anna-Jane and Wilmina-Marianne. When the Major-General died in Granada in 1803 Sir Walter Scott was chosen as the guardian of the children, who became great friends of his daughter, Sophia Scott. Sir Walter thought highly of Mrs. MacLean Clephane and her accomplished daughters, particularly Anna-Jane, and was impressed by their knowledge of the poetry and music of their native land.

Margaret MacLean Clephane married Lord Spencer John Alwyne Compton, heir to the Marquis of Northampton on 24th July 1815, the main arrangements for the wedding being organised by Scott. As heiress, the estate of Torloisk passed with her to the family of her husband, but it was provided that the property should not be held by a Marquis, and when he succeeded to his father, it passed to their younger son, William, and eventually through marriage to the family of the present owner, the Farquharson of Invercauld.[12]

Wilmina-Marianne, the youngest of the three sisters, was married in 1831 to Wilhelm, Baron de Normann, in the diplomatic service of Prussia. Anna-Jane, the middle daughter, died unmarried. The section of the manuscript which is of most interest to us is in her hand. She obtained the music from which it was copied from a "Mr. MacDonald" who had taken part of it down from the playing of Echlin O'Cathain. This gentleman was probably Patrick MacDonald, one of two Sutherland brothers who were pioneer collectors of Gaelic music. Their collection, published by Patrick MacDonald in 1784 after his brother Joseph's early death, consists of 186 vocal airs, among which, MacDonald states, are the last remnants of the music of the harp, and 32 dance tunes.[13]

As a result of the interest in Highland music and poetry at that time Alexander Campbell, a Perthshire man who was an organist in Edinburgh, was commissioned by the Highland Society to tour the Highlands collecting tunes with the aim of rescuing Gaelic music from extinction. His collection consisted of 189 tunes, some of which, with the help of Sir Walter Scott, James Hogg and Professor Wilson, were published in "Albyn's Anthology", along with Gaelic and English words. The rest of his manuscripts have been lost, possibly in the fire which destroyed the Society's offices. Scott, who had been taught music by Campbell, would no doubt have directed Campbell to Mull where he met not only the MacLean Clephane sisters, but also one of their acquaintances, Mrs. Christina Mackenzie of Dervaig.[14]

This lady was the daughter of Dr. Hector MacLean of Gruline, historian of the MacLean family. Her mother was Catherine, daughter of Donald MacLean of Coll. She is said to have married Mackenzie against the wishes of her father who considered the marriage beneath her. She was, by all accounts, a delightful lady who ended her days as a dependent of MacLean of Coll. She was warmly described, as Miss MacLean, by Dr. Samuel Johnson: "She is the most accomplished lady I have found in the Highlands; she knows French, music and drawing, sews neatly, makes shell-work and can milk cows. In short, she could do anything"! She played the spinet and sang for them, and impressed them with her ability to translate 'Erse' poetry.[15]

Alexander Campbell, who also kept a diary of his tour of the Highlands, was no less enthusiastic. He tells us "I spent several days at Dervaig examining the manuscripts of Gaelic poetry and melodies which the father of this lady (Dr. MacLean) and she herself had collected and having marked several pieces for transcription she is under promise to transmit them to one with all possible dispatch. I have in my possession what she gave me on the spot viz a sheet in the hand writing of the present Countess of Compton (late Miss MacLean of Torloisk) containing besides sixteen Highland Melodies three Harp airs (vide No. 3). The same as were played by Murdoch MacDonald Harper to the Laird of Coll. This minstrel was the last of our Hebridean Harpers and died in anno 1739. Mrs. MacKenzie who remembers him perfectly has promised to furnish me with a few biographical notices regarding him and she has likewise engaged to give me some authentic particulars concerning John MacLean the bard of Mull several of whose pieces are in her manuscript collection.

The voice of Harps may yet be heard in the Highlands and Western Islands. As a proof it is well known that the accomplished ladies of Torloisk are admirably skilled in the harp. I myself while in Mull was delighted with the tasteful execution on the improved harp of Mrs. MacLean at Cuinish. This instrument as an accompaniment to the voice is well adapted to support and give affect in what is called musical expression to say nothing of its being of all others the best calculated to exhibit in performance the symmetry and grace of the female form to bewitching advantage. It might be considered rather a romantic if not a wild idea to suggest the possibility of restoring harp music and consequently the re-establishment of the ancient order of Harper in Scotland and the isles. And why not encourage harpers as well as pipers? Premiums so as to excite generous emulation might do great things."

On 23rd August, Campbell writes : "On my way from Treishnish to Sunipole it was pointed out to me the spot where the remains of Murdoch MacDonald the last of our Hebridean Harpers were laid". Since a journey from Treshnish to Sunipol leads past the old graveyard at Calgary, it is probably here that this harper was buried, although an oral tradition has it that he was buried on Coll, and indeed Coll can be seen from this high point in Mull. It is just possible, though less likely, that a burial place on the distant island might have been pointed out to Campbell by his guide, Duncan MacLean, a Gaelic scholar and preacher of outstanding merit, who was at that time tutor at Treshnish.[16]

The harper, Murdoch MacDonald, was, according to John Gunn (1807) brought up by the family of Coll. He is said to have been a pupil of Ruaidhri Dall Morison and subsequently to have been sent to Ireland to continue his studies. Gunn states that he remained with MacLean of Coll until at least 1734 when a payment to him was recorded by Hector MacLean, and that he eventually retired to Quinish, where he died. He was always called Murdoch Clarsair, and his son, who acted occasionally as a servant to MacLean of Coll, was known as Eoin Mac Mhurchadh Clarsair, or John, Son of Murdoch Harper. His grandson was at that time in the service of Col. MacLean of Coll, Hector's nephew. Gunn's information was based on letters from Col. MacLean dated 23rd March 1806, and from Mrs. Mackenzie (Miss MacLean) written the same year. The letters were said to have been lodged with the

Highland Society, but appear to have been lost, possibly in the disastrous fire.[17]

Some details can be verified, however, and though they do not shed a great deal of light on Murdoch's life, they at least serve to confirm his existence. The only contemporary mention is in a list of men delivering up their weapons in 1716 after the first Jacobite Rising. Dated 28th April 1716, it records that at "Breckachie" (Breacachadh) in Coll "along with Hector McLean of Coll younger — Murdoch McMurchie harper, he was not in the rebellion and has no arms". "Angus Roy MacDonald the pyper" at Arnabost on Coll was also listed, who must have served MacLean before the famous Rankine family of pipers.

Murdoch had at least two children : his son John, may be identified with the "John MacDonald alias macmhurchai", whose debt of 10s. was listed by the Coll Kirk Session on 25th March 1779. They apparently considered that there was a probability of recovering his arrears. There was also a daughter, Catherine, who seems to have fallen on hard times. "Cath : McDond (harpers daut)" was recorded living at Penmollach in Quinish, when she received 1/6d. from the Kilninian and Kilmore Kirk Session's distribution to the poor on 19th July 1786. Quinish on Mull was part of the MacLean of Coll's estate. A map of 1801 appears to show Penmollach as the principal house on the estate, possibly just where Quinish House stands today. A Catherine MacDonald is again listed at Penmollach in 1781, 1782 and 1783. She may be the "Cath McDonald in Kilmory an old object now lying sick 7 Feb. 1786", but was back at Penmollach in 1788 and again in 1790, the last record of the lady.[18]

Campbell states that the harp had not ceased in the area until about 1739, when Murdoch died. Christina MacLean Mackenzie, whose musical talents had so impressed Boswell & Johnson, was approached by the Highland Society in 1808 when they were attempting to trace Gaelic manuscripts. She wrote to them: "as to the Highland Music or airs, their music we find was commonly … the … harp for entertainment, with the voice, and the bagpipe for war". According to Gunn, she said that she remembered a number of compositions of the Highland harpers. "These airs she had learnt of her father, who played them on the flute, and had them in all probability, immediately from Murdoch Macdonald, the last of the Highland Harpers, who lived in his neighbourhood". Importantly, in the MacLean Clephane manuscript, comments in the handwriting of Miss MacLean of Torloisk tell us that it contains three harp tunes which were played by Murdoch MacDonald. These are described simply as "Ancient Harp Airs", but it is possible to tentatively identify two of them as variants of two melodies associated with "Rory Dall". Could these be pieces learned as a pupil of Morison?[19]

Contrary to Gunn's supposition, Murdoch MacDonald may not have been the last of the old line of professional harpers in Scotland. William

McMurchy, who was born around 1700, lived in Kintyre well into the second half of the 18th century. He, again, was a versatile musician, reputed to play pipes, fiddle and harp, as well as composing poetry. McMurchy is a common name in Kintyre, and William may well be a descendant of the MacVuirich bards. The only family using the Christian name "William" around that period seem to be at Auchaleck near Campbeltown around 1669-71. Unfortunately the Parish Registers for Kintyre are not complete for that time, but the records of Births commence in 1659, and those for Marriages in 1681. The first William McMurchy noted married Agnes Robertson on 14th March 1728, and they had a daughter, Ann, born later that year on 29th December. There were either no further children, which seems a little unlikely, or the family then removed to another parish, since they do not feature again in the Register of Births. The only other "William McMurchys" to appear in the Campbeltown parish register are both marriages in 1765 and 1769 — rather late if they were the musician in question.[20]

The first certain reference to McMurchy dates from 1745-46, by which time he was one of the pipers to MacDonald of Largie. Largie raised his men and set off to join the Prince, but according to tradition only marched as far as Clachan, where he called on the Minister. The latter was heating wine for punch when he unluckily — or perhaps luckily — spilled the boiling liquid over Largie's foot, which prevented any further attempt by Largie to join the '45. The majority of the Kintyre lairds were supporters of the Government side, and Largie was later persuaded to change his mind, and send his men with the rest to Inveraray. We are told that, when the Kintyre party reached the castle, MacDonald's pipers played alternately and McMurchy, in tribute to the Duke of Argyll, played "The Campbells Are Coming". The Duke, however, was in company with some other gentlemen at that moment, and took no notice of the tune that was played; but when McLeolan (Largie's other piper) played "Fir Chinntire" (Men of Kintyre) the Duke immediately recognised it and said to the gentlemen present "Come we must go out and welcome the Kintyre men". McMurchy was a superior piper, and a good poet, but was grieved that the Duke did not take notice of him and that he did not play "Fir Chinntire".

In the years following the '45 Rebellion, the position of a professional musician must have been very precarious. A poem composed by McMurchy was collected in about 1780 from Captain Alexander Campbell, then Chamberlain of Kintyre. Based on the internal evidence of the poem, it appears that McMurchy was serving overseas in an area where French was spoken. The date is further narrowed with the probability that he was serving with either the 77th Regiment — Montgomery's Highlanders, raised 1757 and disbanded 1763 or, less likely, the 100th Regiment, commanded by Major Colin Campbell of Kilberry, raised 1767 and disbanded 1763. Alexander Campbell, appointed Chamberlain and Baillie of North and South Kintyre in 1767, had also belonged to an additional company of Montgomery's Highlanders, a regiment which was credited with over 30 pipers and drummers. The army had obvious attractions for many of the professional piping families who, like the harpers, had lost their old established sources of patronage. William McMurchy, in the 77th, would have rubbed shoulders with one of the MacArthur pipers. Indeed, the name "John MacArthur" appears among a list of nine names in one of McMurchy's manuscripts — written, it would seem, as a pen-trial. McMurchy's enlistment, however, seems to have been forced on him by difficult circumstances.

> "With looking back on my folly,
> Full of grief and of horror
> That I sold my freedom,
> My family and my peace.
>
> Heavy is this yoke on my neck
> It is beyond my power to endure it
> ......
> The whip of bondage wounding me
> My tender children and my partner
> Without my making provision for their shelter
> Driven to homeless destitution
> That is the pang that pierced me through and through
>
> It is not guile or trickery
> On the part of gentle or simple
> But poverty and hardship
> That drove me into the net
> And the thought that I could support
> With my earnings, my dear ones,
> Or never had I left them
> In the charge of the country".

It has been suggested that McMurchy was aged about 21 at the time of the '45, and in his thirties when he enlisted. But frequent references to him as "old William McMurchy" at the time of his death, and before it, and the other available evidence, make it tempting to suggest that he can be identified with the William McMurchy married in Campbeltown parish in 1728, and that he subsequently moved to serve his patron, MacDonald in Largie. This assumption would put William's age at around 50 at the time of his enlistment, an age for which there are precedents for joining the army; as a piper and a poet, his position as a soldier would have been relatively privileged.

On the disbanding of the regiment, he would appear to have returned to the Campbeltown area. MacIntosh relates how "William McMurchy who lived at Largieside about a century ago was a superior piper and poet. He was visited by a learned gentleman who came in disguise to test McMurchy's power of poetry, the gentleman himself being a poet. McMurchy received the gentleman in a respectful manner and entertained him with a few tunes on the pipes. The gentleman was musing over a verse of poetry, and observing some scones of bread toasting over the fire, got up hurriedly and making for the door, uttered the following :

> "Piobaireachd is aran tur,
> 'S miosa leam na guin a' bhais,
> Fhir a bhodhair mo dha chluais,
> Na biodh agad duais gu brach".

(Piping and raw bread, worse to me than pangs of death. Ye man who deaved both my ears, may you never get a reward.)

McMurchy, dropping the pipe out of his mouth, rapidly said :

> "Stad a dhuine fan ri cial,
> 'S olc an sgial nach boin ri bun,
> Tha mo bhean a t-eachd on Chill,
> Is ultach d'on im air a muin".

(Stop man, give ear to reason, bad is the story that has no foundation. My wife is coming from Chil with a load of butter on her back.)

The gentleman, finding that he had met his match, returned and a friendly conversation took place till McMurchy's wife came home with the butter. The gentlemen partook of the toasted bread and butter and came away wondering that such a man as McMurchy could be found in such a sequestered spot".

McMurchy was not only a literate poet, but a collector and recorder of Gaelic poetry and anything else that he thought worthy of preservation. Based on a similarity of Gaelic script, it has been suggested that he may have been a pupil of Hugh Maclean, a schoolmaster who taught at Kilkenzie in Kintyre around 1699. William noted down many of his own poems as well as compositions by others. One which survives in his own handwriting, among other satires between himself and other poets, is a satire on McMurchy himself. It was composed by a merchant called Bostain MacCairbre. Professor Mackinnon states "A satire in Gaelic usually means foul abuse in more or less faulty rhyme". William is described as a piper, a fiddler, a *harper*, a tailor and schoolmaster, as well as a well-deserved bard, and a man who according to his reviler was enjoying, undeservedly, the confidence of the Laird of Largie.

From the letters concerning the Highland Society's search for Gaelic

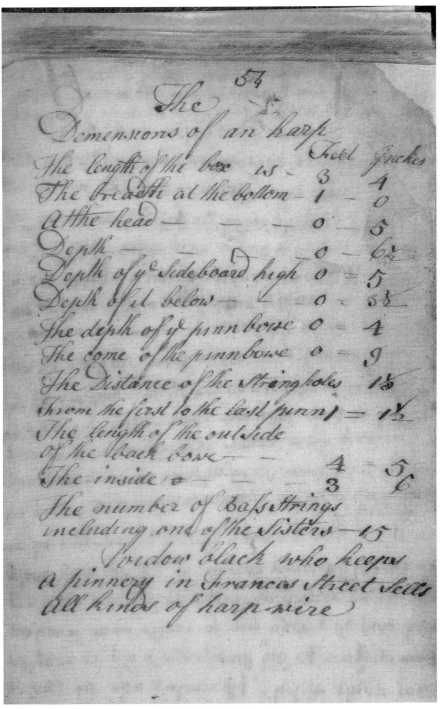

54

The
Demensions of an harp

	Feet	Inches
The length of the box is	3	4
The breadth at the bottom	1	0
At the head	0	5
Depth	0	6½
Depth of y^e Sideboard high	0	5
Depth of it below	0	8½
The depth of y^e pinn bore	0	4
The come of the pinnbowe	0	9
The Distance of the Stringholes		1½
From the first to the last pinn		1½
The length of the outSide of the back bowe		
The inside	4 3	5 6
The number of Bass strings including one of the Sisters — 15		

Jordow Black who keeps
a pinnery in Francis Street Sells
all kinds of harp wire

William McMurchy's M.S.

manuscripts at the begining of the 19th century, some more details about McMurchy can be gleaned. William was the oldest of three brothers. The second brother, James, was described at the time of the correspondence as having died a considerable time since. The youngest brother, Neil, died in 1807. William is described, in a letter dated 20th November 1808, from Limecraigs, the dower house of the Duchess of Argyll, and signed by Argyll's Chamberlain, Duncan Stewart of Glenbuckie, as having died about 30 years before. It also says that he was a remarkable writer of ancient poetry, and that he had been in possession of a Gaelic manuscript collection. The youngest brother, Neil, was said to have been able to recite poetry. Glenbuckie's letter also contains the interesting comment "The eldest of them, William, who was a great genius put all the pibroch and many highland airs to music". This would imply that William was one of the earliest notators of Piobaireachd music -and that also he was possibly the only harper who was able to write down the music for that instrument.[21]

Regrettably, much of this collection seems to have been lost. After William's death, his papers passed to Neil (who is also said to have made a collection of manuscripts). Neil appears to have been a schoolmaster at Whitehouse in the Parish of Kilcalmonel from 1766-1779 before becoming a weaver in Paisley. Neil passed the manuscripts to a grandson of William. When the remainder of the manuscripts were recovered for the Highland Society through the offices of Neil's son, James, a Paisley manufacturer, James expressed his disappointment, since he thought that there should be a great many more of them.

Indeed, the surviving manuscripts, which are in the National Library of Scotland, do not contain any music, but consist mostly of poems (including many of William's own) and proverbs. Some of the poems concern music, particularly that of the pipes, and McMurchy also provides the earliest written source for one of the songs of Ruaidhri Dall Morison. While amongst the miscellaneous material, including a rather potent medical recipe for an unspecified ailment, and a short poem in English on the death of Handel (d. 1759), there is a list of the dimensions of a harp.[22] This was apparently a large, low-headed, wire-strung instrument. It seems unlikely that McMurchy would have written down and kept the measurements of his own instrument. It is possible that this is a description of the harp of Echlin O' Cathain, who was without doubt frequenting that area in the mid 18th century.

McMurchy's death is noted in an ambiguous entry in the Campbeltown Kirk accounts. Under the date 1769 is listed "Willm McMurchy musitioner dead 12 shillings". But the list of debt vouchers to the Kirk passed over to the new treasurer in 1782, and the entry confirms that, in fact, William incurred the debt in 1769, but that his death had taken place before 1782.[23]

By the 18th century the use of the clarsach had declined to the extent that it was used by only a handful of players — and then only rarely as a professional instrument. The fact that it was often used as only one among several instruments played by gifted all-round musicians seems, to indicate that the status of the native harp had sunk to the point that it was no longer viable for a musician to make a career from playing it alone. It was a rare musician who, without patronage or an audience educated to appreciate it, would spend years studying the great body of bardic song with which the clarsach was associated. So the repertoire of the instrument disappeared, to a great extent unrecorded, leaving us only tantalising fragments of great historical interest, and often, also, of great beauty.

14 PUIRT, UIRT AND ORGAIN

Mairg duine do chaill a ghuth	*Woe to the man who has lost his voice*
Agus 'ga bhfuil sruth do dhan	*And who has a flood of song*
Agus nach fhead gabhail leo	*And who cannot sing with them*
Agus nach eol bheith 'na thamh	*And knows not how to hold his peace*
Agus nach seinn cor na port	*And can play neither air nor tune*
Agus nach gabh gan locht laoidh	*Nor utter a lay without defect*
Agus nach sguir da chruit bhinn	*And ceases not from his sweet harp*
Agus nach seinn mar as mian.	*And plays not to his mind.[1]*

We have no examples of the music played on the gut-strung harp of the Lowlands, which are specifically linked with the instrument. In many ways this is not surprising. Apart from some dance music, only a handful of purely instrumental pieces survive in any medieval musical source up to the early 15th century.

We are told, however, in the Melrose Chronicles, of c. 1260, that Adam of Lennox accompanied himself on the harp, while singing motets in praise of the Virgin Mary. The motet form of music was the rage in France from about 1225. It developed from the organum — the religious chant where the parts are sung in harmony — and the conductus, a mainly secular type of part song, where the voices move together in the same rhythm. The characteristic of the motet is the use of polytextuality — each of the parts may sing different words at the same time. The three parts were called "Tenor", "Motetus" and "Triplum". The lowest, the tenor, was often based on a Gregorian chant, while the two upper parts, particularly the motetus in the middle, sang different words and melody, sometimes of secular origin. One finds motetus parts, for example, which have been lifted directly from minstrel or troubadour song. Sometimes, indeed, both sacred and secular texts were combined, for example, a hymn to the Virgin Mary and a poem from a lover to his sweetheart. The use of human examples to reflect divinity was not seen as incongruous and is mirrored also in the art and architecture of the 13th century. The different parts of the motet had melodic independence which grew more pronounced throughout the century, but this was compensated for by the inclusion of repeated rhythmic patterns within the parts (isorhythm), which give the motet its unity.

170 Echoes of these 13th and 14th century conventions may be heard in the later

harp music — isorhythm in the "piobaireachd" style of harp music, such as the "Caoineadh Rioghail" (The Royal Lament) in the Angus Fraser manuscript, and in some of the tunes of the Welsh Ap Huw manuscript, while the repeated rhythmic motifs of some of the 16th and 17th century "Ports" may also reflect this form. The idea of polytextuality may seem confusing to us. However, one should remember that these songs were not intended as public performances but as acts of worship. Any combination of voices or instruments was permitted, though the tenor part was probably most often played by instruments only, the upper parts being taken by voices or instruments. Thus Adam may well have sung the motetus part, while playing Tenor or Triplum, or both, on his harp. This idea of accompanying a voice singing one part with an instrument playing a different melody has obvious implications for Welsh music. It may be possible, in the motet, to trace links with "penillion" singing with the harp.[2]

The influence from the world of minstrelsy on church music did not always meet with approval. Courson castigates prelates in France for allowing "minstrellish little notes" (scurriles notule) to corrupt the performance of the liturgy. These were vocal embellishments or grace-notes, derived from the performance of secular troubadour music, which became popular to the extent that by 1300 they were regularly accepted in the expression of polyphony and, more surprisingly, in plainchant.

One of the most striking examples of the musical virtuosity of this period is a "Sanctus Trope" from a Scottish manuscript compiled in St Andrews around 1230. It has a line for solo voice of extraordinary range and complexity, highly decorated, between plainer choral interpolations.[3]

Clearly, the exchange of ideas and musical forms between the religious and secular worlds, in the 13th century in particular, was very strong. Alan Bruford suggests that in the preceding centuries, with the advent of Christianity, the Gaelic bards had adapted the syllabic quatrains of the Latin hymns and combined them with elements of their native stress metres. Thus they could please their patrons with a new type of song which was not only sonorous and beautiful, but implicitly had the novelty and authority of their Christian models — at the expense, however, of the old pagan traditions of the fili. This blend of native culture with the new religion may have been used in an evangelistic role by the Church.[4] Perhaps this is one reason why the motet, with its convention of polytextuality — two different languages could even be used in the same song — appealed to the religious houses of a multi-cultural Scotland.

In non-religious circles, dance music and other music played in ensemble was certainly widely performed, and it is likely that the harpers took part in this, along with the other musicians of the court. Combinations of harp and lute; harp, lute and organ; or harp and viol are frequently portrayed in illustrations from European sources, from early medieval times until the

Renaissance. The harp would have been used as a drone or chordal accompaniment, or alternatively would have played one of the melody or harmony lines, in the same manner as part-song.

Until around 1450, in the European courts, there seems to have been a general distinction made between "haut" players of loud instruments, such as trumpet or schawm, and those of "bas" instruments, like harp or lute or organ, which had a softer sound. The "bas" instrumentalists were more likely to appear as solo performers, as well as in groups. The records of the Scottish court up to the early 16th century seem to confirm this picture. The combination of harp and tabour, however, is relatively common here, and would suggest that the music, at least on some occasions, was rhythmic, and might have been used for a small number of dancers.

The development of minstrel schools to which even the most advanced of European instrumentalists made frequent visits, from the early 14th to mid 15th century, may have occurred to enable performers to learn and exchange music — possibly different "styles" or "manners" of music or ornamentation which were difficult to notate. Only in this way can one justify the long and sometimes dangerous journeys to the schools, that these musicians undertook.[5] It is clear that only a very small percentage of the music played was ever written down. Similar schools, in the manner of bardic establishments, are likely to have existed in Scotland. Although there are references to Scottish minstrels being sent to Europe, these do not mention any harpers, suggesting that the musical tradition for these instruments centred largely in their own country. Harp and clarsach probably also played the repertoire associated with other instruments, absorbing and exchanging musical influences. This is particularly noticable in the case of lute music. In addition, the harp was undoubtedly used as an accompanying instrument for song, ballad and formal poetry in the Lowlands.

The defeat at Flodden in 1513 sounded the death-knell — in some cases literally — for the Lowland harpers. The court and cultural life of the country was irrevocably altered, and we are left with little evidence of the music played on the gut-strung harp. In the case of the clarsach, however, we are rather more fortunate.

The Highland harper's original function was to provide accompaniment while Gaelic syllabic verse was declaimed or recited. Speculation about the nature of this accompaniment must remain mostly guess-work. In most cultures which have not been affected by European art-music, a version of the melody usually accompanies a singer, but there are exceptions to this. African players of the kora, or other harp-like instruments, often use a series of rhythmic phrases, repeated over and over, and building up into complex patterns beneath the sung melody of their formal music. Some clues that the harpers of Wales, Scotland and Ireland might have used a repeated chordal structure or series of notes on which to base their bardic melodies or to accompany a sung melody, may be found in the early 17th century Welsh manuscript written by Robert Ap Huw. This important manuscript was transcribed from the original of William Penllyn, a harper who lived in the reign of Henry VIII, and gives information which may date from a much earlier period. It is clear that the harp music in it is not purely Welsh, but also had much in common with that of Ireland and Scotland.

It details a number of "measures" on which bardic music was based, given in codes of "I" and "O". These "measures" are also given in musical tablature. It is not certain in which timing, or in which key they should be played since a large number of different tunings were used, but it is possible to make a tentative reading of some of them. One is called "Albann Hyfaidd" — the "Scottish Measure".

Albann Hyfaidd — 1011010001001011

facsimile of original manuscript

suggested transcription

The key in which this sequence sounds most musically convincing seems to be "F major" — which can also be read as "C" with a flattened 7th, similar to a Scottish pipe scale. The notes in the measures could be played as a chord, which was "strong", or played separately as single notes, which were "weak". Four weak "I's" or "O's", made up one "strong" "I" or "O". These patterns should not be thought of as straightforward accompaniment in this basic form, but rather as the underlying musical structure on which a sung or played melody could be built.

Interestingly, an analysis of piobaireachd produced a similar pattern of a and b to the "Scottish Measure".

Thus a b a a
    b a b b
    b a b b] reversal of first part
    a b a a]

This may be pure coincidence but, if so, it is a fascinating one. The names of the Ap Huw tunes indicate that the music was, to some extent, interchangeable between Welsh harp and crwth, as in Ireland it was between cruit and tiompain.[6]

In Scotland, the older verse forms persisted slightly later than in Ireland, though Anglicisation continued to push the Gaelic culture west and north, where there were still poets composing in stressed metres into the 1700's. Hidden by the higher strata of syllabic verse, "amhran" poetry and the less formal bardic metres are likely to have existed in Scotland from the late Middle Ages onwards. Both stressed and amhran verse were probably accompanied, but the harpers found, in the amhran, an ideal form of expression for themselves as poets and musicians. The most notable Scottish example of the harper-bard is Ruaidhri Dall Morison.[7]

Parallel with this existing ancient function as accompanist, there was a general trend throughout Western art music from the late 15th century onwards, towards instrumental music for its own sake. By 1600 it was strongly represented. Melodies which would have accompanied words were played on their own, then modified; musicians composed their own music in the song formats, and then progressed to constructing tunes which were not linked to poetic rhythms. Against this general movement in the 16th century can be set the beginning of the collapse of much of the old cultural background — the Anglicisation of the Scottish Court and its move to London after 1600; the political turmoil of the Highland areas; the growth of specifically Scottish Gaelic forms of expression in dialect, poetry and song; and the waning in importance of the formal language skills of the fili poet, which had been common to both Ireland and Scotland. It is at this point that we find the first surviving traces of Scottish harp tunes, in an area where Highland and Lowland culture met — the Atholl area of Perthshire. This cross-fertilisation, linked with a number of powerful and aristocratic families, seems to have been artistically stimulating.

The "port" type of harp tune can be dated from around the mid 16th century until the mid 17th century. Ports are an identifiable group of pieces, clearly influenced by the European music of the day — and since they were adopted enthusiastically by lute players, they in their turn must have had influence on that instrument. The Ports, in most cases, show distinct characteristics and use a series of musical motifs which are found again and again in their composition. Their irregular phrasing suggests that they were not used as music for song or dance. They have asymmetrical construction, in that the first part is usually shorter than the second. Most are in 4/4 time, but occasionally in 3/4. They frequently begin with an introductory run of single notes, often rising and covering a wide range of the scale, in many cases with octave intervals, and often ending with a drop of an octave. This may represent the remnants, or a formalised rendition, of the tuning prelude commonly played by harpers and pipers. One or two bar phrases are often repeated an octave apart, or in an ascending or descending sequence, both of which are ideally suited to the "stopped" technique of wire strings. This emphasises the wide tonal range of the clarsach. Several tunes include a motif where the same note is repeated, either four or, occasionally, three times. The last phrase of many Ports is a repetitive pattern of descending notes, which tends to tail off rather inconclusively. Some tunes include a phrase which implies a shift in modulation, without the use of an accidental sharp or flat, while some have an actual accidental, usually in the second part. Most of these can be dealt with by pre-tuning a string in one octave, though there have been suggestions that a technique of stopping a string at top or bottom to produce a semitone rise in the note may have been used.

Ports are generally not melodically strong pieces of music. Lowland musicians, however, obviously considered them interesting and worthy of attention. The Ports in the early manuscripts are often very inaccurately notated, which may suggest that they were a fairly new form of music at the beginning of the 17th century — and perhaps one with which the musicians who wrote them down were not entirely familiar. There were clearly more Ports than have survived, since a number of titles turn up in later sources only, showing that these tunes were current until the late 18th century, during which time some, at least, must have been forgotten.

"Ports" do not occur in Irish sources. Only one, "Purth Clarseach" is recorded by Bunting, and this is a version of "Port Gordon". We can find no mention, in Irish collections, of tunes with this word in their title which do not have a Scottish connection. The first record of the word "Port" itself, in a musical context, is in the poem by Donnachadh Mor of Lennox, in the Book of the Dean of Lismore, which dates it to before 1513-40. The poet uses it to describe a form of harp music.[8] "Port", in this sense, is a late entrant into Irish Gaelic, not appearing until around 1600. A poem "Consolations", in which the word "corphort" describes harp music, is thought by Bergin to be later than the early 16th century date given for it by O' Curry. Indeed the rather unscholarly language suggests that it was a product of the Irish bardic tradition in decline, in the late 16th or early 17th century. One of the earliest examples of the word in Ireland is as "gallphoirt" or "foreign tunes".[9] At this time there was a particularly strong wave of Scottish influence into Ireland, mainly into the north of Ireland from central and south-west Scotland, whereas earlier contacts had been predominantly West Highland. Families such as the

x = decoration

Port Robart

Montgomeries, who had strong harping connections, were prominent in the expansion of their estates into Ulster. In Wales, in the Ap Huw manuscript, the term "porth" appears in the title of three tunes and one, strikingly, is called "Alban benporth" — the "Main Scottish Tune". Unfortunately the manuscript does not give the music for this melody. There appears to be a definite Scottish association with the word "Port" at this period.

The earliest dateable "Port" may be **"Port Robart"** which appears in the Wemyss manuscript. This is likely to have been composed for Robert Stewart, second son of John, 11th Earl of Lennox, and his countess, Lady Elizabeth Stewart. The alternative title for this piece of music, given in the Straloch manuscript, is **"Port Preist"** and, indeed, Robert Stewart was a prominent representative of the Church. He was first Provost of the Collegiate Church of Dumbarton, and in 1542 was about to be created Bishop of Caithness, but was deprived of the dignity for having joined with his brother, the Earl of Lennox, in opposition to the Regent Arran. Robert spent the following twenty years in exile in England. On his return to Scotland in 1563, his support for the Reformed Church gained him the Priory of St. Andrews when the Church's property was forfeited to the Crown and distributed between families of rank. He was castigated by the Kirk Session of St. Andrews for allowing a parish to fall vacant and diverting the funds intended to support its minister into "golf, archery and entertainment". His patronage of the arts was well-known. James Lauder's "My Lord of Marche Pavane" was composed for him, as was a hymn "Quam multi Domine sunt", by David Peebles. Stewart married the eldest daughter of the Earl of Atholl in 1578, but she claimed that he was impotent and divorced him in 1581. He elsewhere produced an illegitimate daughter so where the truth lies, one cannot be sure. In 1579 he resigned the Earldom of Lennox, which he had inherited after his brother Matthew's assassination, in favour of his nephew, Esme, Lord D'Aubigny, later the first Duke of Lennox. Robert Stewart accepted the Earldom of March, and was made Bishop of Caithness in 1583. During his absence, the see was committed to Alexander Gordon, son of George, Earl of Huntly. Stewart died in St. Andrews in 1586, aged 70.[10]

The links between this small circle of great families are so close that they must provide the key to the titles of the "Port" tunes. Robert Stewart's mother was a daughter of the first Earl of Atholl, while he himself married Lady Elizabeth, daughter of the fourth Earl. One of her sisters, Margaret, married John Grant, 4th Laird of Freuchie, and died in 1555. Their second son, Patrick, built Muckerach Castle in the 1570's, and married Jean Gordon (? of Echt). Patrick died before 1617. Could he be the subject of the tune **"Port Patrick"**? The Grants are known to have employed "Mulleachan the clairscher" at this period. The Atholl connection with harping is so strong that it is not surprising that more than one **"Port Atholl"** is found in the collections. **"Port Lennox"**, also known as **"The Duke of Lennox Port"** is

Detail of fireplace, Castle Huntly

almost certainly dedicated to Esme Stuart, created first Duke of Lennox in 1581. Esme Stuart's daughter, Harriet, married George Gordon, sixth Earl and first Marquess of Huntly (1562-1636) who is likely to be the subject of one of the tunes entitled **"Port Gordon"** He is the Huntly who defeated Argyll at the battle of Balrinnes, when it was foretold that Argyll's harp would be played in the Gordon territory of Strathbogie — which it was, but as spoils of war.[11] In the magnificent castle that George Gordon built at Huntly, the carved fireplace shows the Royal Arms, including a harp to represent Ireland. It is such a well drawn clarsach that the sculptor must surely have used a real instrument as a model. Most heraldic harps are obviously imaginative depictions. Also shown are the Gordon arms of the Marquess, and those of Lennox, for his wife. Another daughter of the Duke of Lennox, Lady Mary, became Countess of Mar. The records show that at this period the Mar home was frequented by a "woman clairsocher". Musical contact already existed between the two noble households. In 1571, the Countess of Lennox wrote to the Earl of Mar, then Regent, asking him to favour the bishop of Caithness in regard to the benefice of St. Andrews and to be good to certain musicians in the isle of "Inchennen", which was part of her dowry.[12]

PORT BALLANGOWNE.

More than one **"Port Gordon"** exists, however, and the other tune may have a different origin. It appears as variants in the MacLean-Clephane manuscript among the tunes played by Echlin O Cathain, subtitled "Scottish Highland Original adapted to the Harp by Carolan"; in Oswald's "Caledonian Pocket Companion"; in Dow's Collection, and as "Purth Clairseach" in Bunting. Shortly before 1595 Alexander Robertson of Inchmagrannoch married Agnes Gordon, and the tune may mark this occasion. She died in 1634. Many of the early "Ports" can be linked with an event of significance amongst the great families who are known to have been patrons of the harpers. The Atholl family also had links with the Rosses of Ballnagowan — Lady Elizabeth Ross, who died in 1570, was Atholl's sister-in-law. She married John, Lord Fleming, whose son John was created first Earl of Wigtown, and is likely to be the subject of the tune **"The Lament for the Earl of Wigtown — Cumha Iarla Wigtown"**. The Earl died in 1619, and his widow, Sarah Herries, married Hugh Montgomery of Braidstane, whose family had strong connections with harping and harpers in both Scotland and Ulster.

The earliest sources of "Port" tunes, the Skene manuscript, was collected around 1615 by or for John Skene of Hallyards in Midlothian, and is in tablature for the mandora. It contains **"Port Ballangowne"** (perhaps composed for Lady Elizabeth Ross). The next, the Straloch manuscript, was collected between 1620-27 by Robert Gordon of Straloch, who was the first person to receive the degree of Master of Arts at the College of Aberdeen. This manuscript included **"Port Preist"** and three tunes headed simply **"A Port"**. One of them has the postcript **"Finis Port Jean Kinsay"** — apparently a misspelling of "Lindsay".

The Lindsays of Edzell were clearly familiar with the music of the clarsach at the end of the 16th century. They were at odds with the senior branch of the family, the Lindsays of Crawford, although Sir David Lindsay of Edzell had married the daughter of the tenth Earl of Crawford. The wild and profligate twelfth Earl, who succeeded his father in 1607, was imprisoned by his family in Edinburgh Castle, where he died in 1621. He left only one child, Lady Jean Lindsay, who scandalised her relatives by running off with a "jockey with the horn". The Scots word "jockey" comes from "joculator", which by the 17th century meant an itinerant minstrel. It is quite possible that he played a harp as well as some sort of trumpet. Lady Jean ended her days as a beggar until the Restoration, when King Charles II granted her a pension of £100 a year "in consideration of her eminent birth and necessitous condition". Jean may have played the clarsach herself. Indeed, could the figure of "Musica" at Edzell be a portrait of Jean Lindsay as a young girl? The unnatural way in which the sculpture is defaced — the only carving in the series to be so damaged — appears as though it might have been intentionally carried out. Perhaps it was done in reaction to her shocking behaviour. "Port Jean Lindsay" may have been played by her, or may have been composed for her. Prior to

1600, around the time of her birth, her father David attended St. Andrews University.[13]

This link with St. Andrews may have particular significance. There was clearly a strongly musical community in the town with religious, academic and aristocratic connections. Robert Stewart, as Prior of St. Andrews, was based there. John Major, who described the harps of the "Wild Scots", taught at St. Andrews. He died in 1550. Thomas Wood was the compiler of an important Psalter containing distinctively Scottish Psalm settings which also includes illustrations of harps. Wood lived in St. Andrews between 1562-86, as did several other composers, including Peebles and Lauder. George Buchanan was Principal of St. Leonard's College, St. Andrews in 1566, while John Monipennie came from Pitmilly, close by St. Andrews, and was in the town in 1597. Was it around this time that they had the opportunity to observe the "strings of clarschoes of brass wyre and strings of harps of gut"? There are likely to have been close contacts between Atholl musicians and the St. Andrews circle. In 1580, one occasion worthy of particular note is recorded in the Calendar of Scottish Papers — "July 29. St. Andrews. There have been present since the King of Scots' coming to this town, the *Earls of Morton, Lennox, March*, Montrose, Rothes, *Mar* and *Atholl*, Lords Ruthven and *Lindsay*, some other inferior persons of the Council, and sundry attenders". It is highly likely that at least one, possibly several, harpers would have been amongst the "attenders". Here we have a gathering of all the nobles to whose families the "Ports" are dedicated, several of whom are known to have employed harpers. The harper to the Douglas Earls of Morton at this date was Robert Galbraith, who is likely to have been one of the Mac a' Bhreatnaich harpers. The named "Ports" have such a distinctive character, and can be linked so frequently with patrons who lived before 1600, that it is possible to suggest that this particular group of tunes belongs to the late 16th century. Tunes of the same construction, such as the "Lament for the Earl of Wigtown" or "The Fidler's Contemt" do not use the word "Port" in their title, and are probably of a slightly later date.[14]

"**Fuadh na mfilairan — the Fidler's Contemt**" has been associated with Ruaidhri Dall Morison mainly because of his known antipathy to fiddle players, and because it is ascribed to "Rorie Dall" by Dow. Morison, however, does not seem to have been a composer of music. The tune has a typical "Port" construction, and may be an example of an unusual musical convention, represented in the Ap Huw manuscript by titles such as "Hated by Musicians" and "Hated by Crwth Players". Tunes with an aggressive feel to them may have been a recognised form of expression, in the manner of the bardic contests, or flytings — another Welsh title is given as "Alban (Scottish) hyddic". "Hyddic" may be a personal name but can also mean "very nasty" or "very angry". William Matheson suggests that "The Fidlers' Contemt" may be a satirical "take-off" of fiddle music, exaggerating their characteristic Scotch Snap.[15]

Three other early harp tunes occur in the Straloch manuscript. All are headed "**A Port**". One is simply a typical example of these tunes. Another can be identified as a shorter version of the tune which in Dow's collection is entitled "**Cumha Peathar Ruairi**" (the Lament for Rorie's Sister). There is considerable confusion between the sources as to whether the "Port" tunes should be ascribed to O Cathain or Morison — or indeed to either harper.

"**Port Atholl**" and "**Port Gordon**" "and others" were attributed to Ruari O Cathain by Arthur O Neill. Although Ports Atholl and Gordon are included in Daniel Dow's collection, as well as "**Da Mihi Manum**", which is traditionally linked with O Cathain, Dow gives no composer for these tunes. Dow did attribute to "Rorie Dall" four other tunes — "**Lude's Supper**", "**Is eagal leam am bas**", "**Fuadh na mfilairan**" and "**Cumha Peathar Ruairi**" — which led Matheson to suggest that these four tunes should be linked with Morison rather than O Cathain. However, the last tune, the "Lament for Rorie Dall's Sister" (the word "Dall" only occurs in Dow's translation, not in the Gaelic title) is found in the slightly shorter form, as "A Port" in the Straloch manuscript, written between 1620-27, before Morison's birth. O Cathain did have a sister, though whether she died before 1620 is not known.[16] It is odd, if it is one of his tunes, that O Cathain's name is not mentioned in connection with it in the Straloch manuscript since this is the source which tells us that at least one of the tunes was certainly played by him.

At the end of one of the melodies, again simply entitled "A Port", is the postscript "**Finis Port Rorie Dall**". This tune also appears in the Skene manuscript under the title "**Port Ballangowne**". Since the Skene manuscript predates the Straloch manuscript, one might suppose that this is the original title. Whether O Cathain composed it, or simply played the Straloch version of the tune, is not certain. His name is not linked with it in any other source. Balgowan lies between the two main parts of the Lude estate, Inchmagrannnoch and Monzie, on the River Tummel, and would no doubt have been a familiar name to members of the Robertson family. Alternatively, as previously suggested, it may be linked with the Rosses of Ballnagowan.

The assertion that the word "Port" was used by O Cathain as a title for his compositions depends on one late Irish perspective — that of Arthur O'Neill, whose information, though it deserves close study, is not always entirely accurate. It is unlikely that O Cathain, whose earliest dateable visit to Scotland can be put tentatively at 1615, could have composed all the tunes that were adopted so rapidly by a range of instruments in different parts of the country. In several cases, completely separate tunes are found under the same title. For example, there are at least two different "**Port Atholls**" and two "**Port Gordons**". This suggests that more than one composer of the tunes was involved. If Ruairi O Cathain did compose any of these melodies, it would seem that he was adopting a form of harp music which already existed in Scotland at that time, since the earliest dateable "Ports" appear to have been composed around 1570-80. There is of course no reason why they might not have been part of the repertoire of both O' Cathain and Morison.

In addition to those in the early manuscripts, a group of **ten unnamed "Ports"** are to be found in the MacLean-Clephane manuscript. The origins of these tunes are not known, although the MacLean sisters obviously took an interest over many years in the remnants of harp music that survived in their own area, as well as those brought by visiting musicians and collectors. The Clephane side of the family had connections with Fife, so it is possible that the tunes might have come to them from a source linked with St. Andrews. Some of their "Ports" can be identified as known harp tunes in other collections. **"Port 2nd"** is a partial version of "Port Gordon" as in Bowie's book; **"Port 6th"** is "Port Ballangowne"; and **"Port 7th"** is "Is eagal leam am bas" (I am afraid of death). **"Port 1st"** also has close similarities to a tune "The Keiking Glass" which comes from the Skene manuscript.[17] A short **"Irish Port"** is found in the Wemyss manuscript, along with "Port Robart". Since the manuscript was written by the seventeen-year-old Lady Margaret Wemyss, a member of a prominent Lowland family, the word "Irish" in this case is equally likely to mean an "Erse" or "Highland" Port.

The classic "Ports" seem to have been a characteristically Scottish form of harp music which had a fairly short lived fashion between the mid 16th and mid 17th centuries. This type of tune was being overtaken by other forms of instrumental music and, at the same time, the profession of harper was beginnning to die out. The word "Port" persisted in the title of harp tunes though they no longer demonstrated the form of the classic 16th century "Ports". This may indeed have been a reversion to an earlier, more general, use of the word in relation to harp music. By the beginning of the 18th century variants of tunes such as the **"Horseman's Port"** and **"Port Atholl"** appear in collections — a large number of variants suggests that a tune has been current for some time. The Balcarres manuscript (c. 1692-94) contains four different versions of the same **"Port Atholl"**, apparently played by well-known lutanists of the day. The title again connects this tune with central Perthshire.

The later collections show a type of tune more strongly melodic than the early 17th century "Ports", though they still include that word in their title. Their more flowing and tuneful character may be a consequence of their being adapted by the fiddle from older compositions, or it may be a natural development in style. **"Port Atholl"** in Bowie and Oswald is an example, as is the second **"Air by Fingal"**, also in Bowie's book.

The ascription to the eight harp tunes in Bowie's collection reads ... "The following pieces of Ancient music were furnished to the Editor by a Gentleman of Note in the Highlands of Scotland, were composed originally for the Harp and were handed down to him by his Ancestors who learned the same of the famous Rory Daul a celebreted Harper in the Reign of Queen Ann — These tunes are called in our language Ports and were composed either for Religious Worship, or on Heroic Subjects."[18] Bowie is probably referrring to the only Queen Anne to reign in her own right between 1710-1714. Ruaidhri Morison, the Blind Harper, died in 1713 or 1714. "Rory Daul" is credited as the player, but not the composer of the tunes, and the fact that the first three melodies are described as **"Airs by Fingal"** suggests that they were believed to be of some antiquity. The other tunes given by Bowie are **"Port Gordon"**, **"Port Atholl"**, **"Port Lennox"**, **"McLoud's Salute"** and **"The Battle of Sheriff Moor"**. This last tune can be sung to the words of a poem: "Oran air Cath Sliabh an tSiorraimh" which was found among the Robertson of Lude papers. Since the battle took place in 1715, the words and title cannot have been given to it by either of the Blind Harpers. The melody, however, is of the same type as "Tha mo chion air an ur ghibt", used by the Skye poetess Mary MacLeod for one of her compositions. William Matheson suggests that the tune is typical of those used by the harper/bard and that she may well have learned it from Ruaidhri Dall Morison at Dunvegan. The words of her poetry echo one of his own songs. Given this, and the inclusion of "McLoud's Salute", Bowie's informant may indeed have obtained these tunes from Morison. It is most unlikely that such a well-known harper would not have visited Perthshire at some point in his travels, especially when it is noted that Norman MacLeod, the younger son of Iain Breac, had married Anne Fraser, a daughter of Lord Lovat, in 1703, and was living close to Perth under the wing of the Atholl family. Norman inherited the chieftainship of MacLeod on his brother Rory's death in 1699. After Ruaidhri Dall's banishment from Dunvegan there was an unsettled period in his life when we know that he made other journeys around the mainland. Morison is likely to have travelled to see the new chief, and may well have visited Lude.[19]

This more melodic type of tune does not have the recognisable characteristics of the "Ports" and classification usually depends on the title of the piece. Other compositions which may be identified as harp tunes are **"Lude's Lament"** in Oswald's collection, which seems to be an extended version of "Lochaber No More". William Matheson also points out a similarity to "Thig an Smeorach as t-Earrach". Also in Oswald are **"Carrallan's Lament"** and **"Carland's Devotion"**, both of which appear to have been named after Turlough Carolan, though they are not any known compositions of his. This habit of attaching the name of a famous musician to a tune seems to have been — and still is — a common practice. It does not necessarily mean that it was composed, or even played by them. This may explain the inconsistent attribution of melodies to "Rory Dall", especially since the name, belonging to the two different harpers, had been famous in Scotland for over a hundred years.

The clearest example of the naming of a tune must be **"Rory Dall's Port"**, which first appears in James Oswald's "Caledonian Pocket Companion". It is

also included in the MacLean-Clephane manuscript, though not amongst the harp tunes. Although Oswald's collection contains several pieces of harp music, it is not known from what source he obtained his tunes. In London, he belonged to a music society known as the "Temple of Apollo", in which several notable Scottish musicians and noblemen took part. General Reid, closely related to the Robertsons of Lude, and a fine musician himself, was a member, and may have provided Oswald with some of the harp tunes, most of which occur in the later volumes of his work.[20] Another source might have been a fiddle player named Ogilby, who was working in London as a dancing-master in the late 17th century, and subsequently made a successful career in the theatre in Dublin. He "would not tell where in Scotland he was born ...". It is possible that he was related to another fiddler named Ogilby, who was executed for the murder of a harper in Edinburgh in 1594. His descendants might well wish to hide their disreputable family history.[21] James Oswald himself was well-known — not to say infamous — for including his own compositions among melodies that he claimed were much older, for spuriously attributing tunes to historical figures such as David Rizzio, the Italian secretary of Mary Queen of Scots, and for adding his own variations to existing traditional tunes.

"Rory Dall's Port", while it may possibly be based on an earlier melody, is a series of variations, six two-part variations in all, which are likely to be Oswald's inventions. What is interesting, however, is that it was obviously intended to be in the style of a harp tune.[22] Indeed several of the known harp tunes show a similar form — a series of short four or eight bar parts which form a repetitive progression, one to the next. Each part usually ends with the same, or similar, sequence of notes. This type of tune is related to the old clan marches found in both Ireland and Scotland. In Ireland, one of these tunes

"Burn's March" (could the Scottish name be significant?) formed part of the basic repertoire of the apprentice harper. Other examples of these tunes in Scotland are "**The Horseman's Port**"; the *first* and *third* "**Airs by Fingal**" in Bowie; and "**Carrill's Lament**" (again probably named for Carolan) in Oswald.

These are not true variations on a theme, but another group of harp tunes does exhibit this form. The earliest to be notated is "**Port Ballangowne**" in the Skene manuscript which has a complete variation on the melody. How accurate the transcription is, we cannot be sure since this may have been an attempt by a lute player to write down music directly from a harper. The variation is constructed by substituting a group of semi-quavers for some of the main melody notes. On a wire-strung clarsach it is technically much more comfortable, and makes musical sense, to interpret each group of semi-quavers as a series of grace-notes attached to the melody notes, rather than giving them their full notated value. The timing of the tune is not accurately written throughout in any case. If this reading is close to what was actually played, it may give an insight into the early development of the variation form which is now known as "ceol mor".

The Scottish Highland form of variation is given a different treatment from that of classical music, and has reached its height in the "ceol mor" of the bagpipes. This pipe music has achieved its present formal structure over the last 150 years, but it is likely to have existed in a similar form since at least the 16th century. There is no doubt that the clarsach also played music with a theme and variations. It seems to have been an accepted convention that variations could be added to any of the more formal harp airs. These appear to have been constructed in two different ways : either by taking the main notes of the melody, and playing them in a repetitive rhythm, or by taking the main melody notes and adding the same, or a similar, sequence of decorations or grace-notes to each — the decorating motifs usually growing more elaborate with each variation. The first type may have links with the "galliard" which often followed a slow "pavane" in the dance music of the court. The rhythm is usually reduced to a repetitive 6/8 pattern for the first variation. Variations which add grace-notes are common to both pipe and harp music, and can also be seen in the Welsh Ap Huw manuscript.[23]

Tunes with variations of the first type are "**Caoineadh Rioghail**" (The Royal Lament), said to have been composed on the execution of King Charles I in 1649 by John Garbh Maclean of Coll, in the Angus Fraser manuscript; "**Port Patrick**" ; and "**Lude's Supper**" in Oswald.

"**The Lament for the Earl of Wigtown**" shows variations of both the first and second type, as does the "**Lament for the Bishop of Argyll**", which appears in both Dow and, in a different version, in the MacFarlane manuscript (c. 1742). There are several possible candidates for the subject of this last tune. These include Robert Montgomery, son of the Earl of Eglinton who died

around 1558; Neil Campbell, who resigned the see in 1608; and Andrew Boyd, natural son of Thomas, Lord Boyd (a family with Ulster connections) who died in 1636. The most likely, however, is Hector MacLean, who took part in Montrose's campaign for Charles I. He was made Bishop of Argyll in 1680 and died in 1687. He married Jean Boyd, grand-daughter of the aforementioned Andrew, and one of his sons (he is reputed to have had 16 daughters!) was Anndra Mac an Easbuig, a well-known MacLean poet. Anndra is mentioned in "An Account of the depradations committed on The Clan Campbell", which also included a reference to "the harper's son in mull". There were clearly harpers active in the area during his father's lifetime.[24]

A further class of harp tune can be identified in the Failte — the Salute or Welcome. Ruaidhri Morison is described as playing a Salute at the hunting party at Coire-an-Easan, which is likely to have been a version of the tune now played by pipers as **"Cumha Craobh nan Teud** (the Lament for the Harp Tree/Key) but which is also known as **"Corrienessan's Salute"**.[25] Variations could also be played on the ground of this type of melody, as we find with the aforementioned tune and with **"Suipear Tighearna Leoid"** (Lude's Supper) in Oswald. The "Ancient Harp Air III" in the MacLean-Clephane manuscript is similar to Oswald's variation for the tune. "Lude's Supper" is ascribed by Dow to "Rorie Dall" and by Gunn to O Cathain, but Gunn's story of O Cathain attending a feast at Lude in 1650, in the company of the Marquess of Huntly, seems to be an invention of his own. Huntly, at this date, was a

fugitive in the struggle between King and Parliament. It is possible that the tune may mark the regaining of their estates by the Robertsons of Lude from the Ogilvies in 1619. It has a typical "Salute" form.

Many different clans have "Salutes" associated with them. "McLoud's Salute", given among Bowie's harp tunes, is a good example. A similar tune "Failte bheag Mhic Leoid" (MacLouds Lesser Salutation) appears in Dow's collection. A "Failte" is usually more rhythmic and has a livelier character than a "Port". They are usually in 6/8 timing, though sometimes in 4/4. The MacLean-Clephane manuscript contains a short "Failte Chlarsaich", while amongst the ten unnamed "Ports" we also find one tune entitled "Jig", with the instruction that it should be played "Slow". It is clearly of the Failte type, rather than a dance tune. The tune "Failte na Miosg" (Salute to the Musket, or Salute to Drunkenness) also found under the title "Port More" (The Big Port) is a similar type of tune.[26] Ports III and IV in the MacLean-Clephane manuscript have so much in common with "Failte Mhic Dhonail Ghuirm" (McDonald of the Isles Salutation) and "Failte Mhic Cai (Lord Rae's Salutation) in Dow that one can suggest that all four tunes are also harp Salutes. This possibility is strengthened by the dedication of another similar tune as "Gradb Dhoudhaill oig" (Mr. Campbell of Achnabreack's Salutation). The Dougal Og of the title is likely to be the son of Sir Duncan Campbell killed at Inverlochy in 1645, who was brother to the unhappy Florence MacLean of Coll. Dougal himself died around 1660, and was succeeded by his nephew, Sir Duncan Campbell, whose harper, Duncan MacIndeor, may also have served the preceding chief.[27] Other probable harp Salutes included in Dow's book are "Failte Mhic Caoinnich" (Seaforth's Salutation) and "Failte Loch Ioall" (Loch Isle's Salutation). The version of "Port Gordon" given in Dow and in Bunting as "Purth Clarseach" seems to have more of the character of a Failte than that of the early classic Ports.

How the melodies were expressed on the clarsach must remain a matter of speculation. The native musical tradition has always been open to the absorption of outside influences, and Scottish music contains elements drawn from European classical music, and the traditions of Ireland, Wales, England and Scandinavia. Scottish traditional music itself is almost entirely melodic — the only harmony being the drones of the pipes and a little double-stopping on the fiddle. The harp and clarsach have obvious harmonic possibilities, however, but it is difficult to know exactly how the harpers dealt with these.

Three terms which are regularly applied to clarsach music are "cuir" (or cor or uirt), "port" and "orgain". The word "orgain", when it relates to the clarsach, appears to mean the ringing bass harmony line, and is likely to have derived from the use of the word "organum" in the late Middle Ages. "Port" seems to mean a harp melody in general terms, though by the late 16th century it represented a particular type of tune. "Cuir" or "cor" is more of a mystery. The word probably comes from the same root as "chora", and it is tempting to suggest that it may signify the decoration applied to the basic melody line, since we are told in more than one case that a harper could play "puirt is (and) uirt (or cuir) is orgain", or could play "cor" and "port". Where it is used in the Irish poem "Consolations", Bergin translates the composite word "corphort" as "sparkling melodies". "Cor" is also used in the sense of "accompaniment" as in Sileas na Ceapaich's poem to Lachlann Dall. It may also simply mean a different sort of tune. Some tunes in the Ap Huw manuscript include the word "Cor" in their title. Irish harpers, we are told, had to be able to play "goltraighe" (sad music); "geantraighe" (merry music) and "suantraighe" (sleeping music), and the Scottish players must certainly have had a similar repertoire.

The key to playing the music on the wire-strung clarsach must surely be in the decoration and stopping techniques which are as essential to the instrument as are grace-notes to bagpipe music. They not only punctuate the music, but also define the harmonies, depending on which notes are left to ring. Guides to these decorations are found in the Ap Huw manuscript and in Edward Bunting's book, which have been convincingly deciphered in practical playing terms, respectively, by Robert Evans of Cardiff and Ann Heymann in the United States. Similar techniques are likely to have been used by Scottish harpers, though as yet we have found no notated music which gives the grace-notes in the detail of the Welsh and Irish examples. Some of the musical terms, however, are common to the three countries, and some are also applied to pipe music.

By the 18th century, in the MacLean-Clephane manuscript, we have the music of Echlin O Kane, which may have been transcribed directly from his playing by Patrick MacDonald and transmitted to the MacLean-Clephane sisters. These tunes show the rather florid treatment that one would expect from an Irish harper of the period, with triplets, grace-notes and runs inserted in the basic melody. It is comparable to the style of music in much of Bunting's collection. The bass line is given as single notes — chords are very rarely used, though the bass often includes grace-notes. It is possible that the player filled out the chords, but a sparing treatment is in character with the wire-strung clarsach where the sustained ring of the strings makes a full chordal bass line overpowering and unnecessary. On the few occasions when a full chord is found in any of the harp tunes, it marks a moment of particular musical significance in the melody.

It is clear that at no point was the music static — there would be many versions of a tune current at the same time, expressed by each harper in their own way. Since none of the tunes, in either Scotland or Ireland, were written down by the harpers themselves, there is no music that can be seen as completely "authentic" in antiquarian terms. There are, however, many beautiful harp melodies which deserve to be played. Harpers of today, who are familiar with the idiom of traditional music of their own time, should therefore feel comfortable in making their individual interpretation of these. A list of harp tunes and their sources is given in Appendix D.

15 CLASSICAL REVIVAL

Oh! for his Harp as it sounded of yore!
But the Wizard of Song shall awake it no more;
For o'er his pale urn Scotia weeps broken hearted
The best of her Sons was the Minstrel departed![1]

It is ironic that the rich heritage of Gaelic culture should be 'discovered' by the scholars of the Lowlands and the upper classes of Scottish society, just as the last notes of the old line of Highland harpers faded. For most of the population this colourful bardic culture had existed hitherto unsuspected, but it now struck a deep chord with many artists, musicians and poets. And because it had been carried for centuries by oral tradition, it related to the native people and natural landscape in a way that was very much in tune with the philosophical "Zeitgeist".

The Ossianic poems of Macpherson made a tremendous impact in their own country, and indeed throughout Europe, though it is regrettable that the controversy surrounding their authenticity should sometimes have overshadowed the very genuine oral tradition in which they had their basis. The character of Ossian, bard and minstrel of the Fingalian warriors, appears again and again in the art and literature of Scotland at this period, representing the poetic muse of the country. An example of the creativity inspired by the legends was Alexander Runciman's major work, the Hall of Ossian in Penicuik House. This was painted in 1772 and, although it was destroyed by fire in 1899, enough evidence remains, in the artist's own sketches, in photographs and other paintings, to give an impression of the dramatic effect that this grand room must have had. Landscape and figures are intermingled in the wall paintings in a way which expresses the native roots of the epic poetry. The ancient harper features powerfully in the composition. This romantic and historically flawed view of Gaelic Scotland — a rather uncomfortable mixture of Celtic legend interpreted through Classical education — was one which persisted strongly into the 20th century. Still, it was an ideal which at least inspired action in attempts to preserve what remained of the culture, and to resuscitate the elements that had failed.

It was noted in the committee meeting of the Highland Society of London, held on 16th January 1784, that an offer had been received from a Mr. Gwyne (a distinguished Welsh performer on the triple harp) to instruct a Highlander on the Harp. The committee was to put into effect the following resolutions : "That by recommendation of Ensign MacRae of the 42nd Regiment and his letter, Christopher McRae in Kintail in Ross-shire, be sent for and requested under the particular conditions for that purpose determined upon, to repair to London as a fit and most proper person to be presented by Mr. Gwyne and that the Secretary do write to his parents accordingly.

The conditions as follows viz. That the person recommended to Mr. Gwyne be a Highlander and speak the language. That he shall Indent to the Secretary of the Society in London for five years. That at the Expiration of his indenture he shall be obliged to teach another accordingly to the Directions of the Secretary. That when the Term of Indenture is expired he shall and also, any other Indental Professor of the Harp be obliged to return to and reside in Scotland Two years at least.

That from the period of McRaes Arrival in London he shall according to his own good behaviour be entirely at the expense of the Society unless contrary to their most Sanguine Expectations he be disapproved of by the Society".

Gilchrist (Christopher) MacRae duly arrived in London, and at a meeting of 31st May 1784 the committee recommended the Secretary to prepare Indentures, and to inform Mr. Gwyne that MacRae would be sent to his house as soon as it was convenient to receive him. However, at a meeting held on 30th December the Secretary informed the Committee that Mr. Gwyne proposed sending a "young Welshman thoroughly instructed on the Harp instead of receiving the young man MacRae to be perfected in that instrument". The Committee resolved to write to Mr. Gwyne thanking him for his good intentions, but having provided a young man from Scotland, they decided to have him instructed in the best manner possible without giving any further trouble to Mr. Gwyne. The Society duly made enquiries into the cost of having MacRae taught the harp elsewhere, and the Secretary reported on 17th January 1785 that Two Guineas for entrance and Two Guineas for 12 lessons was the smallest charge ever made by any good master. It was resolved that Christopher MacRae be taught the Harp and maintained for the year 1785 at the expense of the Club in persuance of the resolutions entered upon calling him from Scotland. But by 5th March the Secretary was requested to write to MacRae's parents and inform them that as the scheme of teaching him the harp had failed, the Society would either send him home free of expense, or recommend him to some station in the West Indies at his parents option. The Committee also decided that its finances were not in a state to send the Welsh harper mentioned by Mr. Gwyne to Scotland.

However, during the adjournment of the Society during the summer of 1785, it seems that it was possible to send MacRae to Wales. On 1st November the Secretary reported that he was there at Wynstag to learn the Ancient Instrument the Harp under the tuition of the Harper of Sir Watkin Williams

Wynn, according to the former order of the Club and Committee. Unfortunately the Club found that "after an experiment of some months at Wynstag, the young musician's education, maintenance still continue more expensive than it is proper for the club should incur on this occasion, where the accomplishment of the object proposed is attended with great uncertainty, but the attempt accompanied with a certain and considerable expenditure.

That the club being thus disappointed in the original purpose of having this young man taught and maintained at little if any expense". (Mr. Gwyne had apparently originally offered to educate and entertain him at no charge) ... "and that never the less it is incumbant on them to put him into some line of living pursuant to their engagement to his parents and the young man's own merit. Therefore Resolved that Christopher Macrae be immediately recalled from Wales. That he be sent out to Jamaica at the expence of the club with the earliest opportunity and that the members of this committee will recommend him to the protection of their friends in that Island under whose patronage there is no doubt of his success fully proportioned to his own deserving. And that his parents be made acquainted with this resolution". Some of the expenses recorded by the Society are detailed below.

June	1784	By paid for a suit of Lowland cloths, shoes, stockings. Hat for Christopher McRae. £5.14.
July	1784	By paid Christopher McRaes expence for May, June, July £7.19.2 (and similar sums throughout 1784 and 1785).
October	1784	By paid Christopher MacRaes expence for a pair of strong breeches. £-.15s.
Aug. 29	1785	By paid at Ed. (Edinburgh) for the Harpers plaid, hose and for carriage £2.6s.
Sept. 20	1785	A place being provided for Christopher McRae with Sir Watkins Harper at Wynnstag in Wales, pursuant to the original purpose of the Club of his learning the instrument in that country. It became necessary to fit him out with fit articles for a decent appearance on that occasion. His Highland dress is charged above. He had three coats and some waistcoats and breeches and from the treasurers own things for which no charge is made. (Shirts, stocks, shoes and stockings, a great coat, a bonnet with a feather, and a hat are listed at a total cost of £8.15.8). By paid in part coach fare to Wales in the Shrewsbury Fly £11.11
March 1	1786	By given to Christopher McRae to furnish him in cloths for the W. India climate £16.17
March 2	1786	By given to Christopher McRae to pay his passage to Jamaica £12.12.

June 8   1786   By Gow the musicians Bill for Instructing McRae the young
Harper the violin and for music books. £16.3.6.²

(Presumably MacRae had spent his year in London in the study of Scottish
music, if not on the instrument that he had intended to take up. He may well
already have played the fiddle, which had led to his recommendation as a
student for the harp.) So the good intentions of the H.S.L. were frustrated.
It would have been interesting, especially if he were a fiddle player, to see what
MacRae would have made of the instrument.

The Highland Society, based in Edinburgh, had made some useful efforts
to trace what remained of the harpers' music and any surviving instruments.
In June 1805 their minutes record thanks to Brigadier-General Robertson of
Lude for agreeing to furnish the Society with the two harps in his possession.
By 1st November 1805 the harps had been received by the Society, who agreed
that drawings should be taken and tests made on the harps. In January 1806
the Society commissioned Gunn to draw up a description of them, at a fee of
20 guineas, with the intention of publishing his report in the Society's
Transactions. By May 1807 Mr. D. Sommerville had been asked to draw the
harps, and was paid £37.5.6. Although the Secretary announced 'the
publication of the Third Volume of the Society's Transactions, and Mr.
Gunn's Treatise on Harps and ancient music', at the meeting of 19th June
1807, Gunn's report was in fact published separately later that year.³

The Highland Society of London, too, was active in organising piping
competitions from the beginning of the 19th century onwards. During the
early decades of that century it also seemed keen to promote the other national
instruments despite the failure of their earlier scheme. The committee
involved in the 1832 piping competitions put forward the idea that prizes
should be awarded for playing strathspeys and reels on the violin, while
Captain Mackenzie suggested that the Highland Society of London should
encourage "the Old Scottish Harp, an instrument equally as national as the
bagpipe, and now almost forgot. Perth or Stirling might be a suitable place for
the establishment of a School for such a purpose". Mr. MacDonald of Dalness
was ordered to draft a report concerning the violin and harp, and he
subsequently completed and submitted this to the Society. According to
MacDonald : "It has been suggested to the Committee by Gentlemen, whose
musical accomplishments well entitle their opinions to regard, that it is not yet
too late to restore to the Highlands, the use of the Harp, with which it is well
known, they were once familiar.

It is believed there has not existed, for many years a single Harper in the
Highlands of Scotland, and the race is almost extinct even among our Irish
neighbours. Wales has been more fortunate in this respect, and not a little of
the pleasure of the traveller in that splendid country is derived from hearing,
as the Sun is going down behind the Mountains, the beautiful tones of an

instrument with which so many of the glories of the Ancient Britons are connected. Of the extent and capabilities of the Harp, with all its modern improvements, it is not for this Committee to speak. In its present state, it is hardly inferior to any instrument with which we are acquainted; and the whole science of music is open to the Composer for it ... A liberal and carefully regulated scheme would, to all appearances, have the effect of gradually introducing over the country a knowledge of the Science of Musick, our unacquaintance with which has been regarded, in the eyes of Foreigners at least, as a blot upon the National Character.

The Harper as of old would form part of the establishment of the Highland Chieftain, and the delightful recreation of this peaceful Hall, while a new source of enjoyment would be opened to the Peasant, purer than those with which his merry-makings are so often concluded, and drunkenness and its attendants would give place to friendly emulation, and the social prize be awarded, not to the greatest drinker, but to the most accomplished Musician of the Circle".

Perhaps it is not surprising that the well-meaning idealism of MacDonald apparently met with little enthusiasm from the rest of the Society; or at least no action was forthcoming. His vision of peasant pastimes does seem a little unrealistic. Nor is there a record of anything having materialised from the appointment of Malcolm MacGregor as "Caledonian Harp" maker to the H.S.L. in June 1812. MacGregor was a pipemaker in London, and had devised a keyed Highland pipe chanter. He was instructed to fashion harps "after the model of that in the possession of General Robertson of Lude", but does not seem to have produced any instruments.[4]

In Ireland, too, attempts were being made to revive the tradition. The first Irish Harp Society was set up in 1811, at which a number of students were enrolled, and one of these, Edward McBride, was appointed tutor when the second Irish Harp Society was formed in 1819. On 20th August 1821 he reported to the Society that he had four resident pupils, including among these a 'Patrick Byrne (blind) of Co. Meath, aged 23'. This would appear to be Padraig Dall O Beirn, although there is a contradiction between the age given by MacBride and the dates of his birth and death, carved on his tombstone in Carrickmacross, where O Beirn had long lived and was well known. According to these he was born in 1794 and died at Dundalk in 1863, aged 69. In either case, it would seem rather a late age to begin learning the harp so it is quite possible, as Armstrong speculates, that O Beirn had been a pupil of Arthur O Neill, and had already received tuition from him, prior to O Neill's death in 1816.

O Beirn is of especial interest to us since he was the last of the Irish harpers having links with the old tradition to tour in Scotland. His visit coincided with the period of experimentation in Edinburgh with the early photographic processes, and O Beirn was used as the subject of a series of portraits. Four of these pictures have survived, and are now part of the outstanding D. O. Hill Calotype Collection, owned by Edinburgh City Library. The portraits, taken around 1843, were noticed by R. B. Armstrong, who was given permission by the then owner, a Mr. Andrew Elliot of Princes Street, to publish one of them in his book "The Irish and Highland Harps" (1904). Armstrong's attempts to obtain further information about "Byrne" were unsuccessful though he notes the tradition that O Beirn was believed to have played only in private houses and at concerts in Edinburgh and around Fife. Armstrong suggests that O Beirn was about 60 years old at the time that the portraits were taken, but this appears to be an over-estimate.

Another portrait of O Beirn, possibly taken later in his life, was published by F.J. Bigger in 1911, along with a short description of the harper. Bigger, too, was unable to find a great deal of information on his life, adding only that "He was a frequent visitor at the Shirleys of Lough Fea, where his harp was preserved, he only played old Irish airs and when asked to play the new tunes he invariably replied : "I never learned them my son". O Beirn certainly appears to have been a very competent musician, according to a glowing account of his playing in Dublin in 1860. This report was published by Francis O Neill in 1913, and was part of an article contained in the "Emerald" of New York of 19th September 1868, not as O Neill stated, that of 1870.

Fortunately O Beirn himself was interviewed by John Bell, a Scot who resided for some time in Ireland and who took a great interest in the old harpers and their instruments. "Mr. Byrne is a protestant, he is a native (of) Farney near Carrickmacross Co. Monaghan", reads the entry in Bell's notes which appears between "Sally ie red Sally for the trunk. The forepillar of the old harps were many of them of oak and richly carved," and "There is Hempsons harp it is now in the possession of Sir Harvey Bruce". It is clear from Bell's notebook that the comments and information contained in it were obtained directly from Padraig O Beirn around the year 1849. It is probable that the two men first met when O Beirn gave a concert at Dungannon on 9th July of that year, and a poster advertising that concert is bound into the notebook. Interestingly, the illustration of a harp used for the poster was engraved by M. Kirkwood of Edinburgh and may have been a legacy of O Beirn's visit to Scotland during the early 1840's.

While in Ireland, John Bell acquired a reproduction of the harp now known as the Downhill Harp which had been owned by Denis Hempson. The copy passed from John Bell to the National Museum of Antiquities of Scotland in Edinburgh, where R. B. Armstrong was to examine and describe it for his "The Irish and the Highland Harps". Bell's entries also confirm that he obtained the harp after he had met O Beirn in 1849 — "Rainie's Harp was made by James McBride, a wheelwright near Omagh, it is not an ancient Harp, it is the one that Mr. Byrne is to get for me; it was the harp Rainy played upon before George 4th". And again on another page "Joseph Kelly of Barleyfield near

Dundalk gave my harp to Peter Collins, when a boy he used to ride through the house on the harp with his handkercheif in its mouth as a horse" — a reference to the animal head on the prow of the harp.

The harp was in Edinburgh in 1892, according to the museum catalogue, and it was still there when Armstrong examined it, but it has since disappeared and the museum has no idea what has happened to it. The harp was still strung when described by Armstrong, but the measurements given differ from both the entries regarding strings given by Bell. These read "Largest wire to be got in Flower the wire drawers Church St., Dublin, 5 wires of this, 3 wires of the next size, 6 of the next, 7 of the next, 5 of the next, 8 of the next, making 34 in all". (The last three had been changed from 6, 6 and 7). And on another page the note "1/2 lb each of the 3 first numbers of brass wire, 1/4 lb of next which will string the tennor, then there are 2 oz of course and 2 oz of fine treble wire, this constitutes the whole wire".

Bell gives also the "ancient way of tuning the Irish Harp from Mr. Byrne, noted on 10th July 1849 which is as follows : " G on the Violin, Now tune the 5th to G which is D, then you tune the octave below to that D, then you tune the 5th to the low D, which is A, then you tune the octave to that E below, then you tune the 5th to the E above which is B natural, then you tune the 5th to B natural which is F sharp, then you tune the octave to F sharp below, then you sound the G on the violin and B and D, and the octave above which is G which makes a common chord, then you tune all the instrument up and down by octaves".

"The open on the bass string on the Violin is one of the Sisters on the harp. ... The next string below on the harp and it were tuned in unison, for which reason they were called the sisters. These two unison notes are sometimes called and in ancient times were called Ne Cawlee -or the companions, afterwards they were called the Sisters. The harp is tuned by the sister note, so the open on the bass on the fiddle is the note by which the harp is tuned. The Harp is then tuned in 3rds, 5th, 4th and octaves on the principle of the pianoforte, so when you get seven strings tuned the rest are tuned in octaves."

It is regrettable that Bell did not make more extensive notes on the musical terms used by the harpers. O Beirn certainly knew some, and according to a letter from Dr. MacDonnell to Edward Bunting, written while they were still collecting information, prior to the 1840 volume, O Beirn had spent a day with MacDonnell. A Miss Reilly of Scarvagh was said by O Beirn to be the only person then living who had been taught to play through the Irish language, and he would endeavour to collect some technical terms from her, for Dr. MacDonnell. Miss Reilly was probably the Bridget O'Reilly of Virginnia who was listed as a pupil under Arthur O'Neill at the Harp School in 1811.

A further note by Bell explains what happened to O'Neill's own harp. After his death it apparently passed to Rainy, one of his pupils. One Samuel Patrick (described as a bad harper) and some others had taken umbrage at Rainy's wife and "it was burned as a bonfire because Rainy's wife had gone out of the house, the brass pins were pulled out of Rainy's harp and O'Neill's and they sold them for drink". According to another short note "Edward McBride, who taught Mannigal (possibly James McMolaghan, another of Arthur O'Neill's students) and Vallentine Rainnie, all played before George IV in Dublin". It was the harp that Rainy used then that O Beirn had promised to get for Bell.

Most of the information of this period, which relates to old Irish harpers has been obtained from a limited number of sources, of which Bunting, directly or indirectly, contributes the major portion. Two short notes by Bell provide some relative comparisons of Arthur O'Neill's own performance, which may help to widen the perspective : "Cate Martin a woman, a native of Co. Cavan, near Virginia was an older person than Arthur O Nial and played better than ever he did" and "Victory of the Co Meath was a great harper in his day and his harp was the largest of the day, he was an older man and a better performer than Arthur O Neil yet a contemporary". The latter would have been Alexander Vectory of Meath who was listed as one of a number of second rate players who were alive in 1779, according to Echlin O'Cathain's memoirs. Echlin also gets a mention by Bell with another version of a familiar tale "One McKane an old harper went over to the Highlands and in the house of one of the Chieftains he kicked up a disturbance, the Chief had the nails of his fingers cut off and had him shift for Ireland, after giving him a sufficiency of Highland whisky". Carolan receives only one curious mention : "Carolan is still travelling he and Byrne are now the only travelling harpers 9th July 1849". This reference was probably noted down by Bell during O Beirn's concert, and is surely a misinterpretation of some comment made by O Beirn on that occasion. The only remaining entry in Bell's notebook relative to harping simply reads "Patrick Murney is a Harper he plays in Little Donegal St, Belfast in his own house, he is a little fellow of about 25 years old. 27th August 1849".[5]

Irish harpers were not the only wandering minstrels to visit Scotland. A letter, dated 1830, from Joseph Train, an Excise Officer in Newton Stewart, to Sir Walter Scott, described a Welsh harper who frequented Galloway and Dumfriesshire, and who died in April 1816. His name was William ap Pritchard of Llandegai. Train writes : "I had visited a friend at the Ferrytown of Cree, and was returning to Newton Stewart with my friend Captain Denniston, the Author of 'Legends of Galloway', when we met on the way the Blind Minstrel with his harp over his shoulder. He was led by a female whom we afterwards learned was his wife and was followed by several children, some travelling on foot, others seated in a small wicker cart of very rude construction, drawn by a little Cuddy of the old Gipsey kind. As we drew near to them the old man raised his Harp and began to play the popular Air 'Kenmore's on and awa', Willie'. It was a calm evening in the month of April, and the melodious sound of the Harp soon brought a crowd of peasants from the neighbouring fields of Kirroughtree and from the adjacent hamlets of Machermore which, with a fiddle played by one of the younger branches of the Minstrel's family, formed a band that called into action the dancing powers not only of the other children, but likewise of several of the spectators.

The appearance of the Blind Minstrel of Llandegai was somewhat singular. He was seemingly upwards of fifty years of age, of very diminutive stature, the small part of his countenance that was seen above his bushy beard was of a sallow complexion very much pitted by the smallpox, and was nowise improved by his large sightless eyeballs that seemed to roll instinctively as he moved his hand along the strings of the Harp. His habiliments seemed to be just what chance had thrown in his way. On his legs he wore a pair of blue rig and fur hoeshins, partly drawn over the knees of his small clothes, the original part of which had evidently been worn by a person of more capacious dimensions. His vest of red plush cloth with deep pockets before was in every way similar to that kept in the wardrobe at Eglinton Castle, stained with the blood of the unfortunate Earl who was shot by Campbell the Exciseman. The outside colour of the coat was brown, inside blue. It was the only part of his dress that bore any proportion at all to his person. On his head he wore the cap called in old times a Megirkie with a large Roman Letter in front such as was usually wore by Chattering Charlie, the last professional Jester retained as such in the family of Cassilies or I believe in the establishment of any Scotch nobleman ...

... William ap Pritchard was a native of the Parish of Llandegai in Carnarvonshire but his chief residence had always been the South of Scotland. I cannot find that he had been in the practice of attending professionally the Caledonian Hunt Assemblies or the fashionable Winter Balls either in Ayr or Dumfries, but at Merry Makings in Town and at Kirns in the Country. He was the chief "Gut scraper" between Gretna Green and the braes of Glenapp, and like Habbie Simpson, the famous Fiddler of Kinghorn, 'at Bridals he won mony placks'.

For many years he was a constant attendant at the great Annual Fair of Kirkdomminie in Carrick. There he usually laid by his Harp and by the enlivening strains of his Fiddle kept the younkers dancing till after sunset at nearly the longest day. Wandering Willie was noted for giving the longest Reel for a Penny of any Fiddler at Kirkdomminie ... He composed the popular Airs, Culzean Castle, Carrick Shore, the Merry lads of Ayr and Ayrshire Lasses, although the latter Tune has been by some person erroneously attributed to Hugh, the last Earl of Eglinton ...

... After having passed through the Gatehouse of Fleet at nightfall, they solicited lodgings at the farmhouse of Tanneymaws and at several other places on their way to Bearlochan but were refused shelter even in any of the outhouses for the night. At length compelled by necessity these poor houseless wanderers lay down in a gravel pit fast by the great road to Portpatrick nearly opposite the old Mill of Twynhame, but alas ere morn the brow of the pit fell and buried the whole family, seven in number ... They were laid in three graves in Twynhame Kirkyard in that part called 'The Stranger's Corner'. (The ass and the cart were sold to defray the expense of the Funeral. What became of the Fiddle I have not been able to learn, but what remains of the Harp has fallen into my possession.)

The remembrance of this tragic event will be long kept up in the Country by the people superstitiously pointing out the 'Harper's Hole' as a nightly meeting place of many an unearthly group of uncouth figures in human form ..."[6]

Train's description of the blind harper formed the basis of Scott's "Wandering Willie", a character in his novel "Redgauntlet". Another contemporary account of the family's death says that his wife, Ellen Hughs, and their 16 year old daughter played the harp "with eligence and taste" so the whole family may have formed something like a travelling band. William ap Pritchard and Padraig O Beirn mark two extremes of the status of itinerant musicians in Scotland during the first half of the 19th century — the one playing for pennies at country fairs and dying destitute, and the other, feted by Edinburgh society as a last representative of the old order of bards. A strange contrast indeed, but perhaps these extremes had always existed, with the trained bardic harper and poet at the top of the social scale, and the rootless fairground musician at the bottom, both with their own audiences, and both playing their part in the musical life of the country.

Although the professional use of the native clarsach and the gut-strung harp of the Lowlands had, in their day, always been very much a male preserve, the playing of the instrument in aristocratic society, particularly by female amateurs, had apparently been relatively common. It was in these circles that harp playing survived, though the "improved" or "pedal" harp was the instrument normally used by the turn of the century. Campbell's eulogies on its effect in setting off the female form seem to have expressed a common sentiment. Many society ladies chose to have their portraits painted holding a harp, thus demonstrating in one image, their native roots, their elegance and their accomplishments.

A number of the families which had a longstanding link with harping, chose to retain this connection. Lady Grace Menzies, daughter of Lord Grantley, who had married Sir Neil Menzies in 1816, appears in a painting playing the harp, while Jane, "Countess" of Eglinton also holds a small instrument — on her left shoulder — in her portrait of 1777. Erard's of London, Harpmakers to the Queen, sent a bill to Sir Duncan Campbell of Barcaldine in 1835 requesting payment for a "New Patent Double Movement Harp with Light-Tinted Sounding Board", a Brown Leather Cover, a Set of Italian Strings, a String Box and a Packing Case and Wharfage, at a total cost of £137.14.00.[8] On 15th May 1860 "Item no. 2" in a list of Packages forwarded from Holyrood Palace to Taymouth Castle, seat of the Campbells of Breadalbane, is an "old

Irish Harp". A later inventory of the property of the deceased Marquis at Taymouth, made by Christie, Manson & Woods in 1863, includes, in the Gun Room "An Ancient Irish harp, also described as the "Mullagh" or "Curragh" Marsh Kerry Harp", which is now in the National Museum of Ireland. It is thought to date from the early 18th century but precisely when and how it came into the possession of the Breadalbane family is not known.[9] Colin, daughter of Patrick MacDougall of MacDougall wrote in 1820 from the boarding school in York to which she had been sent that she was much surprised that the young ladies at the school were allowed to break the Sabbath by playing on the harp and piano, as well as playing games.[10] Sir Walter Scott also encouraged his daughter Sophia to take up the instrument. However some players, like her friends the MacLean-Clephane sisters, not only acquired the expected level of technical competence on the harp, but took a much deeper interest in the music which had been associated with it in the past.

Lady Elizabeth D'Oyly was born Elizabeth Jane Ross. Her father was Thomas Ross, a Ross of Balnagowan, who served as an Army officer in the Caribbean and in India, and her mother was Isabella Rose MacLeod, eighth child of John MacLeod of Raasay. Both her parents died when she was very young, and she and her sister were brought up by her grandfather on Raasay. Elizabeth was sent for schooling to Edinburgh, where she lived with an aunt who was the widow of John MacLeod. This was a family with a strong piping tradition — John was probably the son of Malcolm MacLeod, said to have been John Mackay's first teacher of piping. It is not surprising to find that Elizabeth too developed an interest in this music — what is unusual is that by her early twenties, on her return to Raasay, she was able to transcribe Gaelic music, and produced a manuscript with the title "Original Highland Airs, Collected at Raasay in 1812 by Elizabeth Jane Ross".

Johnston and Boswell had commented on the social and musical activity in the Raasay household during their visit some 40 years before, and this seems to have continued in succeeding generations. Angus Mackay wrote of Elizabeth "Her musical taste was remarkably good, and she was so fond of Piobaireachd, that she acquired many of the longest pieces from the performance of the family piper, and was accustomed to play them on the piano with much effect". The piper, John Mackay, in fact dedicated to her one of his own ceol mor compositions — "Lady Doyle's Salute". Elizabeth is also likely to have transferred the music for which she had such facility to the concert harp, an instrument with which she was also familiar. Her marriage in 1815 to the English baronet Charles D'Oyley took her to India where they lived until 1838. Her husband was a talented painter, and made several watercolour and pen sketches of their gracious drawingroom, showing his wife seated at the harp. Many of their visitors spoke warmly of her musicianship. Elizabeth kept up her connections with Raasay although much of her life was spent abroad. She wrote a number of songs and poems in Gaelic, some of which were published in Sinclair's "Oranaiche" and in private pamphlets. An oral tradition, quoted by Peter Cooke, tells how during a trip across the water to Raasay she was told about the disruption of the church, and that on hearing this, she dishevelled her elegant hair and wept at the news, beating with her hand on the sides of the boat. It is almost inconceivable that a lady so steeped in the customs and culture of her island home should not transfer the vocal and pipe music that she loved to her harp as well as to her keyboard. The manuscript in her hand which has survived is apparently only part of the music and song that she noted down, but her other collections cannot now be traced.[11]

Not all the many young ladies who were set to learn the harp found such pleasure in it. In 1812 Elizabeth Grant of Rothiemurchus tells of the purgatory of an hour's music practice before breakfast at her home in Speyside : "Our clothes were all laid on a chair overnight in readiness for being taken up in proper order. My Mother would not give us candles, and Miss Elphick insisted we should get up. We were not allowed hot water, and really in the highland winters, when the breath froze on the sheets, and the water in the jugs became cakes of ice, washing was a cruel necessity, the fingers were pinched enough. As we could play our scales well in the dark, the two pianofortes and the harp began the day's work. How very near crying was the one whose turn set her at the harp I will not speak of; the strings cut the poor cold fingers so that the blisters often bled. Martyr the first decidedly sat in the dining room at the harp. Martyr the second put her poor blue hands on the keys of the grand pianoforte in the drawing room, for in these two rooms the fires were never lighted till near nine o'clock — the grates were of bright steel, the household was not early and so we had to bear our hard fate ... our 'al fresco' playing below was not much use to us; we had better have been warm in our beds for all the good it did".[12]

In these circumstances it is amazing that the girls' enthusiasm lasted until 1817 when the family moved to Edinburgh, and they were sent to study with Elouis, a harp teacher in the New Town. Joseph Elouis was born in Geneva in 1751 and is said to have died in Edinburgh around 1821. His Christian name has also been given as Jean, although in his published work he uses the vernacular form 'John'. It is not clear exactly when he first came to Scotland, but he was certainly established in Edinburgh before 1806 when part of John Gunn's report on the Lude harps involved the exercise of restringing the "Queen Mary Harp". At the wishes of the members of the Highland Society, the first attempt was made using brass wire, but Gunn did not consider this satisfactory and fortunately, considering the delicate state of the instrument, the brass strings were replaced by gut. This was undertaken by Mr. Elouis, described as "the celebrated performer on the Pedal Harp". Elouis was probably the last person to perform on the "Queen Mary Harp" when he played a number of airs to an audience of the Highland Society. By 1807 he had already published Volume 1 of "A Selection of Favourite Scots Songs with

Accompaniments for the Harp or Pianoforte, which may be Performed on these instruments either with the Voice or without it as Familiar Lessons to which are added Several Airs with Variations". In the preface to this volume Elouis gives his thoughts on the arrangement of the music — "It is generally allowed that modern embellishments or introductory and concluding Symphonies added to Scottish Airs create a want of unity which destroys their characteristic originality, and lovers of Scottish music observe with regret that most of the best melodies literally sink under the burden of foreign graces and intricate embellishments ... The following accompaniments will betray no desire of shining at the expense of the subject, they contain no arpeggios or showy passages (for the author considers such as incompatable with the simplicity of Scottish Song) and they are the only ones ever published for Harp (It is most probable that Scottish airs were originally composed for the harp) which can be performed on that Instrument and piano with or without the voice".

The first volume contains 50 airs with words plus 3 airs with variations by Elouis and may have had more than one print run since some of the extant copies also contain an advertisement for a second volume of a further 50 airs and a list of subscribers for both volumes. The advertisement is dated 1807. The first volume was dedicated to Lady Montgomery and the second to the Earl of Eglinton. The Earl and Countess of Eglinton, their son Lord Archibald Montgomery, his wife Lady Montgomery, and sister Lady Jane Montgomery (probably the lady with the harp in the portrait) were all subscribers.[13]

Elouis remained in Edinburgh until 1821, first at 21 North Hanover Street and then at 55 Hanover Street. He is not recorded in the Edinburgh Post Office Directory after 1821, although from 1822 a Miss Elouis does occur, residing at 46 Great King Street. This may confirm that he did die in Edinburgh, possibly leaving a daughter. Elizabeth Grant gives another reason for his departure. Elouis's reputation apparently never recovered from committing a dreadful social faux pas — he allowed an unintroduced male friend to sit in on the class. The ladies of Edinburgh withdrew their daughters from his tuition, and he may have had to leave the city for some time.

Harping activity in the capital continued, however, with Elouis's place as teacher taken by Henry Edward Dibden, who taught harp from about 1833, first at 23 Union Place and then at 72 Northumberland Street. He added organ to the instruments on offer in 1840 and by 1845 described himself as a "teacher of Harp, piano and organ". An advertisement in the "Edinburgh Courant" of 23rd September 1843 mentions that the Edinburgh Institution for the Education of Young Ladies provides a "Harp Teacher, Mr. Dibden". He was based at various addresses in the New Town of Edinburgh between 1842-54. At this date his home address is given as Elizabeth Cottage, Jordanburn, and in 1857 he moved to Flodden Lodge, Banner Place, Morningside. From 1862 he is listed as "Teacher of the Harp and Piano" at the Morningside address only, and remained there until 1871, the last reference to him in the Edinburgh papers.

Advertisements in the Edinburgh Courant reflect the popularity of the harp in the busy market for second-hand instruments.

April 10	1841	'Double-action harp (for sale privately)
May 22	1841	Erard harp for sale — among household goods
May 5	1842	Patent harp by ERRARD for sale by auction
Nov. 24	1842	Double-action harp (private)
April 1	1843	Double-actioned harp by SCHWEISE among furniture for sale
May 15	1843	Double-action harp amongst household furniture
Jan. 2	1844	"An Elegant Zebrawood Double Action Harp equal to new: the property of a lady having no further use for it. 35 guineas"
Jan.	1844	Errard — new harp — apply to H. Dibden esq., 22 Northumberland Street

These journals also report some of the musical performances in Edinburgh society:

Mon. 13May 1844   Musical Concert
The Harp that once throu Tara's Halls, Mrs. Bushe, Harpe obligito Mr. Laurie"

The Courant of Saturday 14th October 1843 contains a report on the Edinburgh Musical Festival with "harp obligato by Mr. Chipp".

On Saturday 9th December 1843 there was "A Grand Vocal and Instrumental Concert, duet Harp and Flute by Mr. Dibden and Mr. Bucher". And in April 1844 "Mrs. Crawford, accompanied herself on the harp, sang the Irish ballad 'Savourneen Deelish'".[14]

These were performances, on the fashionable instruments of the day, of classical music, or of Scottish melodies arranged by classically trained musicians in the style of current European music. That there were a few musicians who appreciated that this treatment changed the native character of the tunes is best seen in a comment by Elouis : "I have also rejected introductory and concluding Symphonies, and likewise difficult Accompaniments loaded with superfluous notes and extraneous passages — Symphonies: because it is the decided and well-founded opinion of the first judges, that they form an incongruous and inadmissable contrast of ancient and modern style, which gives a foreign cast to the Scottish Airs, effaces their peculiar and characteristic originality and creates an absolute want of unity — Difficult Accompaniments: because they overpower the Scottish Melodies and give them the appearance of a mere secondary part. That neither talents nor ingenuity can render such Accompaniments compatible with the Scottish Airs is strongly exemplified by those of the great composer Haydn, which although replete with merit, give no idea of Scottish Music; and for that reason, may be compared to a portrait exquisitely painted, but deficient in resemblance".

16 A HARP NEW-STRUNG

Do bheatha chlarsaich a ris,   *(Hail to you O Harp once more,*
An deis domh do thilgeadh uam   *After I have cast you from me)[1]*

In 1892 Lord Archibald Campbell proposed that there should be a new prize at the National Mod, the annual competitive festival of the Scottish Gael which took place for the first time that year. Lord Archibald was President of the Mod, and was anxious to revive the playing of the clarsach. He offered an award for the best Gaelic song with self accompaniment on the clarsach. Only two competitors entered : Miss Kate MacDonald and Miss Lizzie B. Mackay, who were both members of the St. Columba Choir, Glasgow, and the first prize was shared equally by both. The sums of money involved were large enough to be a considerable incentive for potential clarsach players — they were sufficient to purchase a harp at that time. After the 1895 Mod, the Celtic Monthly printed the prize list for solo singing with clarsach accompaniment : "First, Miss Emily Macdonald, Cathcart, £7.; Second, Miss M.A. Mackechnie, Oban, £3. (In comparison, the winners of the Premier prize for unaccompanied singing received, as first prize, a gold medal and £1 and as second prize, £2). These two ladies again won the competition in 1896 with the placings reversed.

An article in the Celtic Monthly of 1898 describes Miss Emily Macdonald as belonging to a very musical family, all members of the Glasgow St. Columba Gaelic Choir. Her sister had won the Gold Medal at the Mod. Emily was invited to perform at the Feis Ceoil in Belfast, and the Oireachtas in Dublin, and apparently also travelled to Brittany. "Her rendering of the Gaelic songs and pipe tunes on the harp ..." we read "... always created enthusiasm". Certainly, the instrument was taken up by other young ladies in Scotland and elsewhere — in 1902 the competition for "the best rendering of a Gaelic song with Clarsach accompaniment" was won by a Miss Amy Murray of New York. The same year saw the introduction of the first competition for the playing of "Gaelic Airs on the Clarsach".[2]

It is not clear from what source the entrants obtained the instruments on which they played. From the published photographs, they appear to be playing gut-strung harps, most of which have been copied from the Queen Mary clarsach. According to Francis Collinson, Lord Archibald Campbell had approached Glen's, the Edinburgh instrument makers in 1892, commissioning them to make two harps modelled on the Queen Mary instrument.[3] Glen's 207 certainly had experience in repairing Pedal harps, and had also examined the surviving ancient harps prior to that date. Robert Glen had deposited a cast of the Trinity College harp in the National Museum of Antiquities in Edinburgh in 1881. Another harp, listed in the same Museum Catalogue of 1892, is described as "triangular-shaped, 45 x 26 in., on triangular stand, five strings remaining — (deposited by) A.B. Johnstone 1860". This harp has since disappeared from the museum.[4]

The Glen family came originally from Fife, and two brothers, Alexander Glen, born in 1801, and Thomas MacBean Glen, born in 1804, settled in Edinburgh. Thomas was employed as a broker until 1833 when he set up a workshop as a pipe and flute maker. His premises in 1838 were at 2 North Bank Street. From 1839 he assumed the general title of Musical Instrument Maker. He retired in 1866, having been succeeded in his profession by his sons John (1833-1904) and Robert (1835-1911), who continued the business, moving to 497 Lawnmarket in 1911. Alexander Glen worked as a furniture dealer and bagpipe maker until he died in 1873, after which his son David (b. 1850) remained at 8 Greenside Place until the workshop was closed down and incorporated into his cousins' business of "J. & R. Glen", which later moved a few hundred yards further down the High Street.[5]

The harps made by Robert Glen were wire-strung and of fine craftsman-ship. At least two still survive. One is in the Highland Folk Museum in Kingussie. It was brought to Morley's, the harp makers in London, in about 1934, "by a man who refused to give any information about it". It was supposed at that time to have dated from about 1650, but is now thought to be one of Robert Glen's copies. At least one other Glen harp is known to be in private hands in England.

Another clarsach was believed to have been acquired in about 1900 by Colonel Edward Malcolm of Poltalloch in Edinburgh, author of a collection of Highland Lore and Legend. This harp is of less competent construction and has suffered subsequently from having its strings fixed to the sound board with large screws. It is again wire-strung, and has been carved with the initials "A.R.L.". The badge on the copper mount also shows the Lindsay crest and motto, so it is more likely to have been made for a member of that family, rather than to be one of those commissioned from Glen by Lord Archibald Campbell. The maker is not known. This harp was purchased on the demolition of Poltalloch House in 1959 and gifted to the West Highland Museum in Fort William by Miss Heloise Russell-Fergusson. She was a noted player of the small harp in the 1940's, in a romantic style, who was proclaimed "Bardess Scotia" after performing at a festival in Brittany.[6]

Lord Archibald also ordered six harps to be made by Robert Buchanan, a piano dealer in Glasgow. He had constructed a harp for his wife, Jessie MacLachlan, who sang to its accompaniment at the 1893 Mod at Oban. It appears that Buchanan had at least some of the harps for Lord Archibald made by H.D. Harnaack, a harp maker in London, whose business was subsequently taken over by J. Morley. These instruments also resembled the Queen Mary harp but had gut strings, and the rounded back of modern pedal harp construction. They also included small brass semi-tone blades at the top of each string to enable the player to change key without re-tuning. Several of these harps are still in existance.

Revival of interest in Gaelic song in the early years of the 20th century was due, to a large extent, to the activities of Marjorie Kennedy-Fraser. She collected a large number of Gaelic songs in the Highlands, and published them in several volumes as "Songs of the Hebrides" (1909 et seq.). The arrangements of the melodies, usually with piano accompaniment, were very different from the original versions, and the words were often adapted — sometimes, indeed, Mrs. Kennedy-Fraser composed her own English words to the tunes, which were then translated into Gaelic by her collaborator, Dr. Kenneth MacLeod. They have merit as art-songs, though not as representations of the direct oral tradition. Her daughter, Patuffa, took up the small harp in 1914 with the intention of using it to accompany her mother's songs, and made her own arrangements for these. She travelled widely throughout Scotland and abroad, playing to the troops in France during the 1914-18 war, in many of the capitals of Europe, and in the United States. The instrument on which she played was a small gut-strung Celtic harp of the type made for the Irish market since 1890 by George Morley of London. Patuffa requested that it should not be painted with shamrocks!

The "clarsach" competitions at the National Mod had been abandoned since 1909 because of a lack of entrants, but renewed enthusiasm began in 1922, when Mrs. Duncan MacLeod donated five harps to An Commun Gaidhealach, to be lent to potential competitors. These may have been harps made by Robert Buchanan. The numbers of players began to rise, and after the Mod of 1931, at the suggestion of Mrs. MacLeod, a meeting was held at the home of Mrs. Ingrams in Dingwall to consider the inauguration of a society for the preservation and re-introduction of the clarsach — the ancient Celtic harp. There were 14 people present, including Mrs. Hilda Mary Campbell of Airds and Miss Heloise Russell-Fergusson. Mrs. Campbell of Airds was proposed as President and took the chair. The meeting decided that a Society should be formed and called "Comunn nan Clarsairean" (The Society of Harpers). The first membership form was headed "Comunn na Clarsaich Albannaich" (The Caledonian Harp Society) and the aims and objects of the Society were set out as the preservation of the Clarsach (the ancient Celtic harp) and its re-instatement in the national life of the Gaelic-speaking people. Lady Elspeth Campbell of Inveraray Castle accepted the invitation to become Chieftainess, and in 1932 the Society notes the generous offer from Lady Elspeth of two clarsachs to be lent to intending competitors at the Mod. These are likely to have been two of the instruments commissioned by her husband, Lord

Archibald. The word "Albannaich" was dropped from the Society's title as being unnecessary, and Mrs. Patuffa Kennedy-Fraser Hood was proposed as the first Honorary Life Member.

Also in 1932, Mr. Henry Briggs, a violin maker of Glasgow, brought the first specimens of harps that he had made, which met with the Society's approval. Attempts to make harps available to those who wished to learn to play, included approaches to An Comunn Gaidhealach for co-operation in the use of their harps. An Comunn gave permission to use their harps (one of those donated by Mrs. MacLeod is unaccounted for) when they were not required by members of Gaelic choirs. The rules for the loan of harps stipulated that after one month a report should be made on the player's progress, which should be repeated after three months, and a promise given by the student to compete at the next Mod. After the Mod all harps were to be returned for re-allocation. The first harps were loaned to Duncan Morrison and Ian Smith in Stornoway, and Betsy MacLeod in Skye. A Summer School was held in Portree in 1933 and another proposed for Arisaig the following year. Harps were being offered to the Society's members by Mr. Briggs from £10.10s. each; by a Mr. Thompson of Glasgow from £10.00 each; and by Morley at £8.10s. if three harps were purchased, or £7.10s. each if six were bought.

In 1933 the Annual Report of the Clarsach Society published its aims as being:

1. To promote and encourage the playing of the Clarsach; 2. To preserve its place in the National life of Scotland, especially among Gaelic-speaking people; and 3. To uphold its title to be the true and most ancient instrumental accompaniment of Gaelic song.

Over the subsequent years, which are fully documented in a history of the Society, commissioned to mark its 60th anniversary, Comunn na Clarsaich has certainly succeeded in widening the appeal of the small gut-strung harp. This growth is due, without doubt, to the hard work and enthusiasm of teachers such as Kathleen Barry Milner in Plockton and Jean Campbell in Edinburgh. The Society now has around one hundred instruments on hire to learners, and a number of fine craftsmen are fully engaged in producing harps. Not every scheme has met with success — an attempt to introduce the instrument to soldiers of the Cameron Highlanders (the regiment of General Sir Philip Christison, who succeeded Mrs. Campbell of Airds as President of the Society) failed after a few years. Harp Festivals, Mods, Summer Schools and teaching courses have flourished, however, and continue to expand the number of players in Scotland and abroad.[7] In addition, pedal-harp has continued to be taught at the Royal Scottish Academy of Music and Drama in Glasgow, notably by Sancia Pielou.

In 1972 Sir Philip suggested that the Constitution would have to be brought up to date, which resulted in an alteration to the third of the Society's published objectives. This now reads — "To uphold its title to be the true and most ancient instruments of Scotland". This marks a notable shift in emphasis in the role of the harp, away from its initial, primarily Highland association, and from its role in the accompaniment of Gaelic song. Several styles of playing have developed, ranging from a basically classical approach, which owes much to the musical conventions of the "improved" harp of 19th century drawingrooms, to one influenced by modern 20th century classical music and jazz. Since the 1970's a style of instrumental playing has also appeared, which is now accepted by other performers in the field as being in the mainstream of contemporary Scottish traditional music.

In almost every case, it is the gut-strung small harp which is used, rather than the wire-strung clarsach. It is not the intention of this book, as a history, to make a value judgement on the quality of the music played at this time. By presenting some of the wealth of background information which has lain buried for so many years, it will perhaps stimulate players of the harp or of the clarsach to pursue their own links with the traditions of the past. We have seen the instruments change and adapt, from the earliest Pictish harps and later gut-strung harps of the Lowlands and Eastern Scotland, or the metal-strung clarsach of the Gaels, taking a valued place in expressing Scottish culture, whether at the Courts of Kings, in the great houses of the aristocracy, or the households of the Highland chiefs. We have seen the different harps used as an essential element in the performance of Gaelic bardic poetry, or as the likely accompaniment for narrative Scots ballads. They have played solo or ensemble music, in the hands of highly trained professionals, itinerant minstrels or enthusiastic amateurs. We have seen the disappearance of the Lowland gut-strung harp, and the death of the great Highland wire-strung clarsach, and the re-introduction of both instruments. The adaptability, particularly of gut-strung harps, is indeed both an advantage and a danger. With knowledge of the harp's past function, background and repertoire, each player may be able to reach truly creative conclusions about the music that they wish to play — preserving the essential character of gut- or wire-strung harp, while extending its potential. New material is constantly coming forward, and further research will no doubt throw fresh light on the music which has sounded quietly but strongly over the centuries. Any evidence is to be welcomed. An informed view of the history of the Scottish harps may help to banish the sentimental "Celtic Twilight" which all too often blurs the dignity and nobility that both these instruments have possessed, as part of the nation's cultural life, during the past one thousand years.

APPENDIX A: HARP MEASUREMENTS

Measurements for the Queen Mary and Lamont Harps were supplied by the National Museums of Scotland. Those for the Trinity College Harp were compiled with the help of Mike Billinge. The Trinity College Harp has undergone numerous restorations over the course of time, therefore to enable comparisons to be made between the three harps, the measurements of the Trinity College Harp are an attempt to reflect its probable original dimensions.

	Queen Mary	Lamont	Trinity College
Total height	$30^3/4"$	$37^1/2"$	33"
Total width	$18^1/2"$	20"	$18^1/2"$
Length of arm	$17^1/4"$	$19^1/4"$	18"
Length of pillar to arm	$27^5/8"$	29"	$27^3/8"$
Thickness of pillar at arm	$1^3/8"$	$1^1/8"$	
Thickness of pillar at bottom joint	$1^1/4$-$1^1/2"$	$1^1/4"$	
Thickness at centre	$2^3/8"$	$3^3/8"$	$2^3/4"$
Thickness of arm	$1^1/2$-$1^1/4"$	2"	
Width of soundbox, top	$4^1/4"$	4"	$4^3/4"$
Width of soundbox, bottom	$11^1/2"$	$16^3/4"$	$12^1/2"$
Depth of soundbox at side	4"	4"	$3^3/8"$
Depth of soundbox in centre	5"	$4^3/4"$	4"
Length of soundbox	$25^1/2"$	$29^7/8"$	$28^1/4"$
Thickness of soundbox	$^1/4$-$^5/16"$	$^{11}/32$-$^3/8"+$	$^1/4"$
Width of pillar, top	3"	$3^1/8"$	$3^5/8"$
Width of pillar, bottom	$3^1/8"$	$3^3/8"$	
Number of strings	30	32	30
Sounding string lengths	$2^7/8$-$23^7/8"$	2-$24^1/4"$	$2^7/8$-$24^5/8"$
Spacing of strings	$^7/16"$	$^1/2"$	$^7/16"$
Length of tuning pins	3-$3^1/8"$	$3^{11}/16"$	$3^1/4"$
Width of centre strings	$1^3/16$-$1^5/8"$	$1^3/8"$	
Diameter of holes	$^{19}/32$-$^{11}/16"$ $1^1/8"$	$^7/8"$ + —	

Construction entirely of hardwood - has been identified as hornbeam (Queen Mary and Lamont Harps).

Soundbox carved from one block, except for back piece.

Harp donated by Miss Russell-Fergusson to the Highland Folk Museum, Kingussie. According to a note in the Russell-Fergusson Collection in the Mitchell Library, Glasgow, the harp was brought to Mr. J.G. Morley, Harpmaker, London, about 1934 by a man who refused to give any information about it. Francis Collinson in his "The Traditional and National Music of Scotland" states that this harp was one of those made by Glen, although it is not clear on what authority he bases this claim.

The harp is certainly a reproduction with a constructed sound box, the soundboard being shaped over wood bridges approximately 3"-4" apart. There are 28 pins with a hole for a 29th. At the time of measuring, there were 15 strings intact but sufficient remained of the others to measure all bar one.

Although some of the gauges are used out of position, it seems clear that the instrument was strung using just four basic gauges of wire*.

1.	0.0164 inches	16.	0.0167 inches
2.	0.0166"	17.	0.0179"
3.	0.0169"	18.	String too short to measure
4.	0.0166"	19.	0.0125 inches
5.	0.0166"	20.	0.0191"
6.	0.0166"	21.	0.0164"
7.	0.0174"	22.	0.0192"
8.	0.0167"	23.	0.0192"
9.	0.0165"	24.	0.0191"
10.	0.0170"	25.	0.0195"
11.	0.0166"	26.	0.0305"
12.	0.0125"	27.	0.0305"
13.	0.0125"	28.	0.0305"
14.	0.0173"	29.	No pin
15.	0.0176"		

* Wire gauge 6, 7, 8 and 12

APPENDIX B
FAMILY TREE OF THE ROBERTSONS OF LUDE

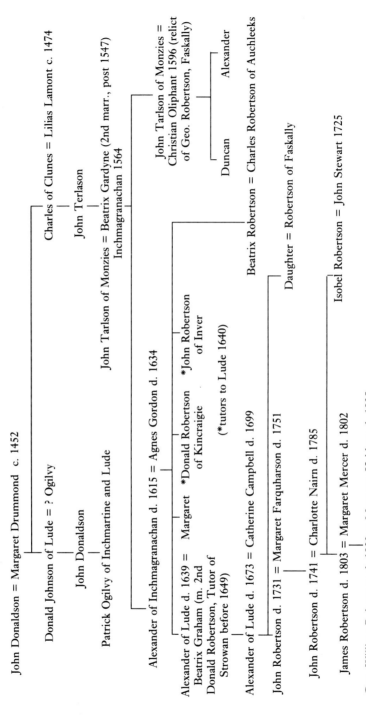

APPENDIX C

FAMILY TREE: ATHOLL/LENNOX/GORDON CONNECTIONS

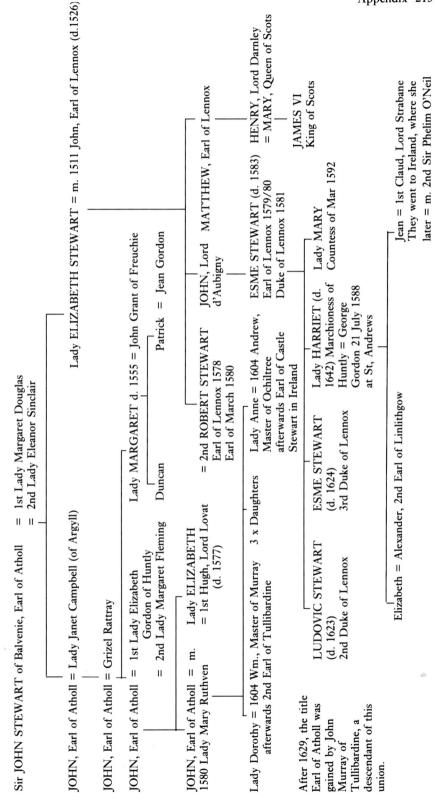

Sir JOHN STEWART of Balvenie, Earl of Atholl = 1st Lady Margaret Douglas
= 2nd Lady Eleanor Sinclair

Lady ELIZABETH STEWART = m. 1511 John, Earl of Lennox (d.1526)

JOHN, Earl of Atholl = Lady Janet Campbell (of Argyll)

JOHN, Earl of Atholl = Grizel Rattray

JOHN, Earl of Atholl = 1st Lady Elizabeth Gordon of Huntly
= 2nd Lady Margaret Fleming

Lady MARGARET d. 1555 = John Grant of Freuchie

Duncan   Patrick = Jean Gordon

JOHN, Earl of Atholl = m.   Lady ELIZABETH
1580 Lady Mary Ruthven   = 1st Hugh, Lord Lovat
(d. 1577)

= 2nd ROBERT STEWART
Earl of Lennox 1578
Earl of March 1580

JOHN, Lord
d'Aubigny

MATTHEW, Earl of Lennox

HENRY, Lord Darnley
= MARY, Queen of Scots

JAMES VI
King of Scots

Lady Dorothy = 1604 Wm., Master of Murray
afterwards 2nd Earl of Tullibardine

3 x Daughters

Lady Anne = 1604 Andrew,
Master of Ochiltree
afterwards Earl of Castle
Stewart in Ireland

ESME STEWART (d. 1583)
Earl of Lennox 1579/80
Duke of Lennox 1581

Lady MARY
Countess of Mar 1592

Lady HARRIET (d.
1642) Marchioness of
Huntly = George
Gordon 21 July 1588
at St, Andrews

After 1629, the title
Earl of Atholl was
gained by John
Murray of
Tullibardine, a
descendant of this
union.

LUDOVIC STEWART
(d. 1623)
2nd Duke of Lennox

ESME STEWART
(d. 1624)
3rd Duke of Lennox

Elizabeth = Alexander, 2nd Earl of Linlithgow

Jean = 1st Claud, Lord Strabane
They went to Ireland, where she
later = m. 2nd Sir Phelim O'Neil

APPENDIX D
HARP TUNES AND THEIR SOURCES

This list includes tunes known to have been composed for the harp and clarsach, tunes known to have been played by harpers, and other tunes linked with the harp by title or melodic characteristics. It is by no means complete, since any of the song-tunes in bardic metre are likely to have been accompanied on the clarsach, but it may provide an indication of the basic repertoire of harpers between the late 16th and early 18th centuries. Alternative titles, or titles of variants, are given in brackets.

Skene M.S. (N.L.S., Adv M.5. 2.15)
c. 1615-1625
    Port Ballangowne
    The Keiking Glasse

Straloch M.S. (lost; partial transcription by Farquhar Graham)
1627-29
    Ane Port
    Port Preist (Port Robart)
    Port Jean Kinsay (or Lindsay)
    Port Rorie Dall (Port Ballangowne)
    Ane Port (Cumha Peather Ruairi)

Wemyss Lute Book (N.L.S. M.S. 2085)
1644
    Port Robart (Port Preist)
    Irish Port
    Da miche manum

Blaikie M.S. (lost; partial transcription)
1683 + 1692
    King James' March to Ireland (Lochaber no more)

Leyden M.S. (copy in Advocates' Library)
c. 1692
    King James' March to Ireland

Crawford of Balcarres M.S. (N.L.S. Acc. 9769)
1692-4
    Da Mihi Manum
    Horseman's Port (x3)
    Port Atholl (I;x4)
    Port Gordon (I)
    The Duke's Port (The Duke of Lennox Port)

Agnes Hume M.S. (Faculty of Adv. 5.2.17)
1704
    Mary Scott (x2; Planxty Scott)

Skene Fiddle M.S. (N.L.S. 5.2.21)
c. 1717
    No 17 — Unnamed (Lochaber no more)
    The Duke of Lennox Port (The Duke's Port)

James Oswald — The Caledonian Pocket Companion
1745-59
    Gilly Cranky
    Port Patrick
    Carrill's Lament
    Lude's Supper
    Lude's Lament
    Port Gordon (II; Bunting 'Purth Clairseach', and Dow)
    Lochaber no more
    The Royall Lament
    Currallan's Lament
    Carland's Devotion
    Da Mihi Manum
    Port Athol (II)
    Rory Dall's Port
    Failtene Moisq (Port More)
    Mary Scot (Planxty Scott)
And several other harp tunes with Irish connections, e.g. Gallaways Lament, McDonogh's Lamentation and The Fairy Queen.

MacFarlan M.S. (N.L.S. M.S. 2084 & 2085)
c. 1740
    Cumh Easpuic Earra-ghaoidheal
    The Royal Lament
    Failte na miosg (Port More)
    Da mihi Manum
    Killicranky
    Galloways Lament
    Mary Scott

N.L.S. M.S. 3091 "Copied from Bremner's Reels 1759"
1765?
    Port Patrick

Daniel Dow — Collection of Ancient Scots Music
1776
    Cumh Ioarla Wigton — Lament for the Earl of Wigtown
    Port Lennox
    Port Atholl (I)
    Cumh Peathar Ruairi — Rorie Dall's Sister's Lament
    Da mihi Manum
    Port Gordon (I)
    The Terror Death — s eagal leam a mbas
    Fuadh na mfilairan — the Fidler's Contemt
    Cumh Easbig Earraghaal
    Suipear thighear Leoid — Lude's Super

Seaforth's Salutation — Failte Mhic Caoinnich
Failte Mhic Dhonail Ghuirm — McDonald of the Isles
Salutation
Failte bheag Mhic Leoid — McLeod's less Salutation
Failte Loch Ioall — Loch Isle's Salutation
Failte Mhic Cai — Lord Rae's Salutation
Mr. Campbell of Achnabreack's Salutation — Gradb
Dhoudhaill oig

John Bowie — Collection of Strathspey Reels and Country Dances
1789
Air by Fingal I
Air by Fingal II
Air by Fingal III
McLoud's Salute
Port Lennox
The Battle of Sheriff Moor
Port Gordon (I)
Port Atholl (I)

MacLean-Clephane M.S. (N.L.S. M.S. 14949 A & B)
1816
(Section B) Port 1st (Keiking Glasse)
Port 2nd (Port Gordon I)
Port 3rd
Port 4th
Port 5th
Port 6th (Port Ballangowne)
Port 7th (Is eagal leam am bas)
Jig
Port 8th
Port 9th
Port 10th

Also 36 tunes from the repertoire of Echlin O Cathain including 'Port Gordon', 'Failte na miosg', etc, described as "Originally Highland Scottish but suited to the harp by Carolan" or "by O Kane".

Fiddle Section   Rorie Dall's Port

Section A
1808-25   Failte Chlarsaich
Ancient Harp Air (I; Is eagal leam am bas)
Ancient Harp Music (II)
Ancient Harp Air (III; Lude's Supper)
Cuachag na 'n Craobh — Ancient Harp Air

Patrick MacDonald — Collection of Highland Vocal Airs
1784
Contains a number of melodies and bardic song tunes described by its editor as "probably being the most genuine remains of the ancient harp music of the Highlands".

A Collection of Irish Airs and Jigs with Variations adapted for Pianoforte, Violin and Violoncello by John Murphy performer on the Union Pipes at Eglinton Castle c. 1810
>Port Gordon (II)

Simon Fraser
1816
>Grant of Sheuglie's contest betwixt his Violin, Pipes and Harp — Mairi Nighean Dheorsa

Angus Fraser M.S. (E.U.L.)

>An caoineadh Rioghail — The Royal Lament
>Craobh nan teud — The Tree of Strings (The Harp Tree/Corrienessan's Salute)
>Easbuig Earraghaidheal — The Bishop of Argyle
>Far-fuadach a chlarsair—The Harper's dismissal (Oran do MhacLeoid Dhun Bheagain)
>Fonn Marbhrann nan teud — Air of the death elegy on the harp (Oran do Mac Leoid Dhun Bheagain)
>Rory Dall Morison (Jig)
>Sheuglie's Harp

Thomas Macindoe M.S. (Mitchell Library, Glasgow, 17361)
c. 1820
>Port Patrick

Angus MacDonald of N. Uist — published in "From the Farthest Hebrides"
1978
>(Said to be harp tunes)
>Oran do Alasdair Mac Cholla
>Caismeachd mhic Iain ic Sheamais
>Alasdair Mac Cholla

Tunes for Ruaidhri Dall Morison's songs, published in The Blind Harper, ed W. Matheson

>Oran do Iain Breac MacLeoid
>A 'Cheud Di-Luain de 'n Raithe
>Creach na Ciadaoin
>Oran do MhacLeoid Dhun Bheagain
>Feill nan Crann

See also tunes in 'Eachann Bacach and the Other MacLean Poets, C. O Baoill; "Bardachd Shilis na Ceapaich — Poems and Songs by Silis MacDonald", C. O Baoill.

APPENDIX E

This list gives all the place-names currently known to the authors with, where applicable, earliest known record and Ordnance Survey map reference numbers.

Names				O.S. Map Ref.
Harperland	nr. Dundonald, Ayrshire	1375	History of the County of Ayr, J. Paterson, Vol 2, p 14	NS 370357
Harpercroft	nr. Dundonald, Ayrshire	1690	"Dundonald" by J.H. Gillespie, Vol I, p 109, 153	NS 365327
Harperland	Spynie, nr. Elgin	1569	Register of the great seal, Vol IV, No 1886	Not identified
Harperland	now Slaphouse, nr. Ayr	1558	S.R.O. GD 1-122	NS 335198
Harperfield	nr. Lesmahagow	1516	S.R.O. GD 33/48	NS 890396
Harperfield (Harperdean)	Haddington	1454	Calendar of Yester Writs, p 108	NT 510750
Harperrig[1]	Midlothian	1573	Protocol Book of Gilbert Grote, ed W. Angus	NT 105612
Harperfwate	Eskdale	1376	Registrum Honoris de Morton, (Ban. Club), I	NY 282910
Harpertoun	Ednam, nr. Kelso	1675	Records of the Baron Court Book of Stitchill, p 78	NT 745394
Harplaw	nr. Largs	N/D		NS 215612
Harperlea	Kinross	N/D		NO 200252
Harperhall	Lanarkshire	N/D		NT 051434
Harper Ridge	North of Coldstream on south side of Tweed			NT 875416
Harpers Hill	Hillfort, nr. Gatehouse of Fleet		Historical Monuments Commission Inventory of Stewartry of Kirkcudbright, No 172	
Harperstone	Greenloaning, nr. Dunblane			NN 843044
Harper-akirhade[2]	Monikie Parish	1471	One of the marches of Affleck described in Register of the Great Seal, Vol II, No 1038	Not identified
Carn a' Chlarsaich	Atholl			NO 069780
Uchd a' Chlarsair	Atholl			NN 814817
Carn a Chlarsair	Muir of Ord			NH 530503
Kinkell Clarsach	Black Isle			NH 554545

Cnoc a Chlarsair	Balmacara	NG 815297
Camus a Chlarsair	Loch Torridon	NG 835550
Eilean a' Chlarsaire	Mull	NM 562297
Fanmor nan Clarsairean	Mull	NM 420444
Lag innis a' Chruiter	Dornie	NG 886268
Dun Cruit	Treshnish Isles	NM 275420
Auchlarsain	between Stuckscarden and Kilblane, Glenshira, nr. Inveraray	NN 125135

Notes and Queries, S.W.H.I.H.R., No XXI, August 1983, p 26

Cnoc a Chlarsair	on the estate of Kilcoy	) Transactions of the Gaelic Society of Inverness,
Harpers Window	in Duntulm Castle, Skye	) Vol V, 1875-6, p 76. None of these have been
Baile chlarsair	Skye	) located, however two of the names have appeared
Gualainn a Chlarsair	Snizort, Skye	) in an alternative source, see below.
Inneal a Chlarsair	Waternish, Skye	)
Guala-a-Chlarsair	Snizort, Skye	Place-Names of Skye, ed A.R. Forbes, p 209
Inneal-a-Chlarsair	Waternish, Skye	Place-Names of Skye, ed A.R. Forbes, p 219
Leac a Chlarsair[3]	Skye	Place-Names of Skye, ed A.R. Forbes, p 233

[1] East Cairn Hill above Harperrig was said formerly to have been called Harpers Hill. It is perhaps coincidence that an adjacent hill, Scald Law, can be translated as "Poets Hill" from old Norse 'Scald', a bard or reciter.

[2] The meaning of "akirhade" is obscure. It is, however, only a century after the recorded presence of "Ade (Adam) Chichariste" at Tillywhandland by Aberlemno, some ten miles further north, so may perhaps represent a mangled scribal attempt to render a Gaelic place-name "achadhade", Adamsfield.

[3] This is probably the graveslab at Glasvin, Glendale

APPENDIX F
HARPERS

This list of harpers has been compiled from contemporary source material. It therefore excludes the following categories:

a) Those musicians whose names have survived in later tradition but for whom there is no firm contemporary evidence.

b) People called Harper who were clearly practising another profession, not that they had necessarily ceased to play the harp.

c) That large number of contemporary references to harpers which fail to give the musician's name.

The list is thus far from being definitive, especially as it is dependant upon the survival of contemporary source material, for which some areas of Scotland are particularly deficient. However, as an understatement of the total number of Harpers it still provides a hint of the importance of the harp in Scotland's musical tradition.

Adam of Lennox	fl 1200-1260	The Chronicle of Melrose, ed A.O. Anderson
Michael (Cithariste) of Carrick	fl circa 1300	Edinburgh University Library, Laing Charters
Patrick)	fl circa 1346	Box 48 No 1869
Andrew) sons of above		"
Duncan McCruiter son of Patrick	fl circa 1385	E.U.L. Laing Charters Box 48 No 1870
William le Harper to Wm de St Clair	fl circa 1285	Records of Wardrobe and House Hold 1285-86, ed B. Byerly and C. Byerly
William Cytharista, probably same as above		Chartulary of Neubotle, ed C. Innes, p 306
Elyas le Harper	1278 x 1296	Calendar of Documents Relating to Scotland, Vol 2, 28 and 224
William Le Harpur of la lawe (1)	1296	Ragman Rolls, printed in the above, p 201
Rogier le Harpur of Hom	"	Ragman Rolls, printed in the above, p 203
Robert le Harpur	"	Ragman Rolls, printed in the above, p 205
Johan le Harpur	"	Ragman Rolls, printed in the above, p 206
Uctins le Harpur (2)	1296	Ragman Rolls, printed in the above, p 208
Ughtred le Harpur	1296	Roll of Esteats, printed in the above, p 225
John le Harpur of Saulton	1296	Roll of Esteats, printed in the above, p 226
James de Coupen	1290 x 1306	Menestrellorum Multitudo, p 77-79, ed C. Bullock-Davies
Thomas Harper (Cithariste)	1315 x 1321	The Register of the Great Seal of Scotland Vol I No 65
Thomas Harper (Citharista) (3)	1328	Exchequer Rolls, Vol I, cxviii
William the English Harper	1360	Exchequer Rolls, Vol 2, 12

Name	Date	Source
(Willelmo, sithariste Anglico)	1358	Exchequer Rolls, Vol I, 559
Andree Harper Strathern	1398 x 1400	Early Records of Aberdeen, ed W.C. Dickinson, p 73
Andrea Harpar Aberdeen	1398 x 1400	Early Records of Aberdeen, ed W.C. Dickinson, p 87, 90
Meg of Abernethy, Harper	1398 x 1400	Early Records of Aberdeen, ed W.C. Dickinson, p 103, 181, 226, 237
William Harper	c. 1360	Index Records of Charters, ed Wm Robertson, p 38
Ade Chichariste	"	Index Records of Charters, ed Wm Robertson, p 56
Nicholas Chicharist		
Joh'i Harpour (of John de Streuelyn)	1357	Extracts From the Account Rolls of the Abbey of Durham, ed The Surtees Soc., p 559
Hugh Harper	1371	The Earls of Cromertie, ed W. Fraser, Vol II, p 320
Adam Harpar	1431	S.R.O. B 65/22 (St Andrews)
Eugenio Klerscharch	1434	Highland Papers, ed J.R.N. Macphail, II, p 175, 177
Duncanum Clarscheouch	1438	Exchequer Rolls, Vol V, p 57
Giolla Criost Bruilingeach	1430 x 1458	Book of the Dean of Lismore
Alan (and his father)	15th C	Grave Slab, Keills, Argyle
John Hathvy	1465	E.U.L. Laing Charters, Box 11, No 364
Thomas Yester	1471	Exchequer Rolls, Vol 8, p 30
Thomas Wardlaw	1458 x 1478	Exchequer Rolls, Vol 6 - 8
Martin MacBhreatnaigh	1471 x 1498	Exchequer Rolls, Vol 8 - 10, and Treasurers Accounts
Pate Harper	1494	Treasurers Accounts
James Mylsone	1496	Treasurers Accounts
Fowlis	1496	Treasurers Accounts
John Harper with ane hand	1497	Treasurers Accounts
John Harper	1503	Calendar of Writs of Munro of Foulis, No 34
Sande (Alexander) Harper	1497	Treasurers Accounts
Pate harper clarscha	1501	Treasurers Accounts
Hew Brabener	1503	Treasurers Accounts
Bragman Harper	1505	Treasurers Accounts
John MacBhreatnaigh	1498	Registrum Secreti Sigilli Regum Scotorum, Vol I, p 30
Rolland MacBhreatnaigh	1505 x 1513	Registrum Secreti Sigilli Regum Scotorum, Vol I, p 173
Adam Dickson	1508	T.A.
Duncan MacGhille Sheanaich (4)	1456	Acts of the Lords of the Isles, ed J. Munro and R.W. Munro, p 92
Muireach MacGhille Sheanaich	1505 x 1528	Exchequer Rolls, Vol 12 - 15

Thomas McAngus	1533	R.S.S.R.S. Vol II, p 212
James Lawson	1539	R.S.S.R.S., Vol II, p 503
Robert Clairsair Lude (4)	1512 x 1540	Book of the Dean of Lismore
Braane McVicar (4)	1512 x 1540	Book of the Dean of Lismore
Thomas Clarsair Mhic Dhughaill (4)	1512 x 1540	Book of the Dean of Lismore
Henry Philip	1506	T.A.
John Haislet	1504 x 1526	A History of Paisley, W.H. Metcalfe, p 122
Donald Hughson	1516	S.R.O. GD 1/945/2 (Caithness)
Dougal Herper	1530	Inventory of Lamont Papers, p 39
Dougal Herperson	1560	Inventory of Lamont Papers, 74
Finlay Roy Harper	1568	Inventory of Lamont Papers, p 86
Jernan Harper	1526	Argyle Transcripts
Robert Galbrayth	1574	T.A.
- Caldell	d. 1594	Edinburgh Burgh Records
Robert MacMillan	d. 1597	Register of Testaments
Andro Callum	d. 1611	Register of Testaments
David MacFeye	1585	Book of the Thanes of Cawdor, ed C. Innes, p 187
Rannald M'Alaster	1596	Highland Papers, ed J.R.N. Macphail, Vol 3, p 78
Anthony McEwin	1588	S.R.O. GD 132/25
Donald MacKean	d. 1602	Account of Earldom of Sutherland, R. Gordon
James Gordon	1612	Glenluce, see text p 96
Mulleachan	1620	The Chiefs of Grant, W. Fraser, Vol 3, p 326
Alastair Reid	d 1639	Chronicles of Atholl and Tullibardine, see text p 149
Murrioch McO'Shennog	1625 x 1636	E.U.L. Microfilm Argyle Transcripts
John Garve MacLean of Coll	1600 x 1685	N.L.S. MS 28.3.12
Dougall Harper alias Mackalaster	d 1646	Inventory of Lamont Papers, p 224
John McEvin	1670	Lude Barony Court Bk, see text p 74
Ralph Potts	d 1661	Holyrood Kirk Session Records, see text p97
Charles Robertson of Auchleeks	1600 x 1640	See text p 149
Harie McGrath	1627	Highland Papers, ed J.R.N. Macphail, Vol I, p 115
William Monteith of Randieford	1620	See text p97
Donald McEntannachie	1685	S.R.O. GD 50/189
Adam Smith	d 1664	Chronicles of the Frasers, J. Fraser, p 453

William Boyd (5)	d 1624	An Historical Account of the MacDōnalds of Antrim, ed G. Hill, p 392
Walter Kennedy (5)	1624	"
- MacNeil (Mull)	1674	Highland Papers, ed J.R.N. Macphail, Vol I, p 281
Neil Campbell	1671	Entries Relating To Campbells in Sheriff Ct Bks of Perthshire, ed D. Campbell, Vol 2, p 107
Duncan McIndeor	d 1694	See text p 119
Roderick Dall Morison	1656 x 1712	The Blind Harper, W. Matheson
Alexander Menzies	d 1705	See text p 143
Daniel Melvile	1709	S.R.O. CH 2/121/7, p 144
James Robertson alias Clarsair	1709	Chronicles of Atholl and Tullibardine families, ed John 7th Duke of Atholl, see text
George Clarsair	1705	"
Duncan Clarsair	1706	"
John Robertson	1709	"
John Robertson	1713	"
John Robertson of Lude	1731	S.R.O. GD 38 and GD 132
Alexander McFarland	1705	Described as "intended harper" in Rothesay Parish Records, ed H. Paton, p 191
Lachlan Dall	d circa 1721-27	Bardachd Shilis Na Ceapaich, ed C. O'Baoill
Murdoch MacDonald	d circa 1739	See text p 162
Grant of Shewglie	d 1746	See text p 153
William McMurchy	d circa 1778	See text p 163

(1) See J.A. Stevenson and R.M. Wood, Scottish Heraldic Seals, 398. "S' Oting le Harp'e"
(2) See J.A. Stevenson and R.M. Wood, Scottish Heraldic Seals, 398. "Walran le Harpeur"
(3) Possibly The Thomas Harper rebel in England 1344, Acts of David II, ed B. Webster, 120.
(4) For a full list of the MacGhille Sheanaich family and other harpers in the Book of the Dean of Lismore, see J. Bannerman "The Clarsach and the Clairsair" and K. Sanger "The McShannons of Kintyre".
(5) Both Scots from Ayrshire who settled in Ulster (at Dunluce), but retained their original lands in Scotland

References

Chapter 1

1   "A Morality Representing the State of a Kingdom by the Figure of a Harp", from the Liber Pluscardenis, ed. F.J.H. Skene (Edinburgh 1877-80) Book XI, 392-400. Probably written circa 1461 by Maurice Buchanan and based on an earlier history by Walter Bower. It has been suggested that the poem may be the work of Robert Henryson (c1430-1500) cf J. Brown ed. Scottish Society in the Fifteenth Century, 200. Carp = sing; suth = true; muth = out of tune; thole = suffer; traist = tried; wyt = blame; bent = begin to play; quyte = even; ay sua quhil = until.

2   cf ch. 10 p

3   J. Carmichael Watson, ed, Gaelic Songs of Mary MacLeod, (1982), 63.

4   A. Carmichael, Carmina Gadelica, Vol 1 (1900) Intro XXX.

5   K. MacLeod, Note on Musical Instruments in Gaelic Folk Tales, in the Celtic Review, Vol VIII, (1912), 341-342.

6   Sound Archive, School of Scottish Studies, (S.A. 195152), Collected from Hugh MacRae, Skye, by J. Ross.

7   O. Swire, The Highlands and their Legends, 218.

8   W. Stokes, ed, Trip Life, 1, 204-5; A.P. Smyth, Warlords and Holy Men, Scotland AD 80-1000, (1984), 81-83.

9   Buchans Ballads of the North of Scotland, II, 201.

10 W. Scott, Minstrelsy of the Scottish Border, II, 251.

11 cf chapter 10, p

12 J.F. Campbell, West Highland Tales, Vol III, (1890), 98.

13 M. Stewart, King Orphius, in Scottish Studies, Vol 17 Part 1, (1973) 1-16.

14 Auchinleck M.S. W.4.1 (Advocates Library, Edinburgh)

15 Ashmole M.S. 61, Bodleian Library.

16 F.J. Child, The English and Scottish Popular Ballads, I, 2-7.

17 Recorded from Calum Johnson, Barra 1969, by A. Kinnaird

18 W. Seton, R.W. Chambers and E.C. Batho, ed, The Chronicles of Scotland, compiled by Hector Boece, Translated into Scots by John Bellenden, 1513, Vol I, (1938), 249.

19 cf chapter 9 p

20 J.F. Campbell, op cite, Vol II, 464.

21 J.F. Campbell, ibid, Vol II, 466.

22 F.J. Child, op cite, Vol II, 139.

23 F.J. Child, ibid, Vol IV, 16.

24 P.S. Shaw, E.B. Lyle ed, The Greig-Duncan Folksong Collection, Vol 2, 290.

25 F.J. Child, op cite, Vol I, 435.

26 P. Underwood, Gazeteer of Scottish and Irish Ghosts, 120.

27 M. Martin, A Description of the Western Islands of Scotland, ed D.J. MacLeod, (1934), 334-335.

28 F.J. Child, op cite, Vol I, 118.

29 L.C. Wimberly, Folklore in the English and Scottish Ballads, 68.

30 J.F. Campbell, op cite, Vol I, 297.

Chapter 2
1   A. MacDonald, Music in the Home Life of the Gael, Transactions of The Gaelic Society of Inverness Vol 33 (1925-1927), 280.
2   F.T. Wainwright ed, The Problem of the Picts, (1980) 129-166; C. Renfrew, Archaeology and Language, (1987), 226-229.
3   C. Sachs, The History of Musical Instruments (1940), 464-465.
4   J. Rimmer, The Irish Harp, (1977), 20; R. and M. Bruce-Mitford, The Sutton Hoo Lyre, Beowulf, and the Origins of the Frame Harp, in Antiquity, XLIV, 1970, 7-13.
5   J. Rimmer, 17; For illustration of the Irish carvings see; H. Richardson and John Scarry, An Introduction to Irish High Crosses (1990), Carndonagh plate 29, Castledermot North Cross pl 38, South Cross pl 40, Clonmacnois pl 65, Donaghmore pl 68, Durrow pl 88, Graiguenamanagh pl 108, Kells, South Cross pl 114, West Cross pl 118, Market Cross pl 122, Kinnitty pl 131 (possible), Monasterboice pl 159, Ullard pl 198, and M. Ryan ed, The Treasures of Ireland — Irish Art 3000 BC — 1500 AD (1983), 66, Shrine of the Stowe Missal detail of the sides.
6   The Royal Commission of the Ancient and Historical Monuments of Scotland, Argyll, Vol 4, Iona, 18-19, 193-197, 204-208.
7   R. Rensch, The Harp (1969), 13-16; Harps and Harpists, (1989), 30-33; R. and M. Bruce-Mitford, ibid, 11-12, where a North British, in particular a Northumbrian origin for the "true harp" is suggested.
8   The Royal Commission on the Ancient and Historical Monuments of Scotland, Argyll, Vol 4, Iona, 102, 222 No 149.
9   J. Hunt, Irish Medieval Figure Sculpture, (1974), No 120 and Plate 181; J. Carney ed, Poems on The Butlers (1945), viii — ix.
10 The Royal Commission on the Ancient and Historical Monuments of Scotland, Skye and the Small Isles, 151.
11 K.A. Steer and J.W.M. Bannerman, Late Medieval Monumental Sculpture in the West Highlands, (1977), 146.
12 A.O.H. Jarman, 'Telyn a Chrwth', in Llen Cymru 6 : 154-75.
13 E.Jones, Musical and Poetical Relicks of the Welsh Bards (1825), 102-103.
14 O. Ellis, The Story of the Harp in Wales, (1980), 15-17.
15 A.P. Smyth, Warlords and Holy Men, Scotland AD 80-1000, (1984); D. Brooke, St. Ninian and The Southern Picts, in Transactions of the Dumfriesshire and Galloway Natural History and Antiquarian Society, 21-42.
16 K. Jackson, The Gododdin, (1969) Appendix; M.P. McDiarmid, The Gododdin and Other Heroic Poems of Scotland, in J. Derrick McClure ed, Scotland And The Lowland Tongue, (1983), 1-7.
17 Stewart Collection, Works of the Highland Bard (1804), 397.
18 J.F. Campbell, West Highland Tales, Vol IV, 164.
19 A.P. Smyth, op cite, 26.
20 D. Brooke, op cite, 21-42.
21 K. Jackson, op cite, 47-67.
22 A.P. Smyth, op cite, 34-35, 216-218.

Chapter 3
1   J.L. Campbell and F. Collinson, ed, Hebridean Folksongs (1969), 93.
2   J.J. O'Meara ed, Gerald of Wales, The History and Topography of Ireland (1988), 99, 103-4; C. Page, Voices and Instruments of The Middle Ages, 228-231; R. Bartlett, Gerald of Wales 1146-1223, (1982). Gerald's praise of Irish music set against a distaste for all other things Irish is mirrored by a Scottish poem on the Highland Army quartered on the south west of Scotland in 1678. Set amidst a general disparagement of the Highland Host is the sole item of praise:

In nothing they're accounted sharp
Except in Bagpipe and in Harpe.
(In J. Elder, (1914), The Highland Host of 1678, Appendix 145-6, poem first printed in 1697).

3   A Buckley, What was the Tiompan, in Jahrbuch fur Musikalische Volks und Volkerkunde 9; 53-88.
4   Proceedings of The Society of Antiquaries of Scotland Vol 103 (1970-71), 104-107 and Plate 17.
5   A. Ross, The Folklore of the Scottish Highlands (1976), 37.
6   M. Remnant, English Bowed Instruments from Anglo -Saxon to Tudor Times, (1986), 42-55; R. Rensch, The Harp, (1971), 68.
7   B. Webster, The Acts of David II, 1329-71, No 102; J. Anderson, The Laing Charters, No 40, 69; K. Sanger, "Harperlands" in the Folk Harp Journal No 49, June 1985.
8   H. McGeown and G. Murphy, Giolla Brighde Albanach's Vision of Donnchadh Cairbreach O'Briain, in Eigse, Vol 7 (1953-55), 80-83.
9   E.C. Quiggin, Prolegomena to the Study of The Later Irish Bards 1200-1500, in Proceedings of The British Academy 1911-1912, 128; O. Bergin, Irish Bardic Poetry, (1974), 66-69.
10 J.R.N. MacPhail ed, Highland Papers, Vol ii, (1916), 175-176; The Exchequer Rolls of Scotland, Vol V, 56; Patent Roll 13 Henry VI art 86, Evidence for an earlier unfamiliarity with the new term of 'clarsair' occurs in Norman French written in 1366, about one hundred years after the first appearance of Scottish Galloglasses in Ireland; — "ministrels Irroies, cestascavoi Tympano fferdanes skelaghes Bablers Rymo clerez ne nullez autras ministrells". (cf The Statute of Kilkenny in H. Berry, Statutes and Ordinances and Acts of The Parliament of Ireland, 446-7).
11 J. Bannerman, The Clarsach and the Clarsair, in Scottish Studies, (1991), Vol 30, 3.
12 A. McKerral, West Highland Mercenaries in Ireland, in The Kintyre Antiquarian and Natural History Society Magazine, No 9, 5-15. Aed O'Connor King of Connacht was responsible for bringing the first Galloglass into Ireland, Aed's father in law was Mac Suibhne of Knapdale in Argyle. The total number of galloglass are unknown, however Professor MacNeill held the view that they constituted a considerable new element in the population of Ireland.
13 J. Rimmer, The Irish Harp, (1977), 40.
14 J. MacKay ed, More West Highland Tales from the Manuscripts of J.F. Campbell of Islay, (1940), 462-472.
15 C. Giblin ed, Franciscan Mission to Scotland, 53-55, (our thanks to Father J.M. Senes for the full translation of the original Latin text.)
16 For discussion of this subject see; — O. Bergin, Irish Bardic Poetry 3-22; G. Murphy, Bards and Filidh, in Eigse Vol 2 (1940) 200-207.
17 J. Maidment ed, Analecta Scotica, Vol I.
18 K.A. Steer and J.W.M. Bannerman, Late Medieval Monumental Sculpture in the West Highlands (1977), 32, 201-213; D. Thompson, Gaelic Learned Orders and Literati in Medieval Scotland, in Scottish Studies Vol 12, (1968), 72-75; K. Sanger, The MacShannons of Kintyre; Harpers to Tacksmen, in The Kintyre Antiquarian and Natural History Society Magazine No 28, 9-15.
19 D. Thompson, op cite, 69; W. Gillies, The Gaelic Poems of Sir Duncan Campbell of Glenorchy (II) in Scottish Gaelic Studies Vol 13 pt 2, (1981), 263-276; W.J. Watson ed, Scottish Verse from The Book of The Dean of Lismore (1978), 32-59; G. Murphy, Bards and Filidh, in Eigse Vol 2, (1940), 202.

Chapter 4

1   From "Thomas off Ersseldoune" Thornton MS. leaf 149, as given in F.J. Child "The English and Scottish Popular Ballads", 1882, 1, 326.

2   G. Lawson, An Anglo-Saxon harp and lyre of the ninth century, in D.R. Widdess and R.J. Wolpert, Music and Tradition, 229-444, (This article considers Masham solely in terms of Anglo-Saxon England, however the Masham area had been subject over this period to various overlords including the Scandinavian Kings of York, cf A.P. Smyth, Warlords and Holymen, (1984), for fuller discussion of this period from a northern viewpoint). Why the Germanic term Harp became transposed from the Anglo Saxon lyre to the triangular frame harp is not clear, however there is general agreement that this happened circa the 11-12th C. It is perhaps not unconnected with the linguistic and cultural changes that occurred after the Norman conquest of England in 1066.

3   D.E.R. Watt ed, Scotichronicon, Vol 2, Books III and IV (1989), 312-313.

4   C. Page, Voices and Instruments of the Middle Ages, (1987), 210-242.

5   A.O. Anderson ed, facsimilie of The Chronicle of Melrose, (1936), 121. There are a number of translations available, most notably that by J. Stevenson reprinted by Llanerch Press (1991). Curiously the translators have turned "motete", which is quite readable in the original, into "molete" in the English editions.

6   J. Stevenson ed, The Chronicle of Melrose, 88, 93; J. Campbell, Balmerino and its Abbey, 156.

7   D.S. Thomson, The MacMhurich Bardic Family, in The Transactions of the Gaelic Society of Inverness, Vol 43, (1960-68), 276-283.

8   W.J. Watson, ed Scottish Verse From The Book of The Dean of Lismore, 248-9. Identified possibly as Duncan 8th Earl of Lennox d? 1425, cf The Companion to Gaelic Scotland, ed D.S. Thomson, (1983), 65.

9   J. Major, Historia Britanniae, 34, where in the Latin text he uses the term "lyra". Later in Book VI when discussing the musical accomplishments of King James he uses "cithara". It is not clear whether he was trying to infer two different types of harp; For English translations see A. Constable, John Majors History of Greater Britain, (1892), 50; J. Gunn, An Historical Enquiry respecting The Performance on The Harp, (1807), 67.

10 K. Sanger, Harperlands, in the Folk Harp Journal No 49. June 1985, 39.

11 B. Byerly and C. Byerly ed, Records of the Wardrobe and Household -controllers book of necessary expenses, 1285-86, No 4348.

12 K. Sanger, Harperlands, in the Folk Harp Journal No 49, June 1985, 39-40; J.A. Stevenson and M. Wood, Scottish Heraldic Seals, 398; J. Stevenson ed, Historical Documents of Scotland, 197; J. Bain ed, Calendar of Documents Relating to Scotland Vol 2, 203, 205, 225.

13 G. Black, The Surnames of Scotland, 344; C. Innes, Origines Parochiales Scotiae Vol I, 111-2; T. Thomson, A. Macdonald and C. Innes ed, Registrum honoris de Morton, (1853), Vol I, LXXVI (Appendix). Among the Morton tenants in the Barony de Butill were "Thome filio Gilberti Waltero Harper et Patricio Walter" at Marnauch.

14 J. Bain ed, Calendar of Documents Relating to Scotland, Vol 2, 201, 226; Wm. Robertson, Index of Records of Charters Granted by David II between 1309-1413, 7 No 65, (This may be the same Thomas Harper who by 1344 was a rebel in England when his lands were forfeited. cf B. Webster ed, The Acts of David II, 1329-71, 120 No 80). A family of clerks and notars using the name Harper in Haddington can be traced from 1430 onwards. "Harperfeld" first appears in 1454, between 1524 and 1531 the name changed to "Harperdeyne" the name it has retained to date, cf C.C.H. Harvey and J. Macleod, Calendar of Writs preserved at Yester House 1166-1625, No 57, 67 A and B, 74, 108, 411, 482 and 522.

15 J. Bain ed, Calendar of Documents Relating to Scotland Vol 2, 189; The Exchequer Rolls of Scotland, (1878-1908), Vol 2, 12.

16 C. Sachs, The History of Musical Instruments, (1940), 264.

17 The Royal Commission on the Ancient and Historical Monuments of Scotland, Argyll, Vol 4, Iona, (1982), 178, 276; National Library of Scotland, MS 10, 000 f. 85v; C. Page, String Instrument Making in Medieval England and some Oxford Harpmakers, 1380-1466, in

Galpin Society Journal, 31 (1978), 44. (It is interesting to note that the earliest Harpmaker listed, in 1366, is located in the north, at York.)

18 National Library of Scotland, MS 18.8.11 f7; Victoria and Albert Museum, Reid Collection of Manuscrips, AL 1693-1902 f IR.

19 Edinburgh University Library, MS DK5, 14 Woods Psalms; National Library of Scotland, The Taill of Rauf Coilyear, Facsimile 1966.

20 D. Thomson, Painting in Scotland, 1570-1650 (1975), 46-48.

21 H. Hargreaves, The Crathes Ceiling Inscriptions, in "Bryght Lanternis" ed J.D. McClure and M.R.G. Spiller, (1986), 373-386.

22 Royal Warrant for Rate of Customs and Valuation of Merchandiser AD 1612, in Ledger of Andrew Halyburton 1492-1503, H.M. General Register House (Edinburgh 1867), 315, 330.

Chapter 5

1 Latin text from J. Gunn, An Historical Enquiry Respecting The Performance on the Harp (1807), 69.

2 H. Edin, Know your Broadleaves, (Forestry Commission Booklet No 20 (1971), 40; J. MacInnes, West Highland Sea Power in The Middle Ages, in Transactions of the Gaelic Society of Inverness, Vol 48 (1972-74), 528; H. McKechnie, The Lamont Clan, (1938), 79; It would seem from "The Old Irish Tree List" (published in Celtica Vol II, 1976, 124) that Hornbeam was unknown in Ireland.

3 R.B. Armstrong, The Irish and Highland Harps, 155-156.

4 J. Rimmer, The Irish Harp, 76.

6 Reproduced in black and white in the Folk Harp Journal No 58, (Fall 1987), 53; Early Music Vol XV No 2, (May 1987), 175, or in colour in Christian IV OG Europa, Kataloget er udgivet af Fonden Christian IV dret 1988 Place XXI, 567.

7 J. Gunn, An Historical Enquiry Respecting The Performance on the Harp (1807), 20.

8 Measurements of the Queen Mary harp pins made by kind permission of the Royal Museums of Scotland using sizers supplied by M. Billinge. Due to the delicate nature of this harp no attempt was made to clear blocked holes, therefore these measurements are a rough guide only.

9 R. Dennys, The Heraldic Imagination (1975) 146, 177, 188.

10 Our thanks to Father J.M. Senes for this suggestion.

11 M. Ryan, Treasures of Ireland, (1983), 180.

12 J. Bannerman "The Clarsach and the Clarsair" in Scottish Studies, Vol 30, (1991) 9-12.

13 K.A. Steer and J.W.M. Bannerman, Late Medieval Monumental Sculpture in the West Highlands, (1977), 58.

14 K.A. Steer and J.W.M. Bannerman, Ibid, 106.

15 cf Ch 3 p35 and Ch 6 p69.

16 John Gunn, op cite, 67-69.

17 J. Monipennie, Certayne Maters Concerning the Realme of Scotland (1603). For the author's identity see — Register of the Privy Council of Scotland, Vol IV, 1585-1592, Introduction lvi, Note.

18 J. Bannerman, The Clarsach and the Clarsair, in Scottish Studies, Vol 30, (1991), 9-12.

19 O. Bergin, Irish Bardic Poetry, (1974), 67-68, 241-242.

20 G. Murphy, Giolla Brighde's Vision of Rolf MacMahon, in Eigse, Vol 4, (19444), 93-94; O'Curry, Manners and Customs, Vol 3, 271.

Chapter 6

1 K. MacLeod, Note on Musical Instruments in Gaelic Folk Tales, Celtic Review 1912 Vol VIII.

2 D. Stevenson, Alasdair MacColla and The Highland Problem in the 17th Century, (1980), 311; R. Pitcairn, Ancient Criminal Trials in Scotland, compiled from the Original Records

and Mss. Vol 3, (1833), 2.

3   J. Dawson, The Fifth Earl of Argyle, Gaelic Lordship and Political Power in Sixteenth-century Scotland, in the Scottish Historical Review, Vol LXVII, i: No 183 (April 1988), 15-17.

4   Acta Dominorum Concilii 1478-95, 172, 204. In another action between the two parties (page 203) Agnes McConell is described as "Agnes of the Illes, spouse of umquhile Thomas Bannatyne of Cames".

5   D. Stevenson, op cit, 308, UlsterJournal of Archaeology, Vol 3 (1855), 105-6; By 1584 one member of a galloglass family had breached the ranks of native Irish Fileadh in the area of Limerick, cf Ulster Journal of Archaeology Vol 7, (1859). 103.

6   J. Munro and R.W. Munro, Acts of the Lords of the Isles 1336-1493 (1986), 295, (in Hewison, Bute in the Olden Times, Vol 2, 383, Agnes M'Connyle or MacDonald of Kintyre and Islay is said to have been the second wife of Thomas Bannatyne); H. McKechnie, The Lamont Clan, (1938), 71-73.

7   Scottish Record Office GD 163A/12. Walter Buchanan of Spittel appears to have been the younger brother of the contemporary Buchanan of that ilk so the relationship to Giles was that of nephew. (cf Moncrieff, Miscellanea Scotica Vol IV, 174-175).

8   J. Gunn, An Historical Enquiry Respecting The Performance on The Harp, (1807), 1, 73-83; C. Bell, Notice of The Harp said to Have Been Given To Beatrix Gardyn of Banchory By Queen Mary And of The Harp Called The "Lamont" Harp, in the Proceedings of the Society of Antiquaries of Scotland Vol XV, (1880-81), 13-33.

9   Genealogy of the Name of Farquharson to 1733, from a copy of the Broughdearg Ms, (Scottish Record Office GD 50/55); SRO GD 132/19.

10   Royal Commission on Historical Manuscripts, Appendix to Seventh Report, No 59, 709; Scottish Record Office GD 38/1/118.

11   J.R.N Macphail, ed, Highland Papers, Vol II, (1916), No XXX, XXXI, 174-177. Among the Lamont Papers, (cf N. Lamont, ed, An Inventory of Lamont papers 1231-1897 (1914), No 42) there is a marriage contract dated 6 January 1461-2, the witnesses include a Donald son of Eugen the poet and Eugen the clerk, who was probably responsible for writing the contract. Both witnesses also gave pledges of twenty cows each as part of the surety to cover the Tocher if the wedding failed to go ahead. These were large sums to cover someone else's Tocher, but do indicate the intrinsic wealth of these two witnesses. Together with their occupations of poet and clerk and use of the forename of Eugen it would seem reasonable to suggest that we are dealing with a branch of the MacEwen bardic family. Eugen or Ewen the poet and Eugen or Ewen Clarsach would have been contemporaries or even alternative aliases for the same person.

12   D.S. Thomson, ed, The Companion To Gaelic Scotland (1983), 170-1.

13   Scottish Record Office GD 132/25; GD 38/1/29; GD 50/159; Atholl, John 7th Duke of, "Chronicle of The Atholl and Tullibardine Families", (1908), Vol II, Addenda XC.

14   S.R.O. GD 132/204; GD 132/495.

15   S.R.O. GD 132/1. GD 132/4. GD 132/7, GD 132/13 and a notebook of Lude traditions now held by the Clan Robertson Centre at Bruar Falls, probably written by Wm. Robertson of Lude in May 1792.

16   S.R.O. GD 132/10; GD 132/12; GD 132/19.

17   R.K. Hannay ed, Rentale Dunkeldense, (1915), 329-330.

18   W.B.D.D. Turnbull, ed, The Chartularies of Balmerino and Lindores, (1841), 33; Royal Commission on Historical Manuscripts Appendix to Seventh Report. No 89, 712. A charter of sale by Patrick Ogilvy of Lude of the lands of "Owrwartmoir" dated at Dunkeld, 9 July 1527 and witnessed by Robert McNair clerk. As Patrick Ogilvy was clearly using the designation "of Lude" during the period that the Book of the Dean of Lismore was compiled it is possible that "Robert Clarsair Lude" was a retainer of Patrick Ogilvy.

19   J. Maitland Thomson ed, Inventory of documents relating to the Scrymgeour family estates, (1912)

20 A. Laing, Lindores Abbey And Its Burgh of Newburgh (1876) 479-483. (The original manuscript is now among the collections of the University of St. Andrews.)
21 R. Nicholson, Scotland — The Later Middle Ages, (1989), 517.

Chapter 7
1   A. Lawson, ed, The Poems of Alexander Hume, (1902), 58. (Also at page 158-"Or to heare the sweet and delicate voices of cunning singers, intermedled with the melodious sound of Lutes, Cisters, Clairshoes, or of other quiet instruments of that Kinde").
2   J. Bannerman, The King's Poet and the Inauguration of Alexander III, Scottish Historical Review Vol LXVIII, 2 : No 186, Oct. 1989, 120-149.
3   C. Bullock-Davies, Menestrellorum Multitudo, (1978), 43-44, 78-79 (Our thanks to Susanne Ferguson for drawing our attention to this reference); A Register of Royal and Baronial Domestic Minstrels 1272-1327, (1986), 21-22; Accounts of the Lord High Treasurer of Scotland, Vol II, 400.
4   J. Southworth, The English Medieval Minstrel, (1989), 69.
5   J. Bain ed, Calendar of Documents Relating to Scotland, Vol 2, 28, 224; K. Sanger "Balvaird" in the Kilt and Harp, Journal of the Scottish Harp Society of America, No 11 Spring 1987, 13; J. Bain, op cit, Vol 4, 474.
6   Exchequer Rolls, Vol I, cxviii; The Surtees Society, Extracts From the Account Rolls of the Abbey of Durham, 523, 528; W. Robertson Index of Records of Charters Granted Between 1309-1413, 38; Register of the Great Seal of Scotland, Vol II, 214-215; W. Robertson, op cite, 56; J. Dalyell and J. Beveridge eds, The Binns Papers, 1320-1864, (1938), Nos. 7, 11 and 12.
7   D.E.R. Watt, ed, Scotichronicon by Walter Bower, (1987), Vol 8, 304-309; J. Stevenson ed, The Life and Death of King James the First of Scotland, (1837), 54.
8   Accounts of the Lord High Treasurer of Scotland, Vol 1, 177, 184; The Exchequer Rolls of Scotland, (1878-1908), Vol 8-13; Registrum Secreti Sigilli Regum Scotorum Vol I, No 237, 238 and 1195. (It is probably with the advent of Rolland, who only received Knockan and not Clutag, that the decline of the family commenced leading to the relative impoverishment hinted at by Glenorchy's satire.)
9   W. Gillies, The Gaelic Poems of Sir Duncan Campbell, in Scottish Gaelic Studies Vol 13 pt 2, (1981), 263-276; Treasurer's Accounts Vol 13, 50, 86, 142, 267.
10 K. Sanger, Aspects of Harping in Lowland Scotland, in the Folk Harp Journal, No 58, Fall 1987, 51-54. One Pate Harper may perhaps identify with a "Patricio Harper" from near "Bardrochata" (probably the place of that name at Colmonell, Ayrshire), who had his cattle stolen in 1508, cf Pitcairn, Criminal Trials, 55.
11 R.B. Armstrong, The Irish and Highland Harps, 142-154. To place the entries into context it is necessary to refer to the edited editions of the Treasurers Accounts.
12 Accounts of The Lord High Treasurer, Vol 3, 403; Vol 4, 93 and 262.
13 H.G. Farmer, A History of Music in Scotland, (1970), 76.
14 S. Donnelly, An Irish Harper And Composer, Cormac MacDermott (?-1618), in Ceol Vol VIII, 41-50; An Irish Harper in the Royal Musick, Ceol Vol VI, 35.
15 A.J. Kempe ed, The Losely Manuscripts, 379-408; R. Evans, Ferniehirst Castle, (1987), 15-16.
16 Accounts of the Lord High Treasurer, Vol III, 367; W.J. Watson, Scottish Verse from The Book of The Dean of Lismore, (1978), 178.
17 C. Innes, ed, The Book of the Thanes of Cawdor, (1859), 238-9.
18 H.G. Farmer, op cite, 177-185.

Chapter 8
1   W. Gregor ed, Ane treatise callit The Court of Venous, Newlie compylit be Iohne Rolland in Dalkeith, 1575, (1884), 52.
2   W. Croft Dickinson ed, Early records of the burgh of Aberdeen, 1317, 1398-1407, (1957),

73, 87, 90-91, 103, 181, 226, 237; P.J. Anderson ed, Charters and Other Writs of the Royal Burgh of Aberdeen, (1890), 313-316.

3 Chambers, Domestic Annals of Scotland, Vol II, 117-119. The Dowager-Countess of Mar — Lady Mary Stewart, married the Earl of Mar (1562-1634), a widower considerably older than her, in 1592.

4 Scottish Record Office, Calendar of Deeds, 1578-1582, No 442.

5 J. Anderson ed, Calendar of The Laing Charters, No 149, 38-39; Pitcairns Criminal Trials, Vol I, 349.

6 Accounts of The Lord High Treasurer of Scotland, Vol II, 443; W.M. Metcalfe, A History of Paisley, (1909), 122; Archaeological and Historical Collections of Renfrew, (1885), Vol I, 124-129.

7 W. Fraser, The Sutherland Book, Vol III, 180-182.

8 Harperford, Parish of Bellie, cf A. Mitchell, Gravestone Inscriptions in Speyside, Bellie 13 T.S; The harps on the plasterwork in the "Kings Room" at the Binns and the second floor main room at Castle Menzies appear to be by the same hand.

9 D.J. Breeze ed, Edzell Castle, (H.M.S.O. publications), 12-19; The Royal Commission Survey of Ancient and Historical Monuments, Fife, Kinross and Clackmannan, 123-124. Figure 247-249.

10 Scottish Record Office, CH 1212; A double marriage of Margaret Pott of Edinburgh to Thomas Watson, and Ralph Pott to Elspeth Clogie recorded in the Canongate Register of Marriages on Thursday 19 August 1647 seems to be an earlier reference to the harper. According to the Canongate Register of Baptisms, (published in the Scottish Antiquary, Vol VIII, (1894), 133)   Elizabeth, daughter to Ralph Potter, indweller in the Canongate, and Elspith Clogie was born 9 June 1648. (possibly the same Elizabeth Potter, described as "poor" interred in Greyfriars burying ground on 21 June 1695). A further child, Robert son of Ralph Potter, harper, and Elspeth Clogie is recorded on 9 April 1650. Assuming the usual flexible 17th century approach to recording names, the death of Elizabeth Logie, wife of Richard Potter, harper recorded in the Register of Interrments in Greyfriars Burying Ground, Edinburgh on 22 December 1658 provides a further reference to the harper. J.G. Dalyell in his Musical Memories of Scotland (1849), 243n, noted this harper but erroneously records the forename as "Thomas".

11 Scottish Record Office, CC 31.

12 Scottish Record Office, CC 48; RD243A-44A; F.J. Grant, ed, The register of apprentices of the city of Edinburgh 1583-1666, (1906), 30.

13 J. Dennistoun and A. Macdonald eds, Miscellany of the Maitland Club, (1840), Vol II, 514.

14 C. Innes ed, The book of the thanes of Cawdor, 1236-1742, (1859), 204, 361-362.

15 R.R. Marshall, The Days of Duchess Anne : Life in the Household of the Duchess of Hamilton 1656-1715 (1973), 73.

16 W. Fraser ed, The Book of Caerlaverock, Vol II, 91-92.

Chapter 9

1 H. Harvey-Wood ed, The Poems and Fables of Robert Henryson, 145.

2 J.R.N. MacPhail ed, Highland Papers, Vol I, (1914), 51-52; W.J. Watson ed, Scottish Verse From The Book of The Dean of Lismore, (1978), 82-87, 96-99, 280; D.S. Thomson, The MacMhuirich Bardic Family, in the Transactions of the Gaelic Society of Inverness, Vol 43, (1960-68), 287.

3 cf Chapter 1 page 6; W. Matheson, The Blind Harper, (1970), Liv-lvi; C. O'Baoill, Some Irish Harpers in Scotland, in the Transactions of The Gaelic Society of Inverness, Vol 47, (1972), 143-144. (This seems to be the earliest recorded use of the term "deuchainn gleusda" in its musical sense, earlier references relate the term to a "pen trial", cf S. Donnelly, "Feaghan Geleash", in Ceol Tire 25, February 1984).

4 C. O'Baoill, op cite, 145-148.

5 R.I. Black, Colla Ciotach, in the Transactions of the Gaelic Society of Inverness, Vol 48,

(1972-74), 238; A.M. Mackenzie ed, Orain Iain Luim, (1973), 36.

6   D. O'Sullivan, Carolan — The Life Times and Music of an Irish Harper, Vol 2, (1983), 160.

7   C. O'Baoill, op cite, 149-150.

8   G. Hill, The Montgomery Manuscripts, (1869), 96-98; According to this account it was an agreement entered into by Donald Ballagh O'Cahan to reveal to Bishop George Montgomery the church lands on the Earl of Tyrone's estates that led to Tyrone, in panic, believing that his more treasonable activities were about to be revealed, fleeing Ireland; the Flight of the Earls.

9   G. Hill, op cite, 25-29. Hugh Montgomery of Braidstane settled his newly gained Irish estates and was created Viscount Montgomery of Ardes on 3rd May 1622. Although the Montgomeries of Braidstane had branched from the main Montgomery line a generation before the senior representative of the family had gained the Earldom of Eglinton, there remained considerable confusion between the two branches of the family, especially in Ireland where Braidstone's descendant, Hugh, 1st Earl of Mount-Alexander and 3rd Viscount Montgomery of Ardes, was often described as "of the Eglinton family". It should be noted that these events fit more closely with the harper Arthur O'Neill's dating of the events surrounding the air's composition.

10 Proceedings of the Royal Irish Academy, Vol XLIII, (1942-43), The Estate of Con O'Neill, No 17 and 18.

11 Da Mihi Manum's first appearance in an Irish source was in 1724, (cf A Collection of the Most Celebrated Irish Tunes, John and William Neal, facsimile edition by N. Carolan, (1986), 3.) Arthur O'Neill in his memoir used the Latin title, the translation being an editorial addition. It is possible that the translations can therefore be attributed to Bunting and were not in common use prior to the 1840 collection.

12 C. O'Baoill, op cite, 152-153; chapter 14 in this book.

13 D. O'Sullivan, op cite, Vol 2, 160; The O'Cathains of Dunseverick in particular would appear to have held Dunseverick from the MacDonnells of Antrim (cf Proceedings of the Royal Irish Academy, Vol 44, Section C, (1937-38), 112-113).

14 cf Ch 13 p158.

15 C. O'Baoill, op cite, 153-156; D.J.. O'Sullivan, The Bunting Manuscripts, in the Journal of the Irish Folk Song Society, Part IV, (1929), 31-36; H.G. Farmer, A History of Music in Scotland, (1970), 257; The air was also used by the poet Rob Donn (1714-78) for his poem "Glengolly", cf H. Morrison ed, Songs and Poems in the Gaelic Language, (1899), 314.

16 C. O'Baoill, op cite, 157-8.

17 Scottish Record Office CH2/121/7/144. Our thanks to Dr. Clarke for this reference; Mitchell Library MS 591705, Seaforth Papers.

18 A. Bruford, The Sea-divided Gael, In Eigse Cheol Tire I, (1972-73), 4-27; D. O'Sullivan, Carolan, 125-126. Carolan does not seem to have been adverse to frequent Scottish borrowings, (cf J. Rimmer, Patronage, style and structure in the music attributed to Turlough Carolan, in Early Music, Vol XV No 2, May 1987, 164-174).

Chapter 10

1   K. MacLeod, Note on Musical Instruments in Gaelic Folk Tales, Celtic Review, 1912 Vol VIII.

2   The Exchequer Rolls of Scotland, Vol V, 56-57.

3   National Library of Scotland, MS 3569; A. MacRae, The History of The Clan MacRae, (1899), 63, 298-303, 325-326, (Lag innis a' chruiter now just marked on the maps as Lagg is approximately halfway between Eilean Donan Castle and the Bards Castle on Loch Long.)

4   A. Mackenzie, History of the Munros of Fowlis, (1898), 32-33.

5   A. McKerral, Two Old Kintyre Lawsuits, (1941), 2-3; H.S. Stevenson, The Shannons of Lephenstrath, in the Kintyre Antiquarian and Natural History Society Magazine, No 11,

3-6; J. Bannerman, The Clarsach and the Clarsair, in Scottish Studies, Vol 30 (1991), 6.

6   K. Sanger, The McShannons of Kintyre : Harpers to Tacksmen, in The Kintyre Antiquarian and Natural History Society Magazine, No 28, 9-15, No 29, 20.

7   cf Ch 6 p73 and note 11: Scottish Record Office GD 50/185/55.

8   N. Lamont of Knockdow, ed, An Inventory of Lamont Papers, 1231-1897 (1914), No 42, 113, 227, 268; H. McKechnie, The Lamont Clan, (1938), 37, 88, 105-106.

9   N. Lamont of Knockdow, op cite, No 786; H. McKechnie, op cite, 176.

10 H. Campbell ed, The manuscript history of Craignish, by A. Campbell (written circa 1720), in the Miscellany of the Scottish History Society, Vol IV, (1926), 265 (see page 270 for a Donald glas M'Oshenag fl 1547 of the Kintyre family of MacGhille Sheanaichs); National Library of Scotland Adv 72-1-37, p 91; J.G. Dalyell, Scottish Poems of the Sixteenth Century, Vol 1, 150-151.

11 N. MacLean-Bristol, Argyll's Hereditary Retainers, in Notes and Queries of the Society of West Highland and Island Historical Research, No XXI, (August 1983), 25-26; A traditional claim that Argyll's harper was called Patrick (Padric Clarsair) can be found in A. Campbell, Records of Argyll, 58-59. However an Instrument of Sasine made to the instance of Colin the 3rd Earl of Argyle to his father Archibald the 2nd Earl dated 1526 has the curiously named witness, Jerman Harper, following after a Godfred Lawmond. (Transcripts from the Argyle Charter Chest, Vol III, p 195, held in the Department of History, Glasgow University.)

12 Scottish Record Office, GD 112/5/87.

13 Scottish Record Office, GD 50/30. Where the harper and his man came from is not clear, however it is worth noting the close relationship at this period between Lady Breadalbane and Lady Weem. The Menzies Baron Court Book, (S.R.O. GD 50/131 p 10) has a record of one "Duncane Makclairssir" around this time.

14 Scottish Record Office GD 112/22/11; GD 112/29/30/5.

15 C. Innes, The Black Book of Taymouth, Under the Bowhouse Book, "Delyverit at the ladyis command out of the meill from the mylne of Balloch to the Bard M'Alaster".

16 D. Wilson, The Kilmichael-Glassrie Bell-Shrine, in Proceedings of Society of Antiquaries of Scotland, Vol 18, (1884), 79-90.

17 A Lucas Deor held the lands of Kilchoan in 1534 and a Michael McLucas Dewar described as a servitor of the Earl of Argyll was in possession in 1559, (S.R.O. GD 103/2/49; GD 50/104/26. Our thanks to Dr. Lorne Campbell for these references. It has been claimed, albeit with an element of doubt, that the ancestor of the MacIndeoirs went to Argyllshire with a daughter of Walter Laird of Buchanan, who married Campbell of Ardkinglas. (G. Black, The Surnames of Scotland, 516). The Buchanans themselves seem to have had access to the bell of St Kessog in the mid 16th century. (Moncrieff, Miscellanea Scotica Vol IV, 176.)

18 K. Sanger, Auchinbreck's Harper, in Notes and Queries of the Society of West Highland and Island Historical Research, No 30 (Feb. 1987), 3-7; Scottish Record Office SC 52. The decree, given at Inveraray.

19 cf Ch 7 p91 and Ch 8 p99; C. Innes, ed, The Book of the thanes of Cawdor, 1236-1742, (1859), 187.

20 W. Mackay ed, Chronicles of the Frasers, 916-1674, (1905), 265, 453. Probably the Adam Smith indweller in Calder whose testament was recorded 16 November 1666. (Inverness Register of Testaments, S.R.O. CC 12. No 58.)

21 R. Gordon, A Genealogical History of the Earldom of Sutherland, (1813), 246.

22 H. Rose, Highland Minstrelsy, in the Transactions of the Gaelic Society of Inverness, Vol V, (1875-6), 78-79. The site lies at the edge of the area between Muir of Ord and Bishop Kinkell called Balvaird, or the township of the Bard.

23 H. Rose, op cite, 77. (For references to harping in poetry relating to the Mackenzies of Applecross, see the Transactions of the Gaelic Society of Inverness, 1984-86, 414-449). A poem said to be by a "Clarsair Mhic Dhomhnuill" and composed while alone in Ireland,

can be found in The MacDonald Collection of Gaelic Poetry, (A. MacDonald and A. MacDonald, 1911, p 392). The authors attribute the patronage to Macdonald of the Isles, however the poem would be more consistent with the period when the line was represented by the Antrim branch of the family.

24 W. Fraser, The Chiefs of Grant, (1888), Vol II, 66, Vol III, 326.

25 National Library of Scotland, MS 28-3-12; N. MacLean-Bristol, MacLean Family Manuscripts (Part 2), in Notes and Queries of the Society of West Highland and Island Historical Research, No XI, (March 1980), 10-18.

26 N. MacLean-Bristol, A Campbell Lament for Inverlochy, in Notes and Queries of the Society of West Highland and Island Historical Research, No XXVII (August 1985), 12-17; Scottish Record Office GD 151 pp 12-13.

27 National Library of Scotland MS 2085 ("The MacFarlane MS" circa 1740), 20; Oswald's Caledonian Pocket Companion (circa 1743-59), Vol VIII, 2. (According to A. MacLean Sinclair, The Clan Gillean, 373, " An Tom Murrain" was still extant in 1899); C. O'Baoill, Eachann Bacach and other MacLean Poets, (1979), 48-49.

28 J.R.N. MacPhail, Highland Papers, Vol I, (1914), 280; Scottish Gaelic Studies, Vol XIV part I, (Winter 1983), 129; Scottish Record Office SC 525

29 N. MacLean-Bristol, Notes and Queries of the Society of West Highland and Island Historical Research, No XXVIII, (March 1986), 25.

30 C. O'Baoill, op cite, 22-23.

31 An Account of the Depredations Committed On The Clan Campbell and Their Followers During The Years 1685 and 1686, Edinburgh 1816, 70

32 The Urquhart stone is now among the collections of the National Museums of Scotland. Having previously been called just Kinkell, the name first occurs as "Kynkelclarsach" in 1527, according to the Exchequer Rolls (Vol 16, 544). W.J. Watson (Place Names of Ross and Cromarty, 115) notes both Easter and Wester Kinkell (now Bishop Kinkell) and suggests that Wester or Bishop's Kinkell, nearer to Muir of Ord or Carn a Chlarsair is the Kinkell Clarsair of the records. G. Laing, (Kinkell — The Reconstruction of a Scottish Castle, 64-68), notes that John Roy Mackenzie purchased the lands of Kinkell Clarsach in 1582 and built the castle sometime between 1594 and 1614. It seems probable that the name Kinkell Clarsach originally encompassed both Easter and Wester Kinkell but subsequently became attached to just the castle which was built at the northern edge of the property.

33 A.M. Mackenzie, ed, Orain Iain Luim, (1973), 8, 18, 48, 72 and 148. The editor's tentative translation of "cruit" to mean violins is probably correct given the instruments limited penetration of the West Highlands and Iain Luim's linguistic conservatism regarding his musical terms. However by the latter part of the 17th century both the instrument and its Lowland name had arrived and begun to vie with and displace the harp from its traditional place, eg the Lament for Murdoch MacRae of Inverinate :

> "Chuala mise clarsach theud
> Fiodhall a's beus ag co-sheinn"
> I have heard the stringed harp
> and the violin in harmony playing with it.
> (B. Macrow, Kintail Scrapbook, 107-109)

The word "organ" in this context is likely to refer to the ringing bass strings, cf chapter 14.

Chapter 11

1 W. Matheson, The Blind Harper, (1970), lxii.

2 ibid, Introduction.

3 I.F. Grant, The MacLeods, (1959), 371.

4 R.H. MacLeod, The End of the MacCrimmon College, in the Piping Times, Vol 29, No

8, (May 1977), 15-18. Wherever the "college" was based, the MacCrimmons were certainly teaching by 1698 when Campbell of Breadalbane sent his piper for instruction. (cf Scottish Record Office GD 112/29/57/6).

5   I.F. Grant, op cite, 375, 376, 489; Transactions of the Gaelic Society of Inverness, Vol L1, (1978-80), 94.
6   W. Matheson, op cite, Introduction.
7   W. Matheson, op cite, lxv, lxix; C. O'Baoill, Bardachd Shilis na Ceapaich, (1972), 175-177.
8   C. O'Baoill, op cite, Introduction, 108-113; Scottish Studies, Vol 18, (1974), 147.
9   Scottish Record Office, CC 23. According to Thomson's Atlas of Perthshire, (1827), Ballinearn lay between Eastertyre and Ballinloan near Logierait, on the north side of the River Tay.
10 National Library of Scotland, MS 1442, f60, f61, f71, f96, f120; Scottish Record Office RS 3/89.

Chapter 12

1   S. MacLean, Obscure and Anonymous Gaelic Poetry, in The Seventeenth Century in the Highlands, (Inverness Field Club, 1986), 93.
2   A. MacDonald, Some Knotty Points in British Ethnology, in the Inverness Scientific Society and Field Club, Vol VII, (1906-1912), 306-307.
3   J. MacInnes, Gaelic Poetry and Historical Tradition, in The Middle Ages in the Highlands. (Inverness Field Club) 1981), 154-155.
4   Perthshire from Mr Stobies Survey — Thomson's Atlas, 1827; National Library of Scotland, MS 1443 f241.
5   S. Gordon, Highways and Byways in the Central Highlands, (1947), 140.
6   J. Kerr, Old Roads to Strathardle, (1984), 9, 48-49.
7   National Library of Scotland, MS 1443, f24, f27.
8   John, 7th Duke of Atholl, Chronicles of the Atholl and Tullibardine Families, (1908), Vol 2, Addenda xc; National Library of Scotland, MS 1439, f9, see too MS 1441, f61, May 12 1715, Rests be John Robertson alias clarser. The earliest written form of the place name "Seomar na teid", (MS 1443, f24), in 1700 equates with the later use of "Chamber or Chalmer" instead of the Gaelic word "Seomar". The use of "Tigh" first occurs in 1727, (MS 1446, f71), it then alternates with Chamber until 1733, (MS 1450, f41) after which the name becomes fixed as "Tighnateid".
9   D. Campbell, The Lairds of Glenlyon, (1886), 119-120.
10 John, 7th Duke of Atholl, op cite, Vol 2, Appendix XIII; Sir N. Paton, Genealogy of the Celtic Earls of Atholl, (1873), 6.
11 John, 7th Duke of Atholl, ibid, XI, xxxiii; A. MacDonald and A. MacDonald, The Poems of Alexander MacDonald, (1924), 232-233.
12 John, 7th Duke of Atholl, ibid, Vol I, 101.
13 Scottish Record Office, CC 2 p 41-42, CC 30.
14 J.A. Robertson, Comitatus De Atholia, (1860), 32, 67-68; Scottish Record Office GD 132/198 and GD 132/192.
15 National Library of Scotland, ADV. MS 72.1.37, 91-92; Scottish Record Office, GD 50/159.
16 D. Meek, The Gaelic Ballads of Medieval Scotland, in the Transactions of the Gaelic Society of Inverness, Vol LV, (1986-88), 55.
17 Some examples of the absorption of these instruments into a Highland family can be seen among the Campbell of Breadalbane manuscripts (1619) — receipts for teaching Sir Duncans bairns the virginals and music, (GD 112/29/10/16). 1613, Letter re virginals from Lady Grantully, (GD 112/39/23/7), and 1620 correspondence with Patrick Davidson master ofthe music school in Aberdeen concerning Lutes and the purchase of (GD 112/39/30/6).
18 R. Kirk, The Secret Commonwealth of Elves, Faunes and Faries, 108.

19 C. Gordon, Letter to John Aubrey From Professor James Garden, in Scottish Gaelic Studies, Vol 8, (1955), 23.

20 Niel Gow's home of Inver and the adjacent estate of Inchmagrannochan had both belonged to Robertson of Lude before their purchase by the Marquis of Atholl around 1698. It is perhaps worth noting that a "James McThomas and son fidlor" in the "town" of Inchmagrannoch appears in a Lude Rental of 1671, (S.R.O. GD 132/541). It would seem reasonable to suggest that these are connected with a Thomas Fidler in Dunfallandie, (Dunfallandy about 4 miles north of Logierait), who appears among the Faskally Papers in 1634, (National Library of Scotland MS 1433, f9). From 1464-1524 Dunfallandie was part of the lands of Coupar Angus Abbey, tenanted by a family McGow, members of whom also used the alternative name of Glashen or McGlashen. The "fiddle" clearly was well established in that part of Perthshire and indeed by 1700 the Earl of Breadalbane was able to dispense "drinkmoney to a violer at Lude" while on a visit, (S.R.O. GD 112/29/52/5).

Chapter 13

1   A. Carmichael ed. Carmina Gadelica, Vol 2, 251.

2   A. MacDonald and A. MacDonald, The Clan Donald, Vol 3, (1904), 254; A.J. Haddow, The History and Structure of Ceol Mor, (1982), 78-81; J.E. Scott, A' Ghlas-mheur, in the Piping Times, Vol 25 No 2 (November 1972), 11-12. (Scott claims the tale "does not appear in any book" however a Gaelic version can be found in an account of the Rankine family of Pipers by Neil Rankin Morrison, in Transactions of the Gaelic Society of Inverness, Vol XXXVII, (1934-36), 64-67. As a source, Morrison should not always be accepted uncritically, cf K. Sanger, Mull and the MacLean Pipers, Piping Times, Vol 42, No 9 (June 1990), 41-42.

3   W. MacKay, Urquhart and Glenmoriston, (1893), 414; Tranactions of the Gaelic Society of Inverness, Vol 48, (1972-74), 40; W. MacGill ed, Old Ross-shire and Scotland, Vol I, 245; W. Fraser, Chiefs of Grant, Vol II, (1888), 156, 265-267. An alternative view of Shewglie's character may be seen in a letter from Lord Lovat to Colquhoun of Luss dated 21 April 1738 where he is referred to as "the little snakeing rogue Shogly", cf H. Taylor, History of the Family of Urquhart, (1946), 235.

4   S. Fraser, The Airs And Melodies of The Highlands and Isles of Scotland (1816), No 3 and Note 3.

5   K. Sanger, Alexander Grant, 4th of Shewglie, Notes and Queries of the Society of West Highland and Island Historical Research, XX, (March 1983), 15-18; C. O'Baoill, Alexander Grant, 4th of Shewglie, Notes and Queries of the Society of West Highland and Island Historical Research, XXIII, (March 1984) 23-24; J.L. Campbell, Some Notes on the Poems of Alexander MacDonald, in Scottish Gaelic Studies, Vol 4 (1929-35), 19-20.

6   C. O'Baill, Some Irish Harpers in Scotland, in Transactions of the Gaelic Society of Inverness, Vol 47, (1972), 161-166.

7   J.L. Campbell, ed, An Account of Some Irish Harpers as given by Echlin O'Kean, Harper, Anno 1779, in Eigse, Vol 6, (1948), 146-148; E. Bunting, The Ancient Music of Ireland, (1840), 78-79; D. O'Sullivan, Carolan, Vol 2, (1983), 159; J. Gunn, op cite, 19.

8   Inveraray Burgess Register, Argyll and Bute District Archives. Our thanks to Murdo MacDonald, Archivist, for this reference.

9   F.A. Pottle and C.H. Bennett, Journal of a Tour to the Hebrides, (1936), 305-306; C. O'Baoill, Some Irish Harpers in Scotland, in Transactions of the Gaelic Society of Inverness, Vol 47, (1972), 160-161.

10 D.W. Soltau, Reise Durch Schottland, Vol II, (1808), 215-216, (translation courtesy of Hans Rehfisch).

11 MacTavish of Dunardry Papers, Argyll and Bute District Archives. Our thanks to Murdo MacDonald, Archivist, for this reference.

12 T. Hannan, The Beautiful Island of Mull, (1926), 69-70; J. MacCormick, The Island of

Mull, 36; A. Munro, Abbotsford Collection of Border Ballads, in Scottish Studies, Vol 20, (1976), 94-97; A. MacLean-Sinclair, The Clan Gillean (1899), 461-462.

13 National Library of Scotland, MS 14949 (b) 1-39; A note to an air in the fiddle section of the manuscript at page 52 reads "Taken by MacDonald from McMurphy of Campbeltown". The Rev. Patrick MacDonald had a connection with Kintyre through his son Donald who was minister of the Kintyre parish of Killean.

14 Transactions of the Gaelic Society of Inverness, Vol 32, (1924-25), 260.

15 J.P. MacLean, History of Clan MacLean, 362; The Celtic Magazine, Vol 12, (1887), 284-286. Both these accounts err in giving her name as "Mary".

16 A. Campbell, A slight sketch of a Journey made through parts of the Highlands and Hebrides to collect materials for Albyns Anthology (1815), Edinburgh University Library.

17 J. Gunn, op cite, 101-103.

18 Scottish Records Office, SC 54/22/52; CH 2/70/1; CH 2/493/1.

19 National Library of Scotland, ADV MS 73.2.26 item 33 (a); MS 14949 (a), and Acc 6658 (MS 266).

20 Scottish Record Office, OPR 501/1A; OPR 507/1A; GD 50/189.

21 K. Sanger, Wm MacMurchy, Piping Times, Vol 34, (Oct. 1981), No 1, and Niel MacArthur, in Piping Times, Vol 38, (June 1986), No 9.

22 R.I. Black, Provisional Catalogue of Gaelic Manuscripts in the National Library of Scotland, ADV 73.2.2, 72.2.12, 72.2.15 and Scottish Record Office GD 328/11; Niel MacMurchy also seems to have held a position as schoolmaster on Gigha circa 1732-45, cf Scottish Record Office E 424/7/6

23 Scottish Record Office, CH 2/50/5.

Chapter 14

1 W.J. Watson, Scottish Verse from the Book of the Dean of Lismore (1978), 248-9.

2 cf Ch 4 p42; A. Harman, Medieval and Early Renaissance Music, (1988), 103-111.

3 Wolfenbuttel Herzog August Biblioteque Codex Helmstedt 628. Heinemann Cat. 677. Facsimile "An Old St. Andrews Music Book", St. Andrews Univ. Pub. No XXX, ed J.H. Baxter, 1931.

4 A. Bruford, Song and Recitation in Early Ireland, forthcoming.

5 M. Gomez, Minstrel schools in the late Middle Ages, in Early Music, May 1990, 213-216.

6 Llawysgrif Robert Ap Huw. The Robert Ap Huw manuscript, British Museum, Additional manuscript 14905.

7 W. Matheson, op cite, 149-154.

8 W.J. Watson, Scottish Verse from the Book of the Dean of Lismore, (1978), 248-251.

9 M. Joynt, ed, Royal Irish Academy, Dictionary of the Irish Language, Section N-P, 196-198.

10 W. Fraser, The Lennox, Vol I, li, 361; A.J.G. MacKay ed, The Historie and Chronicles of Scotland by Robert Lindesay of Pitscottie, (1899-1911), Vol I, l-lv.

11 See Appendix No C.

12 W.K. Boyd ed, Calendar of State Papers relating to Scotland, (1903), Vol 3, 698, (Inchennen or Inchinnan was part of the Lennox estate and lies to the west of Renfrew, between the Black Cart Water and the Clyde).

13 Lord Lindsay, Earl of Crawford and Balcarres, Lives of the Lindsays, Vol 2, (1840), 50-52.

14 W.K. Boyd ed, Calendar of State Papers relating to Scotland, Vol 5, (1907), 469.

15 W. Matheson, verbal communication.

16 C. O'Baoill, Some Irish Harpers in Scotland, in Transactions of the Gaelic Society of Inverness, Vol 47, (1972), 169, Note 10.

17 National Library of Scotland, MS 14949 (b), 62-69.

18 J. Bowie, A Collection of Strathspey Reels, (1789), 32. According to J. Gunn, op cite, 96; The father of the present Mr. Robertson of Strowan, however, who had been constantly

in the practice of hearing General Robertson's (of Lude) great grandfather play this music on Queen Mary's Harp used to play a great number of them on the violin. From him his son, Colonel Colyear Robertson learned, by ear, to play a number of them on the violin, which General Robertson has heard him play, and some of them were taken down in writing from his performance by Bowie, a music seller in Perth. (Quoting from General Robertson's letter to the Highland Society 23 May 1805).

19 W. Matheson, Notes on Mary MacLeod, in Transactions of The Gaelic Society of Inverness, Vol 41, (1951-52), 17-18; I.F. Grant, The MacLeods, (1959), 335-6.
20 M.A. Alburger, Scottish Fiddlers and their Music, (1983), 42-48.
21 M.A. Alburger, ibid, 19-21; M. Wood and R.K. Hannay ed, Extracts from the records of the burgh of Edinburgh AD 1589-1603, (1927), 120.
22 D. Johnson, Scottish Fiddle Music in the 18th Century, (1984), 64.
23 Ap Huw MS, British Museum Additional MS 14905, 34.
24 cf Ch 10 p123.
25 A.J. Haddow, The History and Structure of Ceol Mor, (1982), 136-139.
26 National Library of Scotland, MS 2254, 54.
27 cf Ch 10 p119.

Chapter 15

1 "Dirge" by William Millar, Original National Melodies of Scotland composed by Peter McLeod, (1838), 166.
2 K. Sanger, An Attempt to re-introduce the Highland Harp, 1784-1786, in Notes and Queries of the Society of West Highland and Island Historical Research, No XVII, (March 1982), 8-16.
3 Highland Society of Scotland, Ingliston papers. Sederunt Bk 4, Pt 1, June 1803-December 1808, 151, 161, 174, 176, 183, 270, 274. (Our thanks to Iain MacInnes for extracting these and subsequent entries from the Ingliston papers).
4 Highland Society of Scotland Ingliston papers, Minute Bk 1824 — page 85, 86, 88, 95-101.
5 K. Sanger, Portrait of An Irish harper, in Folk Harp Journal, No 45, (June 1984), 19; Patrick O'Byrne and John Bell, in Folk Harp Journal, No 53, (June 1986), 35-37.
6 W.A.J. Prevost, Joseph Train's Letter to Sir Walter Scott Concerning Wandering Willie, in Scottish Studies, Vol 20, (1976), 117-123.
7 D.P. Menzies, The Red and White book of Menzies, (1894); W. Fraser, Memorials of the Montgomeries, Earls of Eglinton, Vol I, (1859), 392; R. Rensch, Harps and Harpists, (1989), 160.
8 Scottish Record Office, GD 170/560.
9 Scottish Record Office, GD 112/20/5/6 item 103; GD 112/22/58/1 and GD 112/22/58/3.
10 J. MacDougall, Highland Postbag, (1984), 157-158.
11 P. Cooke, Elizabeth Ross and the Piping of John Mackay of Raasay, in Proceedings of the Piobaireachd Society Conference, March 1985; M. Archer, The Connoisseur, Vol 175, (Nov. 1970), No 705, 180-81.
12 E. Grant of Rothiemurchus, ed Lady Strachey, Memoirs of a Highland Lady, (1911), 125, 211, 330-331.
13 J. Elouis, Selection of Favourite Scots Songs with Accompaniments for the Harp or Piano Forte; D. Baptie, Musical Scotland, (1894).
14 Our thanks to Bella Sanger for the extracts from the Edinburgh Courant and the Edinburgh Post Office Directory.

Chapter 16

1 C. O'Baoill, Bardachd Shilis Na Ceapaich, (1972), 114-115.
2 The Celtic Monthly, October 1892, 13; December 1895, 49; December 1896, 55; July 1898, 200; October 1898, 20; January 1901, 63; October 1902, 10.

3   F. Collinson, The Traditional And National Music of Scotland, (1966), 249; National
    Library of Scotland, Acc 83918, Glens Account Book, 139.
4   Catalogue of the National Museum of Antiquities of Scotland, (1892), 317. The missing
    instrument is presumably the harp whose deposit is recorded in the Proceedings of the
    Society of Antiquaries of Scotland, Vol III, 1857-60, 462, when it was described as — "Old
    Harp, about 3 feet in height, which formerly belonged to Mr. Fraser, player on the music
    bells in the steeple of St. Giles Church, Edinburgh".
5   R.D. Cannon, A Bibliography of Bagpipe Music, (1980), 31-39.
6   I. Malcolm of Poltalloch, Highland Lore and Legend, (1938), frontspace, illustration.
7   Clarsach Society Archives, deposited at the National Library of Scotland, Acc 10247, Box
    1 and 2. Minute Bk 1946-57, Minute Bk 1931-37.
8   ibid, Minute Bk 1957-75.

INDEX

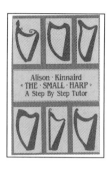